CONSEQUENCES of ADOLESCENT DRUG USE

CONSEQUENCES of ADOLESCENT DRUG USE

Impact on the Lives of Young Adults

BY

MICHAEL D. NEWCOMB

AND

PETER M. BENTLER

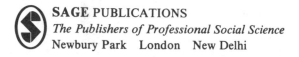

SAGE PUBLICATIONS
The Publishers of Professional Social Science
Newbury Park   London   New Delhi

For information address:

SAGE Publications, Inc.
2111 West Hillcrest Drive
Newbury Park, California 91320

SAGE Publications Ltd.
28 Banner Street
London EC1Y 8QE
England

SAGE Publications India Pvt. Ltd.
M-32 Market
Greater Kailash I
New Delhi 110 048 India

Printed in the United States of America

Library of Congress Cataloging-in-Publication Data

Newcomb, Michael D.
    Consequences of adolescent drug use: impact on psychosocial development and young adult role responsibility/Michael D. Newcomb, P. M. Bentler.
        p.   cm.
    Bibliography: p.
    ISBN 0-8039-2847-5
    1. Youth—United States—Drug use—Longitudinal studies. 2. Drug abuse—United States—Psychological aspects—Longitudinal studies. 3. Drug abuse—Social aspects—United States—Longitudinal studies. 4. Drug abuse surveys—United States.
I. Bentler, Peter M.   II. Title.
HV5824.Y68N49 1988   87-24061
362.2′9—dc19   CIP

SECOND PRINTING, 1989

Contents

362.29
N538c

This book is dedicated to the lives and memories of Margery Newcomb and Charles Vesper, mother and brother of the first author, and to Marion and Werner Bentler on the occasion of their 80th and 85th birthdays, respectively.

Preface

The use and abuse of psychoactive chemicals, including not only illicit drugs but also such widely available substances as cigarettes, alcohol, and prescription and over-the-counter medication, has become recognized as a major national—indeed, international—problem that affects all segments of society. While enough anecdotal evidence on the devastating effects of drug abuse on health, social, and personal functioning exists to merit strong efforts at clinical intervention, as well as prevention, scientific evidence on such consequences in relatively normal and unselected populations is really quite meager. In addition, because abuse of a variety of drugs rather than only a single substance tends to be a common occurrence, evidence for the differential consequences of use of particular substances tends to be even more scarce. This monograph represents a pioneering attempt to evaluate the effects of general and specific drug use during adolescence on young adult functioning.

The range of consequences of drug use that might be studied is enormous, as are the domains of potential predictors of such use and the controls that could be used to eliminate alternative explanations of results. Thus we have been producing a variety of research reports on these topics for the scientific literature. This standard journal-article approach to publication, however, has the drawback that the results are scattered and their interrelations are not easily seen. In contrast, this monograph permits us to present a coherent approach to the area, including not only the empirical results, but also a discussion of the relevant theoretical and practical issues that should make this report relevant to behavioral scientists, as well as to policymakers, educators, and clinicians.

As with any large project, our final synthesis and integration owes a great deal of debt to those who have helped along the way. Since the beginning of our longitudinal project in the mid-1970s, we have had the benefit of numerous professional researchers who are no longer directly involved in the project. These include, but are not limited to, Drs. Lisa Harlow, George Huba, and Joseph Wingard. Julie Speckart has performed double duty in the preparation of this book: She did all typing and manuscript preparation, as well as drawing all of the figures. For these efforts, we extend our warm gratitude. Sandy Yu managed all file preparation and many of the analyses. To her we express our sincere appreciation. A range of other tasks were performed by numerous other people such as Paul Bolten, Belinda Fong, Amy Friedheim, Ingrid Martinez, Phuong Nguyen, Arthur Palisoc, and Edward Win.

This project could not exist without the continuous funding provided by the National Institute on Drug Abuse. This has taken the form of a program project grant (DA 01070) and a research scientist award to the second author (DA 00017). We especially appreciate the support and energy provided by our current grant monitor, Dr. Beatrice Rouse, and her predecessors, Drs. Dan Lettieri and Louise Richards.

This project could also not exist without the cooperation and honesty of our participants. Many have been a part of our project for a major percentage of their lives. Such devotion to our scientific efforts are essential for a project like ours to be as successful as it has been. We ask many personal and sensitive questions of our participants, and it is their willingness to provide candid answers that has permitted us to produce a book with such interesting, useful, and timely findings. We offer our deep-felt appreciation and gratitude to these individuals who have shared their personal successes, as well as tribulations, with us.

Finally, but certainly not least, the first author wants to express his heartfelt appreciation and affection to Kathleen

Andrews. She has offered tireless emotional support and tolerance of his extensive time devoted to writing and analyses necessary to the creation of this book. Similarly, the second author wants to express his deep gratitude to Thea for encouraging this work, and, more generally, for her support of his personal and academic efforts for over a quarter of a century. Thank you both for understanding.

—Michael D. Newcomb
Peter M. Bentler

1

Scope of the Problem and the Nature of Drug Use Consequences

In this book, we report a series of integrated analyses based on our unique study of a large sample of young adults whose personal and social development has been followed in our research program for the past eight years. The goal of the book is to examine the impact or consequences of teenage drug use on the transition into young adulthood, the acquisition of normative role responsibilities, and social integration. While controlling for tendencies toward deviance or lack of social conformity, we assess the influence of using various substances during early and late adolescence on the ability to acquire and perform effectively in a variety of adult roles as young adults. Such roles or behaviors include family formation (i.e., marriage, children), as well as difficulties with this (i.e., divorce) or alternatives (i.e., cohabitation), employment, livelihood, and job stability, reliance on public assistance (welfare, food stamps), sexual behavior, deviance (arrests, criminal activity), educational pursuits, mental health status (i.e., depression, suicide ideation), and social integration (i.e., loneliness, social support). Although drug use in the workplace is certainly one possible consequence of teenage drug use, due to the magnitude of such analyses and a desire to maintain a clear focus on that topic, these results are published in a separate piece (Newcomb, in preparation).

Teenage Drug Use

Drug use among adolescents and young adults has become quite widespread during the past 25 years, with many characterizing the increase as epidemic in proportion (Robins, 1984). For instance, in a recent national survey, 92% of high school seniors reported using alcohol some time in their life, whereas 54% reported marijuana use, and 40% reported using some other type of illicit or hard drug (Johnston, O'Malley, & Bachman, 1986). Although it is not too surprising that many teenagers have experimented at some time with various drugs, problems and concerns begin to arise when this experimental use becomes regular use or even abuse. In this same national survey, 37% reported at least one instance of heavy drinking (five or more drinks) during the past two-week period. In addition, 26% reported use of marijuana within the past month and 5% reported daily use. Thus, for many teenagers, drug use is more than an experimental behavior or simply the result of curiosity. For many adolescents, ingestion of various drug substances has become an important facet of their life-style. It is critical to determine how this behavioral life-style of drug involvement affects a teenager's social and psychological development beyond the years of adolescence.

Adolescence and Young Adulthood

The transition from high school (adolescence) to young adulthood is one of the most important and difficult passages faced by everyone in his or her life. Changes in social environment (high school to college, job, military, or marriage), role responsibility (dependent high school student to independent spouse, parent, coworker), intimacy needs (as lover, spouse, or romantic attachment), community integration (adherence to laws and social norms), and psychological climate (self-feelings, emotional status, stress) can be quite pronounced during this period of development (e.g., Bachman, O'Malley, & Johnston, 1984; Newcomb & Bentler, 1986a). In fact, one frequently mentioned defining feature of adolescence is the rapid and far-reaching changes occurring in virtually all aspects of life and the resultant high-level stress and disequilibrium (e.g., Erikson, 1963, 1968). These challenges are related directly to the developmental tasks confronted by adolescents, such as individuation from parents, establishment of one's own socioemotional support system, and career preparation (e.g., Havighurst, 1952, 1972). Of course, these psychological changes occur in conjunction with aspects of biological maturation (e.g., Brooks-Gunn, Petersen, & Eichorn, 1985; Lerner, 1985).

Upon graduation from high school (or leaving high school should the student fail to graduate), many decisions must be made and life directions set. For instance, the young adult may choose to continue living with parents, or leave home and choose a new living arrangement or environment, such as living alone, with roommates, in a dormitory, with a spouse, or cohabitation. At the same time, essential decisions are made regarding life pursuit or livelihood activities, reflecting changes in role responsibility and practical demands. For some, who are financially able and academically inclined, continuing education in college may be a desired life pursuit. Others may choose to engage in part-time or full-time employment, join the military, become a housewife/mother, or perhaps do nothing.

Thus, during this transition from adolescence to young adulthood, the individual is moving from a rather uniform and stable social environment (attending high school and living with parents) to a world that is increasingly differentiated and diversified in regard to new types of peer relationships (coworkers, roommates), personal responsibilities (career, family, livelihood), options for autonomous functioning, and different sanctions for certain behaviors (cigarette and alcohol use become legal, the right to vote is acquired).

The transition to adulthood is also characterized by a normative succession of social roles, typically progressing from school to work to marriage and family (e.g., Hogan, 1981). Each of these new and differing social roles include varying degrees of traditional (or nontraditional) expectations for attitudes and behavior. As a consequence, the process of entering into these new social role participations and social environments will exert pressure to conform to the existing values of the role, resulting in varying degrees of role socialization (Sarbin & Allen, 1968). Role socialization can be observed in changes in behavior or attitude upon entry into the role or environment (e.g., Yamaguchi & Kandel, 1985a). For example, if a preexisting behavior is at odds with a new role participation, the individual can either socialize to the role by changing the behavior, or retain the behavior by selecting another role more consonant with the behavior. The desired outcome is to participate in a role that is consistent with attitudes and behavior, by either changing the attitudes and behavior or changing the role (Yamaguchi & Kandel, 1985a, 1985b).

These are some of the normative processes that characterize the developmental period from adolescence to young adulthood. It has not been determined, however, if, or in what manner, use of drugs in the teenage years affects this adaptation and accommodation to adult responsibilities and behavior.

The Nature of
Drug Use Consequences

It is generally believed that drug use is bad and often has catastrophic consequences for the individual, his or her family, and society. As such, we may presume that adolescent drug use will interfere with the developmental tasks and maturational growth of young adulthood. We all know this or assume that it is true. Indeed, dramatic case histories popularized in the press make such a conclusion almost self-evident (see, e.g., *Reader's Digest*, 1987). Such cases may be selected to prove a dramatic point, however. They cannot be used to support a causal interpretation because of the absence of information on individuals who may have ingested a drug but had minimal or no negative consequences. Obtaining scientific evidence for drug effects that holds after appropriate control for confounding influences in a sample of randomly selected youngsters growing into adulthood is quite another matter. Moreover, it is more difficult to define what we mean by "bad," or to specify what life areas are generally affected by drug use. An even more difficult task is to prove, in a causal sense, that drug use during the teenage years created certain specific problems for the young adult. Do we know or can we prove clearly that using drugs as a teenager leads to significant and measurable problems later in life or as an adult? Do we have adequate or even acceptable theories to begin understanding and perhaps predicting such outcomes? The answer to these questions is largely no. Very few theories are available to address these issues, data are only currently becoming available to study these issues empirically, and very little has been published as yet. These are the goals of this study: To determine the consequences of teenage drug use on functioning in various critical life areas of the young adult and integrate this information in a theoretical manner.

An extremely large body of data, speculation, and well-refined theories have emerged during the past 20 years to explain the processes of acquiring drug-using behaviors among adolescents. These are very crucial and critical issues and tasks. Certainly, it is imperative to understand the etiological or antecedent factors involved in drug use. Interestingly, however, very little effort has been devoted to determining the consequences of drug use.

Drugs, including psychoactive drugs, have been used by virtually all cultures in many different forms from time immemorial. More recently, public policy has been based on the proposition that the use of mind-altering drugs is bad. This concern, which is largely associated with the epidemic rise in drug use among youngsters and teenagers during the recent past, is appropriate. But as scientists, we must challenge the rather uncritical and unscientific assumption that drug use, in and of itself, is bad and should be prevented, understood, or treated. This may be true. But we need to demonstrate any conclusions in a scientifically rigorous manner, testing explicit theories and causal relationships, and evaluating or controlling spurious influences. How does drug use create bad or problematic outcomes? What areas of functioning are affected? Are there positive effects of drug involvement? These are the types of questions we address in this monograph.

The study of drug use consequences is a new area for the epidemiological study of drug use, as reflected in panel studies of adolescents (such as ours and other important research projects around the country involving Judith Brook, Ann Brunswick, Richard Clayton, the Jessors, Lloyd Johnston, Denise Kandel, Howard Kaplan, Robert Pandina, Gene

Smith, Harwin Voss, and others). The primary initial task of most of these and related projects (e.g., Cherry & Kiernan, 1976; Coombs, Fawzy, & Gerber, 1984, 1986; Fleming, Kellam, & Brown, 1982) has been the development and testing of theories of how drug use is acquired. In other words, they have been etiological in nature and have attempted to explain the essential antecedents of drug use among teenagers. Many important theories have been developed and tested. These have been summarized recently by Chassin (1984), Jessor (1986), Jones and Battjes (1985), Kandel (1980, 1986), Labouvie (1986), Lettieri (1985), Lettieri, Sayers, and Pearson (1980), Long and Scherl (1984), Sadava (1987), and Zucker and Gomberg (1986). These theories have progressed from being rather vague and diffuse to being clear, concise, and well refined. The focus of these theories has been on family and peer influences (e.g., Brook, Whiteman, & Gordon, 1985; Clayton & Lacey, 1982; Fawzy, Coombs, & Gerber, 1983; Fisher, MacKinnon, Anglin, & Thompson, 1987; Huba & Bentler, 1980, 1983a, 1984; Jurich, Polson, Jurich, & Bates, 1985; Kandel, 1973, 1985; Newcomb, Huba, & Bentler, 1983; Newman, 1984; Rittenhouse & Miller, 1984; Vicary & Lerner, 1986; Voss & Clayton, 1984), numerous types of risk factors (e.g., Bry, 1983; Bry, McKeon, & Pandina, 1982; Coombs, Wellisch, & Fawzy, 1985; Dembo, Blount, Smeidler, & Burgos, 1985; Newcomb, Maddahian, & Bentler, 1986; Newcomb, Maddahian, Skager, & Bentler, 1987), deviance, problem behavior, or lack of social conformity (e.g., Akers, 1984; Donovan & Jessor, 1985; Huba & Bentler, 1983a; Jessor & Jessor, 1977, 1978), low self-esteem, depression, or psychological distress (e.g., Aneshensel & Huba, 1983; Kaplan, 1975, 1984, 1985), and stressful life change events (e.g., Castro, Maddahian, Newcomb, & Bentler, 1987; Newcomb & Harlow, 1986; Newcomb, Huba, & Bentler, 1986a). Recently, theories have attempted to grapple with these diverse processes by proposing more complex frameworks that can integrate biological, psychological, and social factors (e.g., Huba, Wingard, & Bentler, 1980; Sadava, 1987; Zucker & Gomberg, 1986) that may be tested in large, interactive models spanning many years (e.g., Stein, Newcomb, & Bentler, in press). More general theories have attempted to account for a broad range of deviant behaviors among the young, such as the structured strain perspective (Cloward & Ohlin, 1960), subcultural socialization (Cohen, 1955; Miller, 1958), control theories (Briar & Piliavin, 1965; Hirschi, 1969; Polk & Halferty, 1966), containment theories (Reckless, 1967; Voss, 1969), labeling theory (Becker, 1963; Kitsuse, 1962), social learning (Akers, Krohn, Lanza-Kaduce, & Radosevich, 1979), and an integrated control-strain model (Elliott, Huizinga, & Ageton, 1985). Discussion of these etiological theories is beyond the scope of this book.

Although a number of longitudinal studies concerned with evaluating the consequences of adolescent drug use on young adult functioning are in progress, as noted above, aside from studies that involve treatment outcomes (e.g., Suwaki, 1983) and hence are not relevant to the present monograph, to the best of our knowledge, only two major studies have so far been published. Halikas, Weller, Morse, and Hoffman (1983) interviewed 100 White regular marijuana users and their non- or lightly using peers in 1969-1970 when they were 18 years of age or older. Drug use and various retrospective measures of childhood personality, behavior, and school problems were obtained. After a six- to eight-year period, 98% of these subjects were reinterviewed and measures of socioeconomic attainment, job and residence stability, divorce and illegitimate pregnancy, and criminal activities were recorded. Although marijuana use was found to have a negative impact on most outcomes, the authors state that "being a regular marijuana user does not have a consistently deleterious effect on outcome variables when early history, especially childhood misbehavior and school behavior problems, and associated use of other illicit drugs are taken into account" (p. 235). In only one analysis—arrests for nondrug crime—did a drug variable emerge as the sole significant predictor of the outcome. Similarly, Kandel, Davies, Karus, and Yamaguchi (1986) followed up 1,004 adolescents from ages 15 to 16 to ages 24 to 25. The consequences of ever using cigarettes, alcohol, marijuana, and other illicit drugs in adolescence on 20 outcomes in five areas of functioning (continuity of participation in the roles of adulthood, educational attainment, participation in deviant activities, health, and extent of use of legal, illegal, and prescribed drugs) were studied. "The measures of time 1 involvement rarely showed any significant regression effects, especially when subsequent drug use variables were entered in the equations" (Kandel et al., 1986, p. 752). That is, with a few exceptions involving small effects manifested with one sex only, there were no deleterious or positive effects of adolescent substance use on functioning at young adulthood. On the basis of prior work in the sample described in the current monograph, we would expect to find more serious and numerous consequences of adolescent drug use than observed in these two previous studies. On the other hand, we would not expect to find as strong effects as have been noted in various cross-sectional or retrospective reports. While we would expect to find results consistent with the observations of Robins, Darvish, and Murphy (1970), for example, that adult Black men who reported having used marijuana as teenagers had more deleterious educational, familial, and antisocial outcomes, our ability more precisely to control for initial levels of confounding variables should lead to some attenuation of raw effects otherwise attributed to drug use.

It does not seem especially relevant to review findings from contemporaneous, rather than longitudinal, panel data sources because of potential confounds such as memory biases (e.g., Baumrind, 1983). Thus Robins et al. (1970) specifically avoided discussing the outcome of men who began drug use as adults in order to avoid interpretational difficulties regarding cause and effect (i.e., whether drug use preceded or followed their adult difficulties). In contrast, although 63%-80% of drug users initiated use after their high school assessment, Kandel et al. (1986) chose to report on the effects of events that occurred during the period from adolescence to adulthood, as reported retrospectively at the time of the follow-up. The correlations and regressions between variables from two different aspects of their follow-up interview, controlling for certain adolescent and follow-up variables, will not be summarized here because they do not involve longitudinally gathered data, in which predictor and consequence measurements are separated by several years, as are the focus of this monograph. Problems such as are noted by Kandel et al. (1986, p. 747) in their own study—"the outcome analyses confound to some extent the antecedents and consequences of drug use"—are avoided by our longitudinal design.

Types of Consequences

The DOMAIN model of drug use, which has been developed at our Center and has been used to conceptualize many drug-related issues (e.g., Huba & Bentler, 1982, 1983a, 1984; Huba, Wingard, & Bentler, 1980), includes four levels of characteristics that may influence or be influenced by substance use. These four domains include biological (such as physiological processes), intrapersonal (within the individual), interpersonal (social), and sociocultural (community systems) factors. Potential consequences of drug use can be discussed in regard to each of these areas that could be affected. Specific areas that need to be addressed within the young adult life period, that are subsumed under these four global domains, include consequences of drug use related to physical health, emotional health, marriage and family formation, deviant attitudes and behavior, sexual behavior and involvement, social integration, educational pursuits, and livelihood pursuits. The available literature reveals that little solid research has been done to explain the impact of drug use on these critical life areas, particularly in regard to adolescent substance use. Although a fair amount of research has emerged regarding the chronic and excessive use of various drugs over lengthy periods of time (e.g., cigarette smokers, alcoholics, heroin addicts), very little has emerged on the consequences of drug use during the critical developmental period of adolescence and young adulthood.

Short-Term Effects

The immediate or short-term consequences and impact of drug use are fairly easy to document and have been fairly well established. On a biological level, it can be demonstrated and measured that drugs affect physiological processes. For instance, acute cocaine intoxication is manifested by localized anesthesia, pupil dilation, constriction of blood vessels, increased heart rate, and elevated blood pressure (e.g., Cohen, 1985; Fischman, 1984; Fischman & Schuster, 1981; Gold, Washton, & Dakis, 1985; Jones, 1984). Adverse health consequences include medical emergencies as measured by cocaine-related visits to hospital emergency rooms. Such visits have increased dramatically in recent years (Adams, Gfroerer, Rouse, & Kozel, 1986). On an intrapersonal level, it is quite clear that drugs have a psychoactive ability to alter or modify various aspects of psychological functioning. Most people get high to feel good and to change some aspects of their sensorium. Tests can be readily made to establish whether these intrapersonal changes affect other aspects of behavior such as operating a motor vehicle, performing job-related tasks, and problem solving. It can also be seen that drug use has an impact upon and changes interpersonal behavior. Everyone can tell when someone is stoned or drunk by the way they behave, act, and react to people around them. Thus drug use can immediately affect personal relationships and aspects of life contingent upon them, such as marriage, friendships, and jobs. Finally, a large number of these short-term effects on the biological, intrapersonal, and interpersonal levels can influence the larger social systems. For instance, Quayle (1983) has noted that on a national level over $30 billion per year are lost due to lowered work force productivity resulting from employee alcohol and drug abuse.

Thus the short-term or immediate consequences of acute substance use intoxication can be readily demonstrated. It does not take sophisticated technologies or expensive longitudinal studies to establish that if someone is drunk and has a car accident, the immediate effects of alcohol consumption may have contributed to the vehicle collision. It is also easy to see that if a teenager is too drunk or stoned to take an algebra final, that the drug use may have caused the failing grade. This type of research can best be approached from a standpoint of traditional experimental design, utilizing specific experimental conditions of varying types and dosage levels of drugs with pre- and posttests of particular tasks of interest, such as driving skill or problem solving. The study of longer-term drug use consequences, however, cannot ethically manipulate drug use levels and experimental conditions. For such questions we must rely on quasi-experimental designs with longitudinal data and specific tests for causal inference.

Physical Health Consequences

Although the focus of this study is not directed toward the determination of physical health consequences of teenage drug use, we would be remiss if we did not discuss this important issue. Below we mention several studies that have examined the impact of adolescent drug use on health status.

Physical health deterioration is a common concern regarding drug use. There is little doubt that excessive and chronic abuse of virtually any drug substance will result in health compromises. It is less clear, however, whether ingestion of various drug substances on an experimental or even regular basis during the teenage years has a noticeable or measurable impact on physical conditions later in life. For instance, in *Healthy People* (1979), the short-term hazards of drug use on adolescent health are considered secondary effects (such as increased risk of traffic accidents), rather than primary effects of the drug use itself.

In one study, Vingilis and Smart (1981) found little physical deterioration in a group of adolescent alcohol abusers. They reviewed 34 cases of teenagers admitted to the Addiction Research Center for alcohol abuse and concluded that physical symptoms of alcohol dependence (delirium tremens, liver damage) were quite rare. Chassin (1984) points out that the "notions of physical addiction (such as withdrawal symptoms) or serious physiological deterioration, will be inappropriate to defining drug abuse within an adolescent sample" (p. 128). On the other hand, teenage drug use may have implications for long-term adult health outcomes through the establishment of habitual behaviors associated with chronic health risks such as cigarette smoking, poor diet, and other life-style imbalances (e.g., Castro, McCreary, Newcomb, Beazconde-Garbanati, & Cervantes, in press; Chassin, 1984). And the consequences of smoking on respiratory impairment seem to be noticeable after two years of smoking more than a few cigarettes a day (Adams,

Lonsdale, Robinson, Rawbone, & Guz, 1984).

Complicating these issues is the fact that most treated adolescent drug abusers (e.g., Beschner & Friedman, 1979) and many teenage users in the general population (Clayton & Ritter, 1985) are polydrug users, which makes it difficult to document physical symptoms related to use of any specific substance (Bentler, 1987a; Bentler & Newcomb, in preparation).

A few recent studies have directly tested the effects of teenage drug use on health outcomes. Over a one-year period during adolescence, hard drug use was found to increase general poor health, whereas later symptom reporting was predicted from earlier cigarette, marijuana, and amphetamine use (Huba, Newcomb, & Bentler, 1987). Newcomb and Bentler (1987b) studied the impact of various types of drug use on numerous measures of health status and health service utilization from late adolescence to young adulthood. They found that teenage drug use did not directly affect physical health conditions or use of medical services, but decreased perceived physical hardiness. Cigarette smoking had the greatest impact on physical symptoms (as well as being one of the substances most frequently used in high quantities), whereas use of hard drugs during adolescence was associated with increased emergency physician visits during the same period. Early cannabis use decreased physical hardiness and increased health problems experienced. Brunswick and Messeri (1986) reported that inhalant and narcotic use decreased physical health over an eight-year period. Unfortunately, several methodological problems (e.g., retrospective assessments of drug use, an undefined baseline measure of poor health, colinearities in their data) limit the usefulness of these results. Kandel et al. (1986) reported that marijuana use in adolescence predicted, for men, the negative consequence of being ill in bed within the last year (initial health status during adolescence was not controlled).

One of the most widely researched drugs in terms of consequences has been alcohol among adult samples (probably second only to cigarette smoking). For instance, Gordon and Kannel (1984) found that male drinkers had lower mortality than nondrinkers (over a period of 22 years), with light drinkers having the lowest mortality. There was a strong association between heavy drinking and stomach cancer. Most other studies have reported higher mortality for heavy alcohol users (e.g., Cullen, Stenhouse, & Wearne, 1982; Klatsky, Friedman, & Siegelaub, 1981). On the other hand, Richman and Warren (1985) found an apparent beneficial effect of beer (specifically) on good health status. Similarly, Kandel et al. (1986) reported that adolescent alcohol use by women predicted less inability to do certain kinds of work because of health reasons in young adulthood. Unfortunately, the latter studies did not control for initial baseline of poor health.

Research literatures are also beginning to develop regarding the long-term effects of illicit drugs such as marijuana and cocaine (reviewed by Nicholi, 1983, 1984). Various effects have been noted on reproductive systems (e.g., sperm, menstrual cycle, fetus), immunological systems, and endocrine systems. Dose-response relations for these negative consequences have not been established.

2

Theories of
Drug Use
Consequences

T he challenge of developing theories to help account for or explain the effects or consequences of teenage drug use forces one to confront the nature of development from a somewhat different perspective than has typically been taken in the drug literature. Etiological theories attempt to predict which factors in a youngster's environment or what features in their psychological makeup will predispose them to engage in drug-using behaviors. Consequence theories, on the other hand, attempt to explain how the use of various drug substances influences or interacts with important features of adolescent development and as a result may alter their psychological makeup, physical condition, or social environment. The nature of adolescent development is certainly not a thoroughly understood phenomenon (e.g., Coleman, 1978; Ellis, 1979). As a result, we begin to grapple with incomplete theories of teenage maturation, while adding the complicating factor of drug use.

Structurally speaking, the teenage years bridge the critical period of life from being a dependent child to an independent adult. As such, it is the life transition in which the bulk of adult behaviors and responsibilities are developed. Adolescence by its very nature and demands is stressful (Starr, 1986). Some research has noted that adolescence, in fact, represents a lifetime peak for the experience of stress as reflected in life change events (e.g., Newcomb, Huba, & Bentler, 1986b). This stress provides the disequilibrium that is essential for growth. It is this challenge that generates new, mature behavior and responsible coping abilities (e.g., Erikson, 1959, 1963, 1968; Piaget, 1962, 1972). Adolescence is the training ground for the acquisition of critical adult competencies and behavior that are necessary to navigate through adult life. These involve education, romantic and sexual involvements, career choices, establishing belief systems, acquiring self-sufficient living arrangements, parenthood, developing support systems, and the numerous other facets that characterize an adult.

The study of consequences of teenage drug use has compelled us to consider the adequacy of many standard adolescent development theories (e.g., see Adelson, 1980, for reviews; Erikson, 1959, 1963, 1968; Freud, 1958, 1969; Lerner, 1985; Piaget, 1972). If these are not rich and complex enough to account for the wide range of developmental tasks and goals, it is unlikely that they will shed much light on how the impact of drug use interacts with this developmental stage. Because most of these theories emphasize general aspects of adolescent development, some theoreticians have specialized the hypothesized processes to account for the role and impact of drug use (e.g., Baumrind & Moselle, 1985). Conversely, several rather general theories of adolescent development have been generated by the need to understand teenage drug use (e.g., Jessor & Jessor, 1977; Kaplan, 1975, 1985).

On the other hand, drug use does not occur in a vacuum, but is typically an integrated and consistent aspect of the teenager's behavioral repertoire. It is usually only one component of a lifestyle (Donovan & Jessor, 1985) of which the totality or various aspects may influence development. When viewed from this perspective, it is difficult to separate out a developmental trajectory from the synergistic influences and resultant consequences, that themselves become new influences that may be impinging upon the path of development. In other words, it is not possible to study the impact of drug use on a developmental course without viewing the drug use as an essential aspect of the course (e.g., Peele, 1986). It is not an influence that occurs in isolation, but has various precursors and outcomes that are consistent with the developmental trajectory. Thus any competent study of drug use consequences must reflect the general ecology of adolescent development and yield results that further the understanding of that critical transition period.

There has been very little theory development regarding the impact of adolescent drug use on later life. The few theories that have been offered are discussed below. Many of these are totally theoretical and have never been empirically tested. Others have been developed to account for the ctiology of drug use, but are rich enough that we have been able to interpolate how they might address drug use consequences. In general, these theories are not mutually exclusive, but are discussed separately below to maintain conceptual clarity.

Impaired Functioning

Common to most theories on the consequences of drug use is the assumption that use of various substances interferes with or impairs physical, psychological, or emotional functioning. This can result from the psychoactive effects of the drug on cognitive, affective, and behavioral processes. It can also arise from the deleterious effects due to the mode of ingestion and/or the metabolizing of the substance by the body on a physical level.

The psychoactive effects of various drugs can create changes and distortions in perception, sensory awareness, cognitive processing, affect, attentional control, and directed behavior, which may interfere with appropriate or adaptive coping or response to environmental tasks or demands (such as job performance or operating a motor vehicle). It is possible that with repeated or continued use, there may be a cumulative effect resulting in a chronic impairment of sensory or neural functioning. This impairment may be evident in a variety of behavioral and psychological manifestations. For instance, we have demonstrated that use of cigarettes and hard drugs was directly associated with dropping out of high school and decreased college involvement, while controlling for academic ability and educational aspirations (Newcomb & Bentler, 1986a). Although the process is not understood clearly, it is apparent that drug use contributed in some fashion to the abandonment of socially valued educational pursuits. We suspect that drug use interferes with or impairs adequate functioning in important developmental roles (i.e., student). It is certainly possible that drug use impairs functioning in other important life roles or activities as well, such as spouse, parent, or provider.

Drug use may also have physical health consequences. Ingestion of various drug substances may interfere with natural metabolic processes and may degrade physical organs or systems. This may occur as a consequence of the route of ingestion or the metabolizing of the substance. For instance, intranasal use of cocaine may destroy nasal passages. On the other hand, a great demand is placed on the stomach, liver, and other organs to process the ethanol in alcoholic substances, often resulting in cirrhosis of the liver or stomach cancer (e.g., Gordon & Kannel, 1984). These results, however, are based typically on a "small subset of heavy consumers of alcohol variously labelled as 'alcoholic', 'excessive', 'immoderate', or 'intemperate' " (Richman & Warren, 1985, p. 254), and leave unanswered the questions of physical impairment in younger drinkers having a less lengthy history of alcohol consumption. Other substances, such as cannabis and cocaine, have received less attention and many questions remain regarding the physical consequences of these illicit substances.

One approach has been to compare common elements between drugs that have received extensive attention in terms of physical consequences and those which have not received such scrutiny. For instance, Clayton and Voss (n.d.) draw the analogy between cigarette smoking and marijuana use to hypothesize the potential physical deterioration that may result from marijuana use. They point out that both substances are smoked, but marijuana smoke is deeply inhaled and retained (a significant mortality factor in cigarette smoking), and more is smoked of a marijuana joint than a tobacco cigarette. They report further that clinical studies of chronic marijuana users have observed respiratory symptoms similar to heavy cigarette smokers (e.g., laryngitis, cough, hoarseness, bronchitis, cellular change), that benzopyrene (a known carcinogen) is significantly more concentrated in marijuana smoke than cigarette smoke, and that more than half of daily marijuana using teenagers also smoke cigarettes daily. They conclude that "the probability is high that the long-term health effects attributable to marijuana will resemble those now attributable to cigarette smoking" and that "the synergistic effects of use of all of these [licit and illicit] drugs on morbidity and mortality rates may be monumental" (Clayton & Voss, n.d., p. 41). And the effects of smoking on respiratory impairment in adolescence are evident after only a few years of smoking (Adams et al., 1984).

On the other hand, it is important to determine whether positive consequences of drug use exist. For example, Richman and Warren (1985) have found that beer consumption was related to reduced morbidity, as has been noted for moderate use of other alcoholic beverages. It is possible that certain substances, most likely used in moderation, may actually reduce stress, enhance well-being, facilitate social interaction, and improve health.

Developmental Lag

Most researchers and scientists identify the period of adolescence as preparatory for the entry into adult life. It is a critical period for the formation of competencies and behaviors that are necessary for the successful acquisition of adult roles, such as spouse, parent, and provider. Baumrind and Moselle (1985) hypothesize that drug use during this important developmental period may impede further psychosocial maturing and create a "hiatus in identity formation." They identify six processes that can occur due to drug use that will result in this developmental delay. Specifically, psychoactive drug use during the teenage years may (a) obscure the differentiation between contexts of work and play (*play*, defined by Piaget [1962], is the use of preexisting schemes of action; assimilation rather than accommodation); (b) promote a false perception of reality and thus reduce reality testing; (c) reinforce the sense of being special and engender egocentric preoccupation; (d) allow the avoidance of realistic and necessary confrontation with environmental demands and responsibilities; (e) consolidate the cultural relativism, negativism, and rebelliousness characteristic of adolescents; and (f) permit the illusory sense of emancipation, while in fact reinforcing regressive parent-child interactions. In these ways, Baumrind and Moselle (1985) suggest that adolescent drug use interferes with the stage-sequential processes of development. As a result, drug-using adolescents may as adults "remain in limbo, suffering from symptoms of diffuse identity, marked by prolonged aimlessness and lack of clarity about goals" (p. 52). These hypotheses have not been tested with data, and thus the theory has no empirical support at this time.

DOMAIN Model

The DOMAIN model of drug use is an interactive framework that hypothesizes general relationships between specific domains of biological, intrapersonal, interpersonal, and sociocultural influences (e.g., Huba & Bentler, 1982; Huba et al., 1980). Drug use is considered an aspect of the Behavioral Styles domain, and is assumed to exert a direct influence or lead to consequences or changes in organismic status, depletion of socioeconomic resources, modification of psychological states (cognition, affect, personality, perception, and consciousness), affect self-perceived behavioral pressure, create shifts in intimate support systems, and change environmental stress.

The main tests of these hypotheses have been between drug use and the domain of psychological status, although some analyses have focused on how substance use can also influence other facets of the Behavioral Styles domain (e.g., deviance). The DOMAIN model provides a useful framework for cataloguing various results and for making general predictions and hypotheses. It does not, however, contain enough specificity to offer precise expectations about how drug use affects later outcomes in more detailed and process-oriented ways.

Etiology Predicts Outcome

Some have suggested that the specific motivation for drug use will determine, to a large extent, the consequences of use. For instance, Carman (1979) believes that "personal effects motivation" for drug use leads to the most problematic users.

In other words, those who indulge in drug use for self-medication purposes, to relieve psychological distress or avoid difficult challenges, rather than for social reasons (peer pressure, to fit in, or disinhibition) will have the greater problems due to their drug use. Baumrind and Moselle (1985) point out that "high-school adolescents seldom have either the commitment or the established work-skills to self-medicate in a disciplined fashion" and that "use of drugs enables adolescents to avoid experiencing the disequilibrating demand characteristics of an environment which would otherwise motivate them to cope, and in the process progressively to acquire more differentiated and integrated systems of action" (p. 55). Thus if drug use is chosen to deal with troubles and life problems, the real issues do not get dealt with and the adolescent will not have acquired the necessary coping skills with which to face life problems in the future. As a result, the particular and specific reasons or motivating factors to use drugs are considered the most important bases for determining the consequences of drug use.

Consolidation of Regressive Coping

Another theory suggests that drug use does not directly cause problems, but allows problems to be dealt with in an inefficient and regressive manner. Hendin and Haas (1985) examined the adaptive significance of chronic and heavy marijuana use among adolescents and young adults. Among college students, they found that marijuana use was not responsible in any direct or simplified way with poor school performance, nor was it used in reaction to poor academic achievement. They did not find that heavy marijuana use was the direct cause of problems, but served to

> help maintain them [the subjects] in a troubled adaptation, reinforcing their tendency not to look at, understand, or attempt to master their difficulties. It served to detach them from their problems, and helped them to regard even serious difficulties as unimportant. Marijuana provided a buffer zone of sensation that functioned as a barrier against self-awareness and closeness to others.

Among adolescents, they noted that marijuana allowed them the opportunity "to avoid choices and challenges associated with growing up." And as adults, they may be obliged by time to make choices for which they are not prepared, resulting in outcomes with which they will not be satisfied. Similarly, Baumrind and Moselle (1985) fear that drug use among adolescents will consolidate and entrench feelings of alienation and estrangement endemic to the teenager.

Amotivational Syndrome

The amotivational syndrome is characterized by "a pattern of apathetic withdrawal of energy and interest from effortful activity, an uncertainty about long-range goals with resultant mental and physical lethargy, a loss of creativity, and social withdrawal from demanding social stimuli" (Baumrind & Moselle, 1985, p. 55). Although these symptoms may occur without the presence of drug use, and in fact are characteristic of the normal adolescent crisis (e.g., Mellinger, Somers, Davidson, & Manheimer, 1976), prolonged use of drugs, and marijuana in particular, may intensify and consolidate these symptoms. Such an expectation is based on neurophysiological action of cannabinoids on the limbic system-cortical connections (e.g., Miller, 1979) and clinical reports (e.g., Baumrind & Moselle, 1985). Amotivational syndrome typically has been operationalized as lowered achievement levels, diffuse career objectives, and abandonment of academic pursuits. Kandel (1978) reviewed relevant research and concluded that these problems generally preceded drug use, and thus could not be a consequence of marijuana use. Baumrind and Moselle (1985) point out, however, that such results do not eliminate the possibility that drug use may consolidate these symptoms and inhibit further development.

Psychosocial Dysfunction

Another perspective is offered by Baumrind and Moselle (1985), who suggest that drug use permits or encourages the avoidance of normal engagement in human relationships and stressful interactions that is necessary for the acquisition of knowledge about the self and others. They contend that to the extent that adolescent drug users attain a feeling of closeness and commitment with others as a result of drug-induced dissolution of boundaries or distinctions, they will fail to acquire the skills necessary to achieve those states without drugs. By basing personal relationships on a private drug experience, adolescents may erode or "stunt" the very relationships they seek to cultivate. (p. 58)

They identify five psychosocial dysfunctions resulting from drug use that may facilitate this process of retarded development. These include escapism, egocentrism, external locus of control, self-derogation, and alienation and estrangement.

Use Generates Abuse

Misuse or abuse of drugs has been considered prima facie evidence for negative consequences of substance use. For instance, drug use in and of itself has been considered a major health problem of national concern (Matarazzo, 1982). Thus one possible consequence of drug use is continued use possibly leading to chronic drug abuse (e.g., Fillmore, 1974). In addition, it has been fairly well documented that heavy use of one substance predicts involvement with other harder substances. For instance, alcohol use precedes cannabis use, which in turn precedes hard drug use including cocaine (e.g., Clayton & Voss, n.d.; Kandel, 1973; Kandel & Faust, 1975; Huba, Wingard, & Bentler, 1981; Newcomb & Bentler, 1986b). More recently, we have found that several miniscquences characterized this stage notion of drug involvement (Newcomb & Bentler, 1986c). Thus one consequence of drug use is the potential or the probability of involvement with harder drugs or polydrug involvement (e.g., Donovan & Jessor, 1983). Each stage of drug use can lead to a family of consequences that may differ from the consequences of use of another drug (e.g., Kandel et al., 1986).

The consequences of chronic drug abuse can be an accumulation of short-term intoxication effects or other consequences that form a long-standing pattern. Such long-term consequences may accrue because short-term negative or problematic results are not attended to or ameliorated, for example, by appropriate coping behavior. In fact, recent research suggests that drug consumption and the experience of adverse consequences of use are only moderately correlated (e.g., Sadava, 1985), suggesting that negative consequences may be insufficient to inhibit further drug use. In other words, heavy consumption or abuse of drugs is a necessary but not sufficient condition to elicit negative consequences. Sadava (1985) suggests, but does not test, that the discriminating feature is a vulnerability to drug-related problems and negative consequences. He speculates that these vulnerabilities may be personalogical in nature and include "other health-risk or deviant behaviors, latent aggressive or depressive tendencies, psychological disorders, [and] differences in personal reactions to alcohol" (p. 396).

Although some studies have examined the personality predictors of adult alcoholism among clinical samples (e.g., Jones, 1968, 1971; Loper, Kammier, & Hoffman, 1973) and problem drinking behavior in adulthood (Donovan, Jessor, & Jessor, 1983), Chassin (1984) points out that

> none of these studies [has] examined the relationship between adolescent drinking [and drug use] patterns and adult alcoholism [drug abuse]. It would be particularly valuable to determine what patterns of adolescent use are associated with later adult drinking (drug) problems or whether particular motivations for substance use in adolescents have long-term negative implications. (p. 130)

Chassin (1984, p. 132) continues:

> There is a need to distinguish patterns and determinants of substance use that is relatively benign from those types of use that are problematic. Adolescent substance use may be problematic if it is associated with immediate negative health consequences, impaired functioning, or psychological distress . . . [or] if it results in either long-term negative physical health outcomes or the development of clinical drug dependence in adulthood. Currently, little information exists concerning the long-range implications of adolescent substance use.

Jessor, Chase, and Donovan (1980) defined an adolescent as a problem drinker if they reported being intoxicated more than six times in the past year or if they reported negative consequences of drinking at least two times in the past year in at least three areas of life (e.g., school, family, or legal problems). Predictors of problem drinking were similar to those of involvement with marijuana and other adolescent problem behaviors. Donovan, Jessor, and Jessor (1983) found that there was greater continuity in non-problem drinking from adolescence to young adulthood than for problem drinking over the same period of time. Greater continuity of problem drinking was found for men (43%) than women (27%). Problem drinkers as adults were, in adolescence, more tolerant of deviance, less religious, and had low values and expectations for academic achievement. Fillmore (1975) found in an educated sample over a 20-year period from young adulthood to middle age, that "the common denominator for predicting later from earlier problems among both men and women consisted of some kind of heavy intake of alcohol whether designated as frequent intoxication or binge drinking" (p. 904).

Problem Behavior Theory

Problem Behavior Theory, as developed and tested by Jessor and Jessor (1977, 1978), hypothesizes that drug involvement is one facet of a syndrome related to deviance proneness or nontraditionality. In a recent paper, Donovan and Jessor (1985) demonstrated that various components of problem behavior among adolescents tend to be generated by one underlying latent construct. This construct was found to account for the interrelationships among problem drinking, illicit drug use, delinquent-type behavior, and precocious sexual involvement. Although the primary focus of this theory has been on the etiological predictors of problem behavior, including drug use (e.g., Jessor & Jessor, 1977), there has been some speculation regarding the possible interinfluences of various problem behaviors. For example, Osgood (1985) used three waves of Monitoring the Future data (e.g., Bachman et al., 1984) to examine the across-time structural relationships between criminal behavior, various measures of drug use, and problem driving. There was a common cause or underlying construct of deviant or problem behavior that remained stable across time, but did not cross-generate between specific types of behaviors. Problem behavior theory and these results suggest that the consequences of drug use are inextricably intertwined with other forms of deviant behavior, and that to study the consequences of drug use is to study also the consequences of general proneness to deviance. In this book, we are challenging this notion by attempting to test for specific consequences of drug use while controlling for general deviant attitudes (e.g., lack of social conformity). Although a somewhat difficult task, as will be seen below, we have been able to differentiate the effects of drug use from those of deviant attitudes, which is essential for determining the specific consequences of drug use.

Self-Derogation Theory

Self-derogation or self-rejection theory is a general developmental model proposed by Kaplan (1975, 1980, 1984, 1985, 1986) to account for a variety of deviant behaviors among adolescents. Although the model is designed as an explanation of drug use and involvement, various features of the theory permit predictions of consequences or outcomes of drug use. For instance, adolescents are presumed to initiate drug use because they have been "unable to meet the expectations that the person, as well as other group members, feels he should meet" (Kaplan, 1985, p. 481), leading to decreased self-worth and increased self-rejection. As a consequence of drug use, the adolescent should experience enhanced

> feelings of self-worth by symbolizing attacks upon the worth of the values according to the standards of which the youth was judged unworthy: by permitting intrapsychic or interpersonal withdrawal from the conventional value system according to the standards of which the youth was a failure, or by permitting the substitution of new (deviant) standards that are more easily achieved than the earlier conventional ones. (Kaplan, 1985, p. 481)

In other words, according to this theory, drug use should increase self-worth, decrease self-rejection, and encourage detachment from traditional roles and attitudes in favor of deviant attitudes and behavior. Of course, this is a gross simplification of a very complex and interactive theory that is only now attempting to grapple with the consequences of drug involvement.

Role Compatibility Theory

Kandel (1984; Yamaguchi & Kandel, 1985a, 1985b) proposes that illicit drug use (in particular, marijuana) is at odds with the acquisition of typical and normative adult roles during the transition from adolescence to young adulthood. These roles typically involve a fixed sequence of school, work, and marriage (e.g., Hogan, 1981). She sees marijuana use as incompatible with adequate or optimal participation in these roles, requiring a resolution of this conflict. This resolution may take the form of role socialization (giving up the deviant behavior) or role selection (changing the role and maintaining the deviant behavior). Using detailed retrospective data, Yamaguchi and Kandel (1985a) examined this role selection/ role socialization hypothesis in regard to the transition to marriage. They found that marijuana use was associated with postponement of marriage and parenthood, and that it increased the risk of marital dissolution. Again using their retrospective data, Yamaguchi and Kandel (1985b) studied these processes as they related to drug use and cohabitation. They found that marijuana use increased the probability of cohabiting. Further, they found that marijuana use indirectly influenced the number of cohabitations by lengthening the postponement of marriage, and thereby increasing the risk of multiple cohabitations. For women, cohabitation reduced marijuana use (role socialization), whereas separation from a cohabital partner was related to illicit drug use other than marijuana.

Precocious Development

A new perspective that we would like to offer is that drug use accelerates development rather than delaying it. In other words, drug users tend to bypass or circumvent the typical maturational sequence of school, work, and marriage and become engaged in adult roles of jobs and family prematurely, without the necessary growth and development to enhance success with these roles. Thus drug users may develop a pseudomaturity that ill prepares them for the real difficulties of adult life. As a consequence, they will have a greater probability of failing at these roles over time.

Despite Yamaguchi and Kandel's (1985a) observation that drug use delays or postpones marriage and family roles, we have found that high school drug use predicts early entry into marriage, cohabitation, and employment (Newcomb & Bentler, 1985). This fits into a role selection theory, because use of drugs (perceived as adult and mature) leads to an enactment of this pseudomaturity by dropping out of school, joining the work force, and developing a sexual relationship (e.g., cohabitation, marriage). Drug-using high school students are often perceived as hip, mature, streetwise, and more adult than their non-drug-using peers. We have also noted the role socialization process occurring, when those who marry early decrease their illicit drug use as a function of their role (Newcomb & Bentler, 1987a). Further, work force involvement (an adult role) did not lead to role socialization, because this activity at a young age was associated with increased drug involvement. We did observe, however, the impact of environmental demand characteristics. For instance, those who joined the military increased their use of tolerated or condoned substances (cigarettes and alcohol), while reducing their use of restricted substances (cannabis and hard drugs). This suggests that the impact of precocious development as a result of drug use is not obviated entirely by role socialization processes (i.e., modifying use). Further, simply quitting drug use will not guarantee the acquisition of important capacities that were not acquired due to the precocious development. Drug use in the military, however, has been characterized as an adolescent misbehavior problem (Beary, Mazzuchi, & Richie, 1983). From this perspective, joining the military may not reflect so much a step toward adult maturity as an extended adolescence with continuing types of teenage problems and acting out.

Our model is in line with Baumrind and Moselle's (1985) notion that adolescent drug use interferes with the critical development of interpersonal skills, coping abilities, and cognitive sophistication, which are necessary to participate effectively in adult roles. In this theory, however, the crucial mechanism is the foreshortening of the critical developmental period, rather than the delay as suggested by Baumrind and Moselle. In other words, there is not simply a gap in development due to drug use, but rather a truncation of vital developmental sequences and the premature immersion into adult roles.

This process is facilitated by the self-perception of maturity and adultlikeness of the drug user, which is then validated by their drug-using peers and confirmed by the respect from their non-drug-user classmates. This respect is not so much based on drug use per se, which many non-drug users will disdain and reject, but by the accoutrements of other desired adult behaviors exhibited by the drug users (e.g., precocious sexual involvement, independence). Much of what constitutes problem behavior in adolescents is not so much true illegal behavior as status crimes. For instance, drinking may be considered a problem behavior among teenagers, but may be condoned, if not encouraged, among adults. Similarly, sexual involvement, a typical feature of normal adult life, is considered by society as a problem behavior among teenagers. Thus it can be easily seen that various behaviors associated with drug use, as well as drug use itself, may be self-perceived and perceived by others as adult and mature among adolescents. This in turn propels that drug user into adult roles prematurely, while forsaking the opportunities of education, trial and error, and the critical experience and learning process of struggling to develop interpersonal relationships, adequate coping styles, and cognitive facility.

One assumption underlying this theory is that precocious development may be generated by an inability or discomfort at delaying gratification. There may be a strong drive and need to grow up quickly and enjoy the positive aspects of adulthood, without waiting until this would naturally occur. As a result, the rewarding aspects of adulthood are sought and coveted (i.e., drug use, autonomy, sexual involvement), while avoiding the more difficult tasks of adulthood that would be gained with experience and maturity (e.g., responsibility, forethought).

The roots of this process may stretch back into childhood. For instance, Funder, Block, and Block (1983) found that four-year-old boys who exhibited the least ability to delay gratification later displayed aspects of ego undercontrol. These qualities included being emotionally expressive, aggressive, irritable, and immature under stress. Among an older age group, Wertheim and Schwartz (1983) found that depressed college males used a present-oriented self-management strategy for handling of events. They preferred to delay aversive events and to choose small immediate rewards over large delayed ones. The authors interpret this to mean that strategies that emphasize short-term positive affective consequences (immediate gratification) may lead to low levels of positive reinforcements over time, creating a life situation characterized by many punishments and few large rewards.

There is some evidence to suggest that physical or biological processes may influence precocious development (e.g., Magnusson, Stattin, & Allen, 1985), which then interact with psychosocial processes (e.g., Brooks-Gunn et al., 1985; Lerner, 1985). For instance, Magnusson et al. (1985) compared early and late maturing teenage girls (based on age at menarche) and found some quite revealing differences between these groups. The early maturing girls ditched school, smoked hashish, drank alcohol heavily, committed thefts, and ignored parental rules more often than late maturing girls. Early maturity was also related to lowered educational attainment in these girls.

It is also probable that precocious development is facilitated by sensitivity and responsiveness to peer pressures consistent with a perception of adulthood, such as the pressure to appear independent, the pressure for recognition, the pressure to appear mature or grown-up, and the pressure to have fun. These four types of pressure have been proposed as components of peer pressure leading to initiation of smoking (Newman, 1984). Compliance with these peer pressures without a concomitant building of competence, a sense of balance for current goals versus long-range goals, and development of mature psychological mechanisms to deal with the tasks of adolescence and impending adulthood, are liable to lead to pseudomaturity rather than the real thing.

Precocious development theory is distinct from problem behavior theory (e.g., Donovan & Jessor, 1985) in that the syndrome of behaviors underlying precocious development may be both positively and negatively valued and are not uniformly seen as problems or deviant. For instance, precocious development theory would predict early involvement in the work force and various types of early independent behavior, which may not be considered problematic, and may perhaps even be desired or condoned behavior. The underlying motivation is to engage in adult behaviors that are rewarding at an age that is generally considered to be premature for such behavior. As with the other theories regarding drug use consequences, very little research has been done that can apply to these hypotheses, let alone directly test them. This is a vital and fruitful area for future research that will bridge the gap between adolescent development theories and research on consequences of teenage drug use. One cannot progress without the other, because drug use in modern society is such a pervasive component of a teenager's life (whether using substances or resisting their use).

Summary

Although the theories reviewed above certainly offer some meaningful direction for empirical research, many have not received any data-based testing. So, although it would be useful to cite various studies that address the hypotheses in these theories, this is not possible due to the scarcity of such studies. Similarly, there has been little general research, let alone theory-based investigations, of the consequences of adolescent drug use. As Kandel (1978) pointed out several years ago, which is equally true today: "Much less attention has been directed to investigation of the consequences of drug use than to the determinants" (p. 27). Several studies, however, have yielded results that either directly or tangentially bear on the issues of drug use consequences. Some of these have been cited above in support of various theories. In the following chapters, we review selectively some research that has shed light on the consequences of teenage drug use, while testing for various impacts of early drug use on later life. The findings are organized around seven areas of life that could possibly be affected by drug use. These include consequences related to family formation, deviance, sexual behavior, education, livelihood, mental health, and social integration.

3

Study Design
and Sample

The Longitudinal Study

This study began in 1976 and was designed to follow a group of adolescents through the teenage years in order to determine the etiological factors in acquiring drug-taking behaviors. A group of 1634 students in the seventh, eighth, and ninth grades provided complete data in the first year of the study in which an excessively large student pool was chosen in order to obtain about 1000 complete sets of student, close-friend, and parent triads who could be linked. Informed consent was obtained from both the teenager and their parents, and a best friend if possible, after the approval had been obtained for participation in the study by the school district, the school principal, and the teacher within the school, who permitted informed consent forms to be taken home. Each participant was informed that their responses were protected legally by a grant of confidentiality from the U.S. Department of Justice. Unfortunately, we do not have detailed information regarding the total sampling frame (or universe of subjects) from which our initial sample was drawn. All students were located at 11 Los Angeles County schools in five school districts and were roughly representative of schools in the county, in terms of socioeconomic status and ethnicity. This comparability was achieved by slightly oversampling lower-socioeconomic status schools, with three high and three medium, but five lower-socioeconomic status schools partici-pating. The oversampling at the school level was done to offset an expected lowered level of voluntary individual research participation among students and parents from the lower-socioeconomic status schools. Our subjects did not seem unusual (except for a larger percentage of girls than boys) in any critical ways, revealed a high degree of heterogeneity and variance on most variables, and appeared quite similar to other samples of that age. At this initial testing with self-administered questionnaires, students provided information regarding their drug use, personality, attitudes toward drugs, peer interaction patterns, and perceived drug use in others.

Data were collected at four other occasions from these same participants during a period of eight years. These retestings occurred at years 2, 4, 5, and 9 of the study. At each testing, the questionnaire was expanded and refined so that, by years 5 and 9, a rather extensive assessment of many life areas were obtained. The year 5 (1980) data were collected when subjects were in late adolescence, either just completing high school or recently graduated. The young adult data were collected four years later when all participants were in their early twenties. This data collection occurred in 1984.

Over the years, the focus of the study has shifted from one of etiology to consequences of drug use. The etiological phase of the study resulted in many important findings regarding the initiation of drug use among teenagers (e.g., Huba & Bentler, 1980, 1983a, 1984; Huba et al., 1981; Newcomb et al., 1983; Newcomb & Harlow, 1986; Newcomb, Maddahian, & Bentler, 1986). These analyses typically focused on the first five years of data. The last follow-up (year 9 in 1984) assessed a wide range of possible outcomes, qualities, or events that might be influenced by earlier drug use. These are the consequences that form the basis of this book.

In 1984, data were collected from 739 young adults from our original sample. This represents a 45% retention rate over the entire eight-year period of the study. This rate of subject loss is not unusual among real-world studies of this type. Various attrition analyses are presented below. The loss of subjects between late adolescence (year 5) and young adulthood (year 9) was not primarily due to voluntary withdrawal from the study (less than 5% actually refused to continue). This loss of subjects was largely the result of the difficulty and frequent inability to recontact all subjects during that very mobile and change-laden period in life from adolescence to young adulthood. In fact, many participants had to be traced to places throughout the country and all over the world. This book is based on the 654 subjects who provided data in years 1, 5, and 9 of the study. Each young adult was paid $12.50 to complete the follow-up questionnaire. Based on the analyses reported below as well as the conditions of anonymity, privacy, and long-term relationship of subjects to researchers under which the data were obtained, we expect our survey to generate valid findings (Johnston & O'Malley, 1985).

Sample Description

Table 3.1 presents the sample description for all 654 subjects, and males and females separately at the young adult follow-up. In the sample, 70% were women and 30% were men. Current age ranged from 19 to 24 years old, with a mean of 21.9. About 34% of the sample were from minority backgrounds (Black, Hispanic, and Asian), 93% were high school graduates, and average income was between $5,000 and $15,000. Women reported having had more children than did the men in the sample. The most frequent current life pursuit was full-time employment, followed by attending a university, and then junior college. The "other or none" life pursuit category included predominantly women who were full-time housewives and/or mothers. The most typical living arrangement was staying with parents. Men were more likely to live with roommates and less likely to be married than women. The "other" living arrangement category was split between being single parents (living with son or daughter) and living with other relatives who were not one's parents (e.g., sibling, cousin, grandparents).

When these participant characteristics were compared to national surveys of young adults (e.g., Bachman et al., 1984; Miller et al., 1983) and other samples of young adults (e.g., Donovan et al., 1983; Kandel, 1984), very similar patterns were noted. This group of young adults does not appear markedly different from young adults in general regarding life activity or living arrangements. The main difference is that the current

TABLE 3.1
Description of the Sample as Young Adults (1984)

Variable	Male	Female	Total
N	192	462	654
Age			
Mean	21.86	21.90	21.90
Range	19-24	20-24	19-24
Ethnicity			
Black	12%	16%	15%
Hispanic	8%	11%	10%
White	70%	64%	66%
Asian	10%	9%	9%
High school graduate			
yes	94%	93%	93%
no	6%	7%	7%
Number of children			
none	96%	80%	85%
one	3%	18%	14%
two	1%	1%	1%
three	0%	1%	0%
Income for past year			
none	3%	12%	9%
under $5,000	31%	34%	34%
$5,001 to $15,000	51%	44%	45%
over $15,001	15%	10%	12%
Living situation			
alone	3%	4%	4%
parents	52%	46%	48%
spouse	7%	21%	17%
cohabitation	9%	9%	9%
dormitory	8%	5%	6%
roommates	16%	11%	12%
other	5%	4%	4%
Current life activity			
military	7%	1%	3%
junior college	9%	13%	12%
four-year college	24%	20%	21%
part-time job	14%	14%	14%
full-time job	46%	47%	47%
none or other	0%	5%	3%

sample has a greater percentage of women than men, as it had since the study began.

Although it may seem unusual to have such a large percentage of the sample living at home as young adults (52% of the men and 46% of the women), recent evidence indicates that this reflects a U.S. national trend. For instance, based on data from the U.S. Census Bureau, Glick and Lin (1986) found that 45% of 20- to 24-year-olds were living with their parents in 1984. This percentage is quite similar to that obtained in our sample and emphasizes, that at least on several indices, our young adult subjects are fairly characteristic of national norms.

Attrition Analyses

In the first year of the study (1976), 64% of the sample were female and 36% were males, whereas in high school (1980) 68% were females and 32% were males. This indicates that the differential representation by sex in the young adult sample (1984) was also evident in the original sample and was not solely a result of differential attrition.

A series of analyses were run to determine whether the attrition in sample size from 1976 (year 1) to 1984 (junior high school to young adulthood) was due to any systematic influence. Those who were able to be located and who provided completed questionnaires in 1984 were compared with those who were not assessed in 1984 in terms of data obtained in 1976. These groups were contrasted in terms of 13 different drug substances and also 25 personality traits from the 1976 data set. Using the Bonferroni procedure to adjust for multiple simultaneous comparisons, not one of these 38 variables was able to differentiate significantly the new sample from those lost at the .05 level of significance. The average (absolute) point biserial correlation for these 38 tests was .04, whereas the average squared correlation was .002. The largest difference accounted for less than 1% of the variance between groups and was not significant when using the Bonferroni method to correct for capitalizing on chance. These analyses indicate that very little of the attrition rate between 1976 and 1984 was due to self-selection based on drug use or personality traits. To tease out any remaining differences, a step-wise multiple regression analysis was run using the 38 1976 drug use and personality variables as the predictor pool, and retention in 1984 as the criterion variable. Using this procedure, nine variables were chosen to differentiate the groups. Although significant, this equation, created by selecting all of the best predictors, was only able to account for less than 5% of the variance between groups. Those who continued in the study reported more beer use, less cigarette use, less attractiveness, more generosity, more intelligence, more vulnerability, less liberalism, less orderliness, and more trustful qualities in 1976 than those who, for reasons discussed above, did not continue in this study.

In a hierarchical fashion, we then added sex and ethnicity (as dummy variables) to the attrition prediction equations. Sex accounted for 1% of the unique variance in attrition (equivalent to its zero-order association with attrition), and ethnicity accounted for less than 3% of the unique attrition variance. Although quite small, these additional effects indicate that those who were most likely to continue in the study were female, White, Asian, and not Black. There were no differential effects for Hispanics. These attrition effects, however, were surprisingly small, considering the lengthy period of the study and the loss of subjects.

These extensive analyses indicate that the loss of subjects between 1976 and 1984 was only slightly due to systematic self-selection or other influences based on personality, drug use, ethnicity, or sex (Newcomb, 1986a).

Of the 739 current subjects, 654 had provided data in 1980, representing a 73% recapture rate from the previous data point. A series of analyses were run to determine whether the attrition in sample size from 1980 to 1984 was due to any systematic influence. We compared those we were able to locate and who provided completed questionnaires in 1984 with those we failed to assess in 1984 in terms of data obtained in 1980. We contrasted these groups in terms of the 26 different drug substances and 23 personality, emotional distress, and social support scales from the 1980 data set. Using the Bonferroni procedure to adjust for multiple simultaneous comparisons, not one of these 49 variables was able to differentiate significantly the new sample from those lost at the .05 level of significance. The average (absolute) point biserial correlation for these 49 tests was .03, while the average squared correlation was .002. The largest difference accounted for only

1% of the variance between groups and was not significant when using the Bonferroni method to correct for capitalizing on chance. These analyses indicate that very little of the attrition rate between 1980 and 1984 was due to self-selection based on drug use or personality traits. To tease out any remaining differences, a step-wise multiple regression analysis was run using the 49 1980 drug use and personality variables as the predictor pool and retention in 1984 as the criterion variable. Using this procedure, five variables were chosen to differentiate the groups. Although significant, this equation, choosing all of the best predictors, was only able to account for less than 3% of the variance between groups. This rather trivial (in terms of magnitude) result indicates that those who continued in the study reported more hard liquor use, more amyl nitrate use, less cocaine use, less ambition, and more leadership qualities in 1980 than those who for reasons discussed above did not continue in the study. These extensive analyses indicate that the loss of subjects between 1980 and 1984 was not largely due to systematic self-selection or other influences based on personality, emotional distress, social support, or drug use.

Comparisons of
Drug Use Frequencies

One constant concern in longitudinal drug studies is that the heavier drug users tend to drop out over time. This damages the sample in terms of representativeness, decreases the variance on drug use items, and seriously questions the results obtained from such a restricted sample.

Using the 1982 data provided by the NIDA-sponsored National Household Survey of Drug Use (Miller et al., 1983) and the recent 1985 data from the same project (NIDA, 1986), we compared the lifetime prevalence and current prevalence between our longitudinal sample and these nationally representative stratified random samples. We focused on the 18- to 24-year-old age group in these national samples, because they were closest in age to our young adult sample.

The Household Surveys assessed 10 classes of drugs that were used for nonmedical purposes without a physician's prescription. These 10 categories of drugs included the legal use of alcohol and cigarettes, the illicit use of marijuana, hallucinogens, cocaine, and heroin, and the nonmedical use of stimulants, tranquilizers, sedatives, and analgesics. An additional scale was created for any nonmedical use of the last four drugs in the 1982 sample. Using the definitions provided in the National Household Survey (Miller et al., 1983) for each substance use category, we created similar categories from our drug use questionnaires. Table 3.2 provides a comparison of our sample and the National Household Survey sample on the lifetime prevalence of all drug use categories.

Our lifetime prevalence estimates are quite conservative. These were calculated on four waves of data over the eight-year period of our study. The first wave (1976) determined lifetime prevalence, whereas all other assessments were based on the previous six months. A subject was considered a user of a particular substance if he or she acknowledged any use of the drug at any of the four assessments. Thus it is extremely likely that a good deal of experimental use went undetected in our design; for 6.5 years during adolescence and young adulthood, we have no assessments of their drug use.

Also included in Table 3.2 are point-biserial correlation sex differences on the lifetime prevalence rates from our sample. Males were coded "1" and females were coded "2," so that a positive correlation would indicate that the women had the higher prevalence rate. As apparent in the table, none of these correlations was significant. Thus, in our sample, lifetime prevalence of drug use was equivalent between men and women for all types of substances.

We contrasted our lifetime prevalence rates with those of the 1982 National Survey using confidence interval estimates provided in the National Survey. There were no significant differences in lifetime prevalence of drug use between our sample (indicated as UCLA) and the 1982 national sample for use of hallucinogens, heroin, sedatives, analgesics, and cigarettes. The UCLA sample reported significantly higher lifetime prevalence of use for marijuana, cocaine, stimulants, tranquilizers, alcohol, and any nonmedical drug use. On no drug

TABLE 3.2
Comparison of Lifetime Young Adult Drug Use Prevalence Between the 1982 and 1985 National Household Surveys and the 1984 UCLA Longitudinal Sample

Drug Category	1984 UCLA	r_{pb} Sex[a] Difference	Difference[b] Test	1982 National	Difference[b] Test	1985 National
Illicit use of						
marijuana	68.9	.03	>	64.1	>	60.5
hallucinogens	22.9	-.05	=	21.1	>	11.5
cocaine	40.3	.00	>	28.3	>	25.2
heroin	2.1	.00	=	1.2	=	1.2
Nonmedical use of						
stimulants	30.3	.04	>	18.0	>	17.3
tranquilizers	21.6	.04	>	15.1	>	12.2
sedatives	17.1	.02	=	18.7	>	11.0
analgesics	10.5	.02	=	12.1	=	11.4
any nonmedical use	40.5	.03	>	28.4	NA	NA
Legal use of						
alcohol	96.9	-.04	>	94.6	>	92.8
cigarettes	77.5	.00	=	76.9	=	76.1

a. Point-biserial correlation mean sex difference. A positive correlation indicates that the females had the higher rate.

b. Based on confidence interval estimates provided in the *National Survey:* > indicates that the UCLA sample had a significantly larger prevalence; = indicates that the prevalence rates were not significantly different; and < indicates that the national sample had a significantly larger prevalence.

did the national sample report a higher lifetime prevalence than our sample.

We next performed the same comparisons for the more recent 1985 national data (NIDA, 1986). Very similar results as those discussed above were found for the lifetime prevalence rates, with two exceptions: The UCLA sample reported significantly higher lifetime prevalence rates for hallucinogens and sedatives compared to the 1985 national survey.

We then looked at the current prevalence rates, which are presented in Table 3.3. In this case, the 1982 national sample was based on use during the past year, whereas our sample reported use during the past six months. Again, these results for our sample are quite conservative because of the different time frames. There were no significant differences between the 1982 national sample and the UCLA sample for current use of marijuana, hallucinogens, heroin, tranquilizers, and analgesics. The UCLA sample reported significantly higher current prevalence than the national sample for use of cocaine, stimulants, any nonmedical use, and alcohol. The national sample reported significantly higher current prevalence for use of sedatives and cigarettes. Only slight changes from these patterns were noted for the current prevalence rates in the 1985 survey: The UCLA sample reported significantly higher current use of marijuana and hallucinogens than the 1985 national sample, whereas no differences were found now for the use of sedatives and alcohol.

It is possible that drug use was higher in the western region of the United States where our UCLA sample was obtained. Regional breakdowns were provided for several drugs in the 1982 National Survey. These prevalence rates were compared to our sample and in all cases were not significantly different.

These careful comparisons with nationally representative samples indicate quite clearly that we have retained large portions of drug users in our sample; at least equivalent to national and western regional averages. Thus results based on our sample cannot be considered distorted because of losing the more deviant drug users from our sample. In fact, we have been fortunate to have retained many drug users in our sample, with many current and lifetime prevalence rates significantly

TABLE 3.3
Comparison of Current Young Adult Drug Use Prevalence Between the 1982 and 1985 National Household Surveys and the 1984 UCLA Longitudinal Sample

Drug Category	UCLA (past 6 months)	Difference[a] Test	1982 National (past year)	Difference[a] Test	1985 National (past year)
Illicit use of					
marijuana	42.8	=	40.4	>	36.8
hallucinogens	8.5	=	6.9	>	3.6
cocaine	33.8	>	18.8	>	16.2
heroin	.4	=	.5	=	1.0
Nonmedical use of					
stimulants	18.0	>	10.8	>	10.1
tranquilizers	6.9	=	5.9	=	6.4
sedatives	4.2	<	8.7	=	5.1
analgesics	4.7	=	8.7	=	6.7
any nonmedical use	22.1	>	16.1	NA	NA
Legal use of					
alcohol	90.0	>	83.4	=	87.2
cigarettes	39.1	<	47.2	<	45.0

a. Based on confidence interval estimates provided in the *National Survey:* > indicates that the UCLA sample had a significantly larger prevalence; = indicates that the prevalence rates were not significantly different; and < indicates that the national sample had a significantly larger prevalence.

higher than the national averages and equivalent to regional trends.

Changes in Drug Use

Frequency of use for 26 different drug substances was assessed during adolescence (year 5, 1980) and when the subjects were young adults (year 9, 1984). Comparing these reported levels of use, there were significant increases in use for cigarettes, caffeine, beer, wine, liquor, amphetamines, non-LSD psychedelics, cocaine, and nonprescription cold medication. Of these, the largest increments were for caffeine, all alcohol substances, and cocaine. Significant decreases in use were evident for use of marijuana, hashish, minor tranquilizers, barbiturates, sedatives, LSD, inhalants, and PCP. Clearly the most dramatic change in illicit substance use is the increase in cocaine use. As adolescents, 18% of the sample reported any use of cocaine in the past six months. As young adults, this number had increased to about one-third of the sample. Interestingly, the significant increase in cigarette smoking was not due to new people beginning use, but rather reflects an increase of use among those already smoking. Even though there has been a significant decrease in cannabis use between adolescence and young adulthood, over 40% of the newly assessed subjects reported marijuana use during the past six months. As adolescents, about 80% reported using some alcoholic drink in the preceding six-month period, whereas when these individuals were in their early twenties this figure rose to about 90%.

Although these figures indicate that some quite important changes in drug use have occurred between adolescence and young adulthood, it is also important to determine the stability of use over this period of time. Drug substances were averaged into five drug use categories: Cigarettes (1 item), alcohol (3 items), cannabis (2 items), hard drugs (15 items), and nonprescription medication (4 items). The correlation between adolescent cigarette use and young adult cigarette use was .63, whereas this correlation for alcohol was .53, .60 for cannabis, .48 for hard drugs, and .33 for nonprescription medication. Because varieties of drug use have been found to reflect a general factor of drug use, we used a latent construct of general adolescent drug use to predict a latent factor of general young adult drug use. General drug use at each point was assumed to be reflected by cigarette use, alcohol use, cannabis use, hard drug use, and nonprescription drug use. It was found that adolescent drug use accounted for 60% of the variation in young adult drug use. In other words, there was a moderate degree of stability as well as change in levels of substance use from adolescence to young adulthood, and the nature of this stability and change are important areas for future investigation of this data set. More details regarding patterns of stability and change in drug use over time in this sample are presented elsewhere (Newcomb & Bentler, 1986c, 1987a).

4

Constructs
and Measures

One of the key features of this longitudinal study of drug use consequences is a heavy reliance on the distinction between constructs and measures. In general, theories make statements about constructs. For example, the proposition that Social Conformity inhibits Drug Use is a proposition relating two abstract concepts of conformity and drug use, rather than a proposition about the effects of a specific measure of social conformity (e.g., law abidance, operationalized in a particular way based on particular items on a questionnaire) on a specific measure of drug use (e.g., cannabis use during the last month, operationalized with a given frequency rating scale). From the conceptual point of view, then, our research is attempting to evaluate propositions about constructs (which we write with capitals in order to make them distinct). In practice, of course, theoretical statements or hypotheses about constructs must be tested with observed variables, or measures, that are more or less adequate indicators of such constructs. In fact, care must be taken to design the study to assure that appropriate indicators of given constructs are available and have appropriate statistical properties (Bentler, 1978), so that latent variable methodologies can be utilized (see Chapter 5). There is no guarantee, for example, that outcome variables that were not specifically designed to capture the essence of certain constructs would empirically serve to identify latent variables when factor analyzed. Such a difficulty was encountered by Kandel et al. (1986).

In this chapter, we present the constructs that are used consistently in the subsequent empirical chapters that develop models for the impact of drug use on various areas of life. In order to familiarize the reader with the range of constructs included in the analyses of each chapter, a summary of the constructs used in each chapter is provided in Table 4.1. This table is organized according to chapter and is broken down into constructs from adolescence (in the left-hand column) and young adulthood (in the right-hand column). Details regarding the measured variables that are used as indicators of each construct, as well as various psychometric properties of these variables, are given in the Appendix.

Summary of All Constructs

There are nine empirical chapters in this book, each concerned with the impact of teenage drug use on a different area of life. Thus different constructs have been selected in each chapter to capture the specific area of life addressed in that chapter. For instance, in Chapter 8, concerned with Deviant Behavior, four constructs were chosen to represent potential consequences of teenage drug use in young adulthood. These four young adult constructs include Drug Crime Involvement, Violent Crime Involvement, Property Crime Involvement, and Criminal Activities (see Table 4.1). There were four predictor and control constructs selected from adolescence. These include Drug Use, Social Conformity, Criminal Activities, and Deviant Friendship Network. We suggest that the reader familiarize him- or herself with the constructs included in each chapter in a general way by examining Table 4.1. As will be evident, two constructs from adolescence are included consistently in each chapter. These are Drug Use and Social Conformity. Because these constructs are of such vital importance to all of our analyses, a detailed description of them is provided below.

Constructs Used in All Chapters

Two latent constructs, as reflected in six measured variables or scales, are included in all chapters except Chapter 14. These

TABLE 4.1
Constructs Included in Each Chapter

Adolescence	Young Adulthood

Chapter 6—Drug Use and Social Conformity

Drug Use	Drug Use
Social Conformity	Social Conformity

Chapter 7—Family Formation

Drug Use	Relationship Satisfaction
Social Conformity	Family Formation
Family Support	Relationship Importance
Parental Divorce	Cohabitation History
	Divorce Past 4 Years

Chapter 8—Deviant Behavior

Drug Use	Drug Crime Involvement
Social Conformity	Violent Crime Involvement
Criminal Activities	Property Crime Involvement
Deviant Friendship Network	Criminal Activities

Chapter 9—Sexual Behavior

Drug Use	Birth Control Effectiveness
Social Conformity	Dating Competence
Early Sexual Involvement	Satisfaction with Intimacy
Frequency of Sexual Events	Number of Relationships
Number of Sexually Active Friends	Frequency of Intercourse
Satisfaction with Opposite-Sex Relationships	Contracted Venereal Disease
	Abortion Occurrence

Chapter 10—Educational Pursuits

Drug Use	Educational Aspirations
Social Conformity	College Involvement
Academic Potential	Work Force Involvement
Income	Graduated from High School

Chapter 11—Livelihood Pursuits

Drug Use	Income
Social Conformity	Job Instability
Academic Potential	Job Satisfaction
Income	Collected Public Assistance
	Amount Worked Past Year

Chapter 12—Mental Health

Drug Use	Psychoticism
Social Conformity	Depression (CES-D)
Emotional Distress	Emotional Distress
	Purpose in Life
	Suicide Ideation

TABLE 4.1 Continued

Adolescence	Young Adulthood
Chapter 13—Social Integration	
Drug Use	Social Support
Social Conformity	Loneliness
Social Support	
Chapter 14—Large Integrated Model of Specific Drug Effects	
Alcohol Use	Family Formation
Cannabis Use	Relationship Satisfaction
Hard Drug Use	Drug Crime Involvement
Control Constructs	Criminal Activities
Social Conformity	Satisfaction with Intimacy
Family Support	Number of Relationships
Social Support	College Involvement
Criminal Activities	Job Instability
Early Sexual Involvement	Income
Academic Potential	Suicide Ideation
Income	Psychoticism
Emotional Distress	Loneliness

include Drug Use and Social Conformity from the adolescent data. Table 4.2 provides univariate statistics and mean sex differences for all scales that are used to reflect these two factors. Information is given for the mean, range, number of items in each scale, variance, skew, and kurtosis. Mean sex differences are tested with point-biserial correlations with women scored "2" and men scored "1." Thus a positive correlation indicates that the women had the larger value, whereas a negative correlation indicates that the men had the larger value. Point-biserial correlation mean difference tests are identical to the standard t-test, but have the advantage of providing the proportion of variance accounted for by the difference when squared.

Adolescent Drug Use

The Drug Use latent construct is reflected in three measured scales: alcohol frequency, cannabis frequency, and hard drug frequency. Each of these measures is a combined, multi-item scale from two time points in adolescence. The first is year 1 of the study when all subjects were in the seventh, eighth, or ninth grades. At that time, each participant indicated their lifetime

TABLE 4.2
Summary of Variable Characteristics for Measures Used in All Chapters

Latent Construct/ Measured Variable	Mean	Range	Number of Items	Variance	Skew	Kurtosis	Sex Difference[a] r_{pb}
Adolescence							
Drug Use							
alcohol frequency	2.41	1-5	6	4.80	.21	−.89	−.05
cannabis frequency	1.66	1-4.75	4	3.10	1.39	1.12	−.04
hard drug frequency	1.10	1-3.52	21	1.03	4.83	34.54	.05
Social Conformity							
law abidance	13.15	4-20	4	16.24	−.23	−.75	.15***
liberalism	9.96	4-19	4	6.92	.23	−.05	.02
religious commitment	15.57	4-20	4	15.21	−.75	−.18	.12**

a. A positive correlation indicates that the women had the larger value, whereas a negative correlation indicates the men had the larger value.

*p < .05; **p < .01; ***p < .001.

frequency of use for 11 different drug substances on five-point anchored rating scales that ranged from never (1) to regularly (5). These 11 items were averaged into three scales: alcohol (including beer, wine, and liquor), cannabis (including marijuana and hashish), and hard drugs (including cocaine, stimulants, sedatives, hallucinogens, inhalants, and narcotics). During late adolescence, in year 5 of the study, subjects provided frequency of use during the past six months for 21 different drug substances. Responses were given on seven-point anchored rating scales that ranged from never (1) to more than once per day (7). These 21 items were averaged into three scales analogous to those created from the early adolescent data: alcohol (including beer, wine, and liquor), cannabis (including marijuana and hashish), and hard drugs (including minor and major tranquilizers, sedatives, barbiturates, antidepressants, amphetamines, nonamphetamine stimulants, LSD, other psychedelics, amyl nitrate, other inhalants, heroin, other narcotics, cocaine, and PCP). Alcohol frequency is the average of the early and late adolescent scores on alcohol, cannabis frequency is the average of the early and late adolescent scores on cannabis, and hard drug frequency is the average of the early and late adolescent scores on hard drugs. Thus these drug use frequency measures provide combined information about the use of drugs in early adolescence and also in late adolescence. This should yield a fairly reliable measure of drug use involvement during the teenage years. Univariate statistics for these three frequency measures are given in Table 4.2.

These drug use measures form the central core of the analyses to follow. They represent the causal or antecedent condition against which changes in life functioning between adolescence and young adulthood are gauged. The separate measures of alcohol frequency, cannabis frequency, and hard drug frequency are assumed to reflect a general tendency toward Drug Use, identified as a latent construct. In the analyses to follow in subsequent chapters, we test for the impact of this latent factor of Drug Use on life functioning, as well as the specific impact of alcohol, cannabis, and hard drug use, as measured variables. Thus we can determine the influence of a general propensity to use drugs (the Drug Use factor), in addition to the influence of the three specific types of drug use (alcohol, cannabis, and hard drugs). In Chapter 14, we examine an even more differentiated group of substances.

Teenage drug use has been found to be acquired in a sequence of increasing involvement that progresses from one substance to another (e.g., Hays, Widaman, DiMatteo, & Stacy, 1987; Huba et al., 1981; Kandel & Faust, 1975; Newcomb & Bentler, 1986c). In general, high levels of alcohol use precede initiation to cannabis use, whereas high levels of cannabis use precede commencement of hard drug use (including cocaine; Newcomb & Bentler, 1986b). Our general Drug Use factor reflects this increasing involvement notion by tapping a continuous latent tendency to be involved with drug use, ranging from no use of any substance to high levels of use of all types of drugs (alcohol, cannabis, and hard drugs).

Social Conformity

The Social Conformity latent construct was assessed during year 5 of the study when subjects were in late adolescence. This latent factor was identified by three measured variable scales: law abidance, liberalism, and religious commitment (Stein, Newcomb, & Bentler, 1986a). Each of these scales consists of four self-description items in a five-choice semantic differential format, with opposite adjective phrases as anchor points (Huba & Bentler, 1982). Each scale asked the subject to rate him- or herself nearest the adjective phrase, "which describes you most of the time." The law abidance scale consists of these four items: (1) return incorrect change—willing to keep extra change, (2) might use a false ID—afraid to get caught, (3) might shoplift—wouldn't know how or want to, and (4) goodie-goodie honest type—not quite so honest. In scoring, the polarity of items 1 and 4 was reversed. The liberalism scale consists of these four items: (1) support women's liberation—don't feel women need or want it, (2) see cops as law enforcers—see cops as "pigs," (3) think police should carry guns—think cops shouldn't carry guns, and (4) approve of many protests—approve of few protests. In scoring, the polarity was reversed for items 1 and 4. The religious commitment scale consists of these items: (1) am not religious—am a religious person, (2) believe in religion or the Bible—believe in science, (3) feel that prayers are answered—feel that praying is a waste, and (4) think religion is outdated—think religion is not outdated. In scoring, the polarity was reversed in items 2 and 3.

This construct has been found to be a good predictor of teenage drug use (Huba & Bentler, 1982, 1984) and the development of this characteristic has been traced through adolescence (Huba & Bentler, 1983a). This construct reflects a degree of adherence to traditional values and conformity to societal norms. It does not represent conformity to one's particular peer culture. It is a continuous latent construct, which at the low end reflects a rejection of traditional values and societal norms, and an embracing, or least tolerance, of deviance, radical social change, and disadherence to social control (e.g., laws). As such, low scores represent a tendency toward deviance, nontraditionalism, or problem behavior.

Sex Differences

There were no significant sex differences on any of the three Drug Use scales. On the other hand, women were more law abiding and had more religious commitment than the men on these adolescent measures. Point-biserial correlations for these mean difference tests are given in Table 4.2.

5

Methodological Considerations and Analytic Approach

ll of the results to be reported in this book can be viewed from an empirical, predictive frame of reference. We attempt to determine to what extent various young adult behaviors and characteristics, especially drug use consequences, can be predicted from information obtained during early and late adolescence. Within such an empirical approach, perhaps the major novel feature of this longitudinal study is our extensive reliance on "latent" variables (as will be discussed below). At the very least, we are using these latent variables to correct for the unreliability of typical measured variables, so the predictions more accurately reflect unattenuated influences across time. We are striving to provide a set of analyses that go beyond the merely predictive, however, that also will allow stronger interpretations of a "causal" nature. In this approach, we do not imply that our "causal modeling" methods provide as strong a basis of inference as might be possible if one could study consequences of adolescent drug use into young adulthood using experimental methods. The reality is, however, that experimentation with random assignment of subjects to experimental conditions cannot be used, and we must rely on statistical controls to eliminate potential alternative explanations of results. Some concepts relevant to our causal modeling approach are the following.

Causal Inferences

We adopt some minimal, but necessary, conditions for interpretation of results within a causal framework. Three typical criteria for causation are (e.g., Clayton & Tuchfeld, 1982; Hirschi & Selvin, 1973) that (a) a statistically reliable association must exist between the cause and the effect, (b) the cause must precede the effect in a temporal sequence, and (c) the association between cause and effect must not be spurious (the result of a third factor that antecedently predicts both). These three conditions must be met before a causal inference can be established, and critiques (e.g., Baumrind, 1983) have not shown that these conditions are unnecessary or incorrect. In addition, a fourth criterion is commonly incorporated in our own work to strengthen the causal inference (e.g., Reichardt & Gollob, 1986). This additional condition stipulates that an earlier measure of the consequence variable should be included with the hypothesized causal or predicting factor at initial measurement. Such a design allows a control for contemporaneous associations, incorporates the stability of the consequence factor over time, and guarantees that the across-time effect represents a change in the consequence variable as a result of the causal or predictor variables, with initial status on the consequence variable controlled. Such a design is sometimes considered to be essential for appropriate inference (e.g., Bentler & Speckart, 1979; Gollob & Reichardt, 1987; Reichardt & Gollob, 1986). Mulaik (1987) discusses some of the broader philosophical issues associated with several conceptions of causality. Our interest focuses on the relatively narrow, but important, issues associated with appropriate statistical controls that make a causal interpretation at least potentially possible, even though these controls may be for unknown reasons insufficient to guarantee an appropriate causal inference.

The long-term consequences of drug use and the impact of drug use on developmental achievements (i.e., family formation, career), which are the focus of this book, tend to be more difficult to demonstrate in a scientifically rigorous manner than short-term or immediate effects. Immediate effects can, in fact, be studied quite well using experimental methods because most induced problems of a short-term nature are reversible and thus ethical constraints do not argue against experimentation. In contrast, long-term effects that could have serious lifelong implications—for example, failure to make the transition to adulthood successfully—cannot ethically be induced and must be studied in naturally occurring circumstances. As a result, these types of consequences have rarely been considered in the drug literature.

As compared to studies of drug use etiology, many more factors must be considered when attempting to account for a particular outcome and then establishing that a specific outcome occurred as a sole result of a specific type of drug use. This more difficult task of verifying drug use consequences across several years has largely been ignored in the literature in favor of determining the etiological factors of drug involvement. Drug use etiology is certainly an important process deserving of detailed research. Etiological studies of drug use, however, are more straightforward than consequence studies of drug use. In etiological studies, the task is to establish that drug use initiation (or an increase in drug involvement) is predicted directly (or indirectly) from an earlier influence. A universe of potential predictors of drug use exist, many of which meet the criteria of causality (as reviewed above). The study of consequences of drug use, however, attempts to evaluate whether a single causal variable—substance use—leads to a wide range of possible outcomes. Each of these possible outcomes has a universe of potential predictors, which also need to be controlled in order to prove that drug use significantly and uniquely contributes to the outcome. Thus the complexity of consequence studies is substantially greater than that of etiological studies: Consequence studies have many possible outcomes with many potential causes, while etiological studies have only one, or a few, possible outcomes (using drugs) with many potential causes. This level of complexity may be one of the reasons that so little research has been directed toward determining the consequences of adolescent drug use.

An example of the complexity of drug consequence research can be seen in the amount of effort, and years of study, it has taken to prove that cigarette smoking, by itself and holding all other factors constant, causes specific types of physical deterioration (Richmond, 1979). Cancer or cardiovascular disease are readily diagnosable under most circumstances. It is more difficult to determine the adequacy of adopting adult roles, the quality of life, and degree of successful social integration of adults—areas that can plausibly be affected by using drugs during adolescence. Thus when studying drug use consequences, it is vital to have a wide range of good measures at multiple time points in order to test and control for spurious influences. Similarly, it is valuable to have consistent and reliable measures of drug use. Finally, the outcome measures need to include detailed assessments of many life areas that could possibly be affected by earlier drug use. All of these components are included in our study of drug use consequences, which form the basis of this book. While we cannot claim that we will have controlled all possible potential confounding influences when evaluating the consequences of drug use—and we are to that extent vulnerable to critique based on arguments of having omitted some key control variable to rule out spuriousness—the range of variables included in this study (see Chapter 4) is sufficiently broad and based on prior work and theories in the field that we believe that few major omissions have been made. Thus we expect that "causal" interpretations of the statistical results are liable to be appropriate in most instances.

Analytic Method

Our primary method of analysis is latent-variable structural modeling (e.g., Bentler, 1980, 1986a; Connell & Tanaka, 1987; Judd, Jessor, & Donovan, 1986; Jöreskog, 1977; Bentler & Chou, 1987; Bentler & Newcomb, 1986a). We have chosen this approach for several reasons. First, this method permits us to examine the relationship among constructs that are unobserved (latent) and that are not influenced by errors of measurement. As a result, the latent factors or constructs become quite powerful and reflect the essence of the concept or tendency underlying the chosen indicators. Two or more measured or observed variables are necessary in order to identify a latent construct. These must be chosen extremely carefully to maintain conceptual clarity, and should be highly intercorrelated.

A second advantage of latent-variable models is that they are multivariate and can represent a complex ecology of variables in an elegant and parsimonious fashion. Multiple causes or consequences can be studied simultaneously. In this instance, numerous factors may be affecting young adult development or outcomes other than drug use and these other predictors can be included in the model to determine the unique contribution of drug use over and above these other plausible influences.

Third, latent-variable models are ideally suited for longitudinal analyses, because they permit the control of baseline associations among variables. Thus a significant regression effect noted across time is automatically interpretable as a partialed relationship that reflects the unique impact of one variable upon the other. To accomplish this, all variables within a particular time—in this case, adolescence or young adulthood—are allowed to correlate freely. No regression effects are imposed within occasion; these are only included across time.

Fourth, latent-variable models are confirmatory in nature and must be guided by appropriate hypotheses. At the minimum, these hypotheses concern the indicators of the latent constructs and which constructs to include in the models under study. A great deal of work must be invested prior to testing a model with these methods. For example, an adequate range of high quality, theoretically relevant indicators must be used if latent variable effects are to be studied. Although there are some empirical aspects to structural modeling, in general, it is not an exploratory procedure.

Another advantage of these methods is that they allow for the testing of relationships among various types of variables. Associations and effects can be studied among any latent or observed variables or the residuals of these variables (Bentler, 1987a; Bentler & Newcomb, in preparation), provided the model is identified. Thus we are not constrained to look only for standard effects between latent constructs, but can study the effects of specific variables in addition to the general factor that they represent. In particular, we are not going to constrain our models to be of the LISREL type (Jöreskog & Sörbom, 1985). Standard LISREL models do not permit a study of various types of nonstandard effects that we anticipate observing in these data. With a latent variable LISREL model, no paths are allowed between measured variables, no path is allowed from a measured variable residual to a common factor, and so on. Because we use the Bentler-Weeks (1980) model, as implemented in the EQS program (Bentler, 1986b), and designs and variables adequate to studying nonstandard effects, we do not anticipate the problem encountered by Kandel et al. (1986) of having to abandon the search for exclusive effects of specific types of drugs.

As in path analysis, the empirical quality of latent-variable models can be evaluated by several overall fit indices. Thus the adequacy of the total model can be evaluated against the observed data. In the analyses of this book, two methods are used to assess the fit of the models. The first is the p-value associated with the chi-square statistic, based on its degrees of freedom. The chi-square statistic represents a measure of the deviation between the covariance matrix obtained from the model being tested and the observed data. It assesses the null hypothesis that the model being evaluated is correct in the population. More formally, the p-value estimates the probability of observing a statistic as large or larger than the one observed, given that the model is true. Thus the larger the chi-square relative to the degrees of freedom, and thus the smaller the p-value, the more likely the model is a poor representation of the data. If one uses the standard .05 critical value to evaluate the null hypothesis, models associated with observed p-values less than .05 would be rejected. Thus a well-fitting model should have a p-value greater than .05 indicating acceptance of the null hypothesis that the hypothesized model is correct in the population. In this case, the estimated model will also adequately reproduce the observed data. The chi-square value is not a totally adequate measure of fit, because it is a linear function of the number of subjects in the sample. Thus, in large samples, it is often quite difficult to obtain a nonsignificant p-value because even small residuals between model and data may be cause for rejecting a model. As a consequence, in addition to the p-value, we use the normed fit index (NFI; Bentler & Bonett, 1980). This is a statistic that ranges in value between zero and unity and indicates the proportion of the sample covariations that is accounted for by the hypothesized model, starting with a null model where no covariance effects are imposed. We typically hope to have this value higher than .90. This index, or a variant that adjusts for number of free parameters, remains one of the better measures of goodness of fit (Wheaton, in press).

Sequence of Analyses

In each chapter we follow a specific sequence of analyses in order to arrive at a final model that adequately fits the data and is substantively meaningful. Details of these analyses for each chapter are given in the Technical Summary section at the end of every empirical chapter. All latent-variable structural modeling analyses are performed using the EQS and EQS/PC computer programs (Bentler, 1986b). As noted in Chapter 4 and in the Appendix, several of the variables are nonnormally distributed, that is, they have large skews or kurtoses. Non-normal data are best analyzed using procedures that do not rely on the assumption of multivariate normality (e.g., Bentler, 1983; Browne, 1984). Unfortunately, it is not feasible to run large models (like the ones represented in this book) with these methods. As a result, we must use normal theory maximum likelihood estimation procedures, realizing that our nonnormal data violate an assumption underlying this method. Comparisons between methods using data with varying degrees of violations of normality, however, indicate that maximum likelihood is quite robust (e.g., Harlow, 1985; Huba & Bentler, 1983b; Huba & Harlow, 1986; Muthen & Kaplan, 1985; Tanaka & Bentler, 1985). In particular, the estimates are consistent and hence are technically perfectly acceptable— indeed, they are perhaps at least as good as distribution-free estimates. The standard errors and chi-square statistics, however, may be influenced by violation of assumptions. This depends on the model and the parameters involved (Shapiro, 1986). In our initial models, which are confirmatory factor analysis (CFA) models, the chi-square test is most likely correct regardless of the distribution of variables, and the standard errors of factor loadings should be similarly correct (Amemiya & Anderson, 1985; Anderson & Amemiya, 1985; Satorra & Bentler, 1986). The chi-square statistic is probably also all right in most of the more general models, providing that the model contains enough of the key variables such that the predictors and residuals are independent (Mooijaart & Bentler, 1987). Unfortunately, a diagnostic that would permit evaluating robustness in our specific models (Satorra & Bentler, 1986) was not available at the time this research was completed. Thus we shall rely on the normed fit index, which should not be affected by violation of assumptions, so the adequacy of a model can always be evaluated. Consequently, we do not feel that our results will be adversely affected by the use of maximum likelihood estimation and testing, which is currently the most common method used in such analyses.

Our first step in each series of analyses is to determine whether the observed variables that we have hypothesized to be indicators of certain latent constructs in fact reflect them reliably. This is accomplished using confirmatory factor analysis. In this CFA model, only hypothesized factor loadings are allowed (all others are held at zero) and all latent constructs are permitted to correlate freely. There are times when only one variable is available to represent a construct. In such a case, the variable itself is used as the construct, even though it is not latent and is influenced by measurement error. Residual variables for repeatedly measured items or scales are allowed to correlate across time. Factor intercorrelations for this initial CFA will be presented in a table. These factor or latent construct intercorrelations are an important result of our analyses. These represent the "true" associations among the latent or unmeasured factors that are disattenuated of measurement error. As a result, these correlations tend to be substantially larger than can be seen in the product-moment correlations among the manifest or observed variables. These correlations also provide the first occasion to examine the substantive association among constructs, and to establish which ones are significantly related, and in what direction, to others.

Due to the relatively large sample size (N = 654), the initial highly restricted CFA model will rarely be an acceptable approximation to the data according to the p-value. If the fundamental aspects of the model are good, however (i.e., hypothesized factor loadings are sizable and significant), the NFI will typically be around .90 or larger. This would indicate that most of the critical features or hypotheses of the model tend to be acceptable, but that several smaller, nonhypothesized relationships (parameters) need to be included in the model to achieve an acceptable fit (nonsignificant p-value of the chi-square test). These additional parameters are empirically determined by modification indices, primarily by Lagrange Multiplier tests (Bentler, 1986c; Bentler & Chou, 1986; Lee & Bentler, 1980; Satorra, 1987). Two types of modifications to the model may be made to improve the fit. These are covariances or correlations among residuals (uniquenesses or errors of measurement) and additional factor loadings. These types of modifications will be made to the initial CFA, resulting in a final CFA model that should adequately reflect the data according to both the p-value and the NFI. Factor intercorrelations for this final CFA model will be presented side by side in a table with those from the initial CFA. Standardized factor loadings will be included in a figure that graphically depicts the relationship between the observed variables and latent constructs. By convention, latent constructs are depicted as circles, observed variables as rectangles, and residual variables (particularly, their variances) as numbers in small circles.

In most of our models, due to their large size and many subjects, quite a few correlated residuals may need to be added in order to achieve a model that fits the data. These typically reflect one of two types of phenomena: small relationships in the data that we were not able to hypothesize a priori or else sample-specific associations that would not be expected to cross-validate. In either case, we do not believe these are worth interpreting in the CFA models, nor feel, based on hundreds of other models we have worked with, that they distort the fundamental features of the model that are theoretically driven. For each model we perform some further tests to ascertain whether this later belief is substantiated. This is described next.

In order to determine whether the model modifications may have disturbed the critical basis of the model, the factor intercorrelations between the initial and final CFAs will be correlated. If the fundamental nature of the model has not been affected, this correlation should be quite high (i.e., greater than .95). This is important to determine because the structural or path models among latent variables are largely based on the factor intercorrelations. If these have changed substantially from the initial to final CFA, the resultant structural model will be altered as well, and could thus modify the substantive meaning of the final model. Because both matrices of factor correlations are reported, for each model, an ambitious reader can also perform two independent path analyses of these latent variables. Even though such a path analysis will not have a statistical basis, its major features should mirror the major effects reported between latent factors in our simultaneous analysis of the entire model.

The last step in the sequence of analyses will be to develop a structural or path model that includes significant across-time associations of a presumably causal nature. We do not start with the final CFA model with all correlated residuals. Rather, we keep its measurement model (factor pattern), but drop all the non-a priori or empirically determined across-time cor-related errors. These across-time correlations may in fact represent causal effects over time that we would want to capture as regression paths rather than simply as correlations. In the initial structural model, all adolescent constructs are allowed to correlate freely, each young adult construct is predicted from all adolescent constructs, and all young adult factor residual variables are allowed to correlate freely. Across-time correlated residuals between repeatedly measured variables are included.

Specific types of across-time Lagrange Multiplier indices are then consulted to establish whether any across-time drug effects of a nonstandard (i.e., non-LISREL) type exist in the data. First, we would test for the influence of adolescent General Drug Use (as latent factor) on young adult measured variables. Next, we would evaluate the consequences of residual drug variables in adolescence on young adult factors and measured variables. Other nonstandard across-time effects are then evaluated. It is expected that such nonstandard effects would replace the empirically determined across-time "correlated errors" of the CFA model that were deleted in the initial structural model, except those for repeatedly measured variables. Based on Lagrange Multiplier modification indices and the significance level of the parameters, paths are added until an adequately fitting model is achieved that only includes significant effects. Although there may be some overfitting at this stage, paths are then deleted by the Wald test to omit multivariately statistically unnecessary parameters. Such a procedure has been recommended (MacCallum, 1986).

The final model will be reported in a consistent manner. A figure will present the associations among the latent constructs (or single-variable "factors"). The across-time associations between latent constructs and observed variables or between observed variables will be summarized in a table. This table and figure will reflect the entire model and are presented separately only for clarity—they are in fact interrelated aspects of the same model. This final structural model provides the culmination of the analysis sequence and captures the substantive findings of the variables under study. Our report will emphasize parameters of the standardized solution because, in view of problems associated with unstandardized solutions (e.g., Bielby, 1986; Sobel & Arminger, 1986; Williams & Thomson, 1986), "we might be best off limiting interpretations of covariance structure models to those that can legitimately be made on the basis of standardized parameter estimates" (Bielby, 1986, p. 63). For a discussion of the merits and problems of standardization, see Kim and Ferree (1981).

Control Variables

The quality of our causal inference will hinge strongly on the adequacy of controls for extraneous and spurious influences. Drug use has been frequently associated with deviance, problem behavior, or nontraditionalism (e.g., Akers, 1984; Brook, Whiteman, Gordon, & Cohen, 1986; Donovan & Jessor, 1985; Huba & Bentler, 1982, 1983a, 1984; Jessor & Jessor, 1977, 1978; Kandel, 1984; Kaplan, Martin, & Robbins, 1984; Maddux & Desmond, 1984). Deviant attitudes often precede drug involvement, are highly correlated with drug use, and thus may represent a spurious factor in tests for drug use consequences. For instance, if a relationship is found between early drug use and later criminal behavior, it is quite possible that both events are the result of general deviance rather than drug use somehow causing criminal involvement. In order to eliminate this possibility, a factor of Social Conformity will be paired with the Drug Use factor in all analyses to control for the influence of deviant attitudes.

Figure 5.1 graphically depicts a prototypical example of our general design for assessing drug use outcomes and consequences. The figure shows only the latent variables, that is, it omits the measurement model that relates these variables to the measured variables. Notice that all adolescent constructs are correlated (the two-headed arrows), as are the residual variables in young adulthood. To control for the spurious influence of Social Conformity, this construct is permitted to predict the outcome constructs. Thus the dotted lines from Drug Use to Outcome A and Outcome B represent partial regression paths controlling for Social Conformity and all other adolescent constructs (via their intercorrelations). Thus if one of those dotted lines represents a significant path, this would indicate that drug use influenced the outcome within the context of a variety of relevant controls, especially Social Conformity.

Other types of spurious effects are also possible. These tend to be more specific to certain outcomes, however, and the same set is not included in all models. In each model, adolescent control variables are chosen to reflect the specific types of young adult outcomes being examined. For instance, divorce is

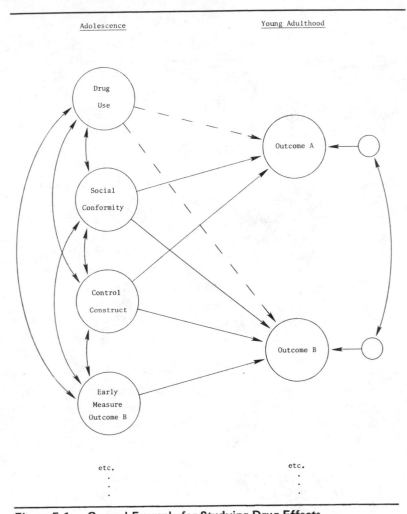

Figure 5.1.   General Example for Studying Drug Effects
NOTE: Two-headed arrows represent correlations and single-headed arrows
are across-time regression effects.

certainly affected by factors other than drug use. It is
important to include other plausible adolescent predictors of
divorce, such as parental divorce and family support. Thus, for
each outcome, we have attempted to include other factors that
may be predictive in addition to drug use.

Where possible, we have included identical variables from
the adolescent and young adult assessments in the models. This

represents the ideal case where all young adult outcome variables were previously measured in adolescence. This situation is represented in Figure 5.1 as Outcome B. The path from Early Measure Outcome B to Outcome B represents a stability effect for that construct. This captures the notion that attitudes, behavior, and events tend to be consistent over time. In order to demonstrate that Drug Use affects Outcome B over time, it is necessary to include this stability effect and the baseline association between Drug Use and Early Measure Outcome B in the model.

For several reasons it may not be possible to have identical measures at all time points for each possible outcome in which we are interested. Some may not have a legitimate baseline because the behavior or activity may not have occurred normatively as yet during adolescent development. For instance, prior job stability or frequency of being fired from a job could not be measured for high school students who have not yet held a job. Similarly, marital stability could not be assessed from a group of adolescents who have not been married. On the other hand, some measures simply were not assessed in our adolescent questionnaires. In these cases where no identical prior measure is available, we will include adolescent constructs that can help approximate the nonexisting earlier measure. Where possible, we will include a more general construct that should control broadly for baseline associations. This type of situation is depicted in Figure 5.1 as the Control Construct and Outcome A (which has no parallel earlier measure).

Gender Differences

In most of the analyses presented in this book, results are presented for the combined samples of men and women (with the exception of Chapter 9 on sexual behavior). This was done for several reasons. First, previous analyses of this data, that have tested for differential effects by sex, have failed to find different processes occurring for men than women (e.g., Newcomb et al., 1986; Stein, Newcomb, & Bentler, 1986b). For instance, Stein et al. (1986b) used a multiple-group covariance structure model to test for gender differences in how drug use and social conformity influence each other over time. Factor correlations and structural paths were found to be invariant by sex. Another reason for combining the men's and women's data is that separate models would be more unstable due to the smaller sample sizes (particularly for men). This could severely distort the reliability of the results. Finally, mean sex differences on most measures are quite small (see the Appendix) and should only minimally affect the results. For example, there were no differences in drug use by sex in Table 4.2, which is consistent with reports by others that sex differences in substance use is becoming smaller (e.g., Kaestner, Frank, Marel, & Schmeidler, 1986).

For these reasons, data from the men and women were combined for the analyses. We do not claim that there are no differential effects by sex, only that these tend to be quite small for this sample. Due to the larger percentage of women than men in the sample, the results could be considered more influenced by women than men, although as discussed above, we would not expect large differential effects by sex. In addition, our primary concern is to provide a stable model of drug use consequences, which called for combining men and women to utilize the entire sample for parameter estimates.

6

The Reciprocal Influence of Drug Use and Social Conformity: An Example of Our Analytic Approach

I n this chapter, we use a small model to illustrate the sequence of analyses that we use in the seven substantive chapters to follow (7 to 13). Chapter 14 is somewhat different because it includes a large integrated model that tests for the impact of several different types of substances. Even so, the general sequence of analyses remains approximately the same throughout.

In each chapter, a general review of the problem or area of impact is presented, including other relevant research that has addressed similar issues. The next section, called "Design of the Model," describes exactly which variables and constructs are included in the analyses and the rationale for their inclusion. This section also includes the two tables and two figures that summarize the empirical analyses and describe the operationalization of the models. The next section of every chapter provides an "Interpretation" and integration of the substantive results. Finally, the "Technical Summary" section provides the details of the analyses. This is the more technical part of the presentation and can be skimmed by those readers who are more interested in the substantive findings.

The substantive example in this present chapter relates to the reciprocal impact between Social Conformity and Drug Use over the four-year period from adolescence to young adulthood. In the analyses to follow in subsequent chapters, Social Conformity is routinely included as a construct during the adolescent time period. This is done in order to control for the possible spurious influence of general deviance on the consequences of teenage drug use being tested. In other words, we want to know what the effect of earlier drug use on young adult functioning is, over and above the tendency for drug use simply to reflect an aspect of deviance or lack of Social Conformity. Thus Social Conformity is an antecedent control variable in these analyses.

It is also interesting to determine, however, how Social Conformity and Drug Use affect each other over time. Donovan and Jessor (1985) have demonstrated that various measures of problem or deviant behavior are generated by an underlying latent tendency toward nontraditionalism. As such, no causal priority is posited between them, because all types of problem behavior (i.e., drug use, precocious sexual involvement) are merely symptoms of the underlying syndrome of nontraditionalism. Other research has found that deviant attitudes or personality tendencies appear to increase drug involvement during adolescence (e.g., Huba & Bentler, 1984; Newcomb et al., 1986). On the other hand, little evidence has been found to suggest that drug use itself makes a person more nontraditional or deviant. In other words, deviant attitudes seem to change behavior (drug use), but that behavior does not modify attitudes (nontraditionalism or lack of social conformity).

When various types of deviant behavior have been investigated over time, the specific types of behavior tend to be stable (consistent or unchanging) as does a general construct (latent factor) of deviance reflected in these specific types of behavior (Osgood, 1985). The specific types of behavior, however, did not cross-generate over time. In other words, engaging in one type of behavior at an early period did not cause an increase in a different type of deviant behavior at a later period. These findings suggest that the syndrome notion may be an accurate portrayal of the process or phenomenon of deviant behavior, although attitudes may function somewhat differently (Bentler & Speckart, 1981). In this chapter, we test whether a causal priority exists between deviant attitudes (lack of Social Conformity) and a particular deviant behavior (Drug Use) across the span from adolescence to young adulthood.

Design of the Model

The model tested in this chapter uses two latent constructs from the adolescent time period and two from the young adult age. The constructs are identical at both times: Drug Use and Social Conformity. In this instance, all young adult consequent variables are perfectly matched by earlier parallel measures. Three observed variables are used as indicators of the Drug Use constructs at both times. These three measures include alcohol frequency, cannabis frequency, and hard drug frequency and were constructed as described in Chapter 4 on measures. Three observed variables are also used to reflect the Social Conformity constructs at each time. These three variables include law abidance, (lack of) liberalism, and religious commitment. These and all other measures are described fully in Chapter 4 and in the Appendix.

The statistical and methodological details related to the development of this model are provided in the "Technical Summary" section at the end of this chapter. Figure 6.1 depicts how the latent constructs were identified by the measured variables in the final confirmatory factor analysis (CFA) model. Table 6.1 presents the factor intercorrelations for the initial and final CFA models. The final structural model is depicted in Figure 6.2 and Table 6.2. The figure presents the relationship among latent factors, whereas the table reports the nonstandard effects that include at least one measured variable. Figure 6.3 provides a complete summary of information from both Table 6.2 and Figure 6.2, and is included to provide a demonstration of all the features in the final structural model. This is discussed more completely in the "Technical Summary" section.

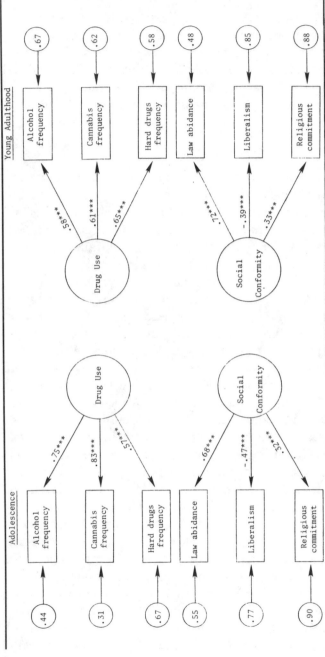

Figure 6.1. Final Confirmatory Factor Analysis Model for the Drugs and Social Conformity Variables

NOTE: Large circles represent latent factors, rectangles are measured variables, and the small circles with numbers are residual variances. Factor loadings are standardized and significance levels were determined by critical ratios of unstandardized estimate to standard error estimate (*p < .05; **pp < .01; ***p < .001). Not depicted in the figure are two-headed arrows (correlations) joining each possible pair of factors. Values for these correlations are provided in Table 6.1.

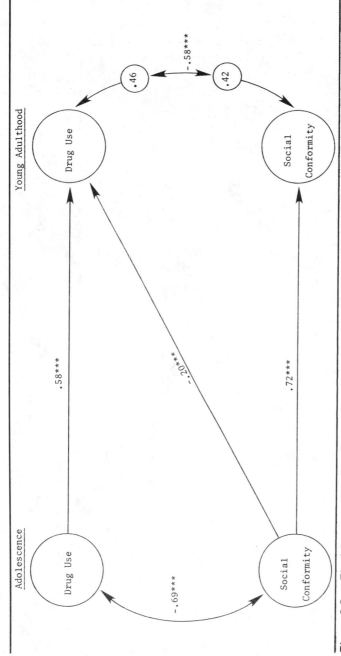

Figure 6.2. Final Structural or Path Model for the Drugs and Social Conformity Variables

NOTE: The measurement portion of this model is not depicted for simplicity. Two-headed arrows reflect correlations and single-headed arrows represent across-time regression effects. Parameter estimates are standardized, residual variables are variances, and significance levels were determined by critical ratios (*p < .05; **p < .01; ***p < .001). Nonstandard effects for this model are given in Table 6.2.

81

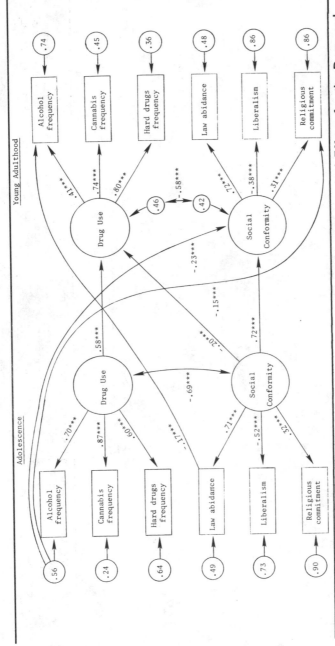

Figure 6.3. Final Structural Model Including Measurement Model and Nonstandard Effects for the Drugs and Social Conformity Variables

NOTE: Large circles reflect latent factors, rectangles represent measured variables, and small circles with numbers are residual variances. Two-headed arrows are correlations and single-headed arrows represent regression effects. Parameter estimates are standardized and significance levels were determined by critical ratios (*p < .05; **p < .01; ***p < .001).

TABLE 6.1
Factor Intercorrelations for the Initial (upper triangle)
and Final (lower triangle) Confirmatory Factor Model

Factor	I	II	III	IV
Late Adolescence				
I Drug Use	1.00	−.77*	.71*	−.53*
II Social Conformity	−.76*	1.00	−.68*	.80*
Young Adulthood				
III Drug Use	.78*	−.79*	1.00	−.73*
IV Social Conformity	−.54*	.82*	−.86*	1.00

*p ≤ .001.

Interpretation

The confirmatory factor analysis provides correlations among the latent constructs that are disattenuated for measurement error. As such, they represent an estimate of the true or error-free association among the constructs. In the Drug Use and Social Conformity model developed in this chapter, we found that in the final CFA model, Drug Use and Social Conformity were correlated −.76 during adolescence and −.86 during young adulthood (these correlations are given in Table 6.1). The stability correlation between adolescence and young adulthood for Drug Use was .78, while for Social Conformity, this correlation was .82. The cross-lagged correlation between adolescent Drug Use and young adult Social Conformity was −.54, whereas the correlation between adolescent Social Conformity and young adult Drug Use was −.79. These rather high correlations support our earlier decision to include Social Conformity as a control variable, because there appears to be a great deal of overlap between these deviant attitudes (a lack of Social Conformity) and Drug Use. This result also supports a large body of previous literature that has found a strong relationship between drug involvement and other deviant attitudes and behaviors (e.g., Donovan & Jessor, 1985; Jessor & Jessor, 1977, 1978; Newcomb, Maddahian, & Bentler, 1986).

As a technical point, it should be noted that, to conserve space, we do not provide the reproduced correlations among factors in the final structural model. The reader could compute these, if desired, from the data in the figures. In this example, it

TABLE 6.2
Direct Across-Time Causal Paths
Not Depicted in Figure

Adolescent Predictor Variable		Young Adult Consequent Variable		Standardized Parameter Estimate[a]
Observed Variable	Latent Variable	Observed Variable	Latent Variable	
alcohol frequency (R)[b]			Social Conformity	−.23*
alcohol frequency (R)		religious commitment		−.15*
law abidance		alcohol frequency		−.17*

a. Significance level determined by a critical ratio of the unstandardized parameter estimate divided by its standard error.
b. (R) denotes variable residual.
*p < .001.

will be noted that Drug Use and Social Conformity in adolescence correlate −.69 in the final model, but −.76 in the final CFA. In general, such within-adolescence correlations will be close but not identical to the CFA correlations. The within-adulthood correlations will rarely be similar, because they represent residual correlations in the structural model, but ordinary correlations in the CFA. Here they are −.58 and −.86, respectively. And, to conserve space, we have also been forced to omit the final factor pattern; this is generally very close to the final CFA factor pattern.

The final structural model revealed that among the latent constructs there was no direct association between adolescent Drug Use and young adult Social Conformity. In other words, early drug-using behaviors did not generate more deviant attitudes, in general, over time. On the other hand, earlier deviant attitudes or lack of Social Conformity increased drug involvement over the same period of time. Three additional significant relationships were found across time (Table 6.2). Early law abidance generated subsequent decreased use of alcohol, and the residual of adolescent alcohol use decreased young adult religious commitment and the general factor of Social Conformity. These effects of alcohol use on later religious commitment and Social Conformity represent the only drug use consequences apparent in these analyses, except for the strong tendency for those who used drugs in adolescence to continue using drugs as young adults. Thus an additional consequence of adolescent drug use is the involvement with drugs as a young adult.

The consequent effects of the early alcohol use residual is an interesting one. The fact that these "causal" relationships were based on the residual of the alcohol variable implies that the type of drug use is specific just to high use levels of alcohol after the effects of general drug use (the Drug Use factor) have been controlled. There are at least two ways to interpret these results. The first is that the decrement in religious commitment and Social Conformity is a direct effect of alcohol use only and not general drug use. Thus early high levels of alcohol use tend to increase deviant and nontraditional attitudes. A second interpretation, not incompatible with the first, relates to the fact that some researchers have found that high levels of alcohol use and problem drinking occur subsequent to use of cannabis and hard drugs, and reflects a high level of drug involvement, particularly among adolescents (e.g., Donovan & Jessor, 1983). If this were true, our present findings would indicate that a high degree of involvement with drugs, as reflected in frequent alcohol consumption, leads to increased deviant attitudes and a decrease in religious commitment.

In general, the results of these analyses corroborate earlier research with adolescent populations that has found that deviant attitudes increase drug involvement, but that has rarely found that earlier drug use increases deviant attitudes or behavior. For instance, Huba and Bentler (1984) found that low law abidance predicted increased drug use and deviance over time, whereas drug use influenced later deviant behavior to a much lesser extent. In other analyses of these data, early drug use did not increase deviant attitudes over a three-year period (Newcomb & Bentler, in press). We did find drug use effects for the specific use of alcohol, however, suggesting that, at least for alcohol, there is an impact of early use on changing attitudes and religious commitment in a nontraditional direction.

Ingestion of large quantities of alcohol as a teenager appears to be a portent for decreasing traditional values as young adults, leading to more liberalism, less law abidance, and especially decreased religious commitment. Conversely, the broader effect of holding deviant or nontraditional attitudes during adolescence appears to be a facilitation of greater drug involvement as the teenager makes the transition into responsible roles as a young adult. As a result, in the analyses to follow in subsequent chapters, where an outcome is found to be significantly generated from Social Conformity (or the variables that are used to reflect this construct, i.e., law abidance, liberalism, and religious commitment), we can imply that drug use may inversely covary with Social Conformity as aspects of an integrated life-style. For instance, if Social Conformity leads to a decrease of specific behavior, it is possible that a decrease in drug use may accompany the decreased behavior, reflecting a consistency in life-style.

Because the focus of this study is on the consequences of teenage drug use, we have not routinely included young adult drug use in the models: doing so would shift the focus of our research to one of testing etiology or antecedents of young adult drug use. Such analyses have been presented elsewhere (e.g., Newcomb & Bentler, 1986a, 1987a). These and other studies (Kandel et al., 1986), however, indicate that one of the primary consequences of teenage drug use is young adult drug use. In fact, in one set of analyses, 60% of the variance in young adult drug use was predicted from adolescent drug use (Newcomb & Bentler, 1987a). This is an important result and represents a critical consequence of teenage substance use. It may also help explain some of the later consequences of early drug use, because drug use continuity can help provide an explanatory mechanism for later consequences. For instance, if teenage drug use predicts later arrests for drug crimes, continuing use of drugs may well provide the causal link.

In the following chapters, the sequence of analyses presented above in regard to Drug Use and Social Conformity is applied to seven different areas of life that we believe could be affected by teenage drug use. These areas include family formation (Chapter 7), criminality and deviant behavior (Chapter 8), sexual behavior and involvement (Chapter 9), educational pursuits (Chapter 10), livelihood pursuits (Chapter 11), mental health status (Chapter 12), and social integration (Chapter 13). Chapter 14 includes analyses on a large model that incorporates many of the significant effects found in the other models and tests for effects of using several specific types of drugs during adolescence.

Technical Summary

Confirmatory Factor Analyses

The first step in our data analyses is to assess the adequacy of our hypothesized measurement model. In other words, we need to demonstrate that the variables we have chosen to reflect the latent factors with which we are concerned in fact reflect these constructs in a statistically reliable manner. This is accomplished via a confirmatory factor analysis (CFA).

An initial confirmatory factor model was run that (a) fixed all factor variances at unity, (b) allowed all constructs (latent factors) to correlate freely, and (c) included across-time correlations between residual variables on repeated measures (i.e., between the residuals of adolescent alcohol frequency and young adult alcohol frequency). This initial model did not adequately reflect the data (χ^2 = 137.24, d.f. = 42, p < .001), although the Normed Fit Index (NFI) was sufficiently large (.95) to suggest that minor modifications should yield an acceptable model. Factor intercorrelations for this initial model are presented in the upper triangle of Table 6.1.

By examining the Lagrange Multiplier modification indices (Bentler, 1986c; Bentler & Chou, 1986), correlations between nine pairs of residuals were added to the model. No additional factor loadings were necessary. These modifications resulted in a model that adequately reflected the data (χ^2 = 34.42, d.f. = 33, p = .40, NFI = .99), or could not be rejected as a plausible explanation of the data. Factor intercorrelations for this final confirmatory factor analysis model are presented in the lower triangle of Table 6.1. All hypothesized factor loadings were significant. Standardized factor loadings and variances of the residual error variables in this final CFA model are graphically depicted in Figure 6.1. The large circles represent the latent constructs, the rectangles are the measured variables, and all small circles with numbers in them are variances of the residual variables. The single-headed arrows that go from the large circles to the rectangles are factor loadings, depicting the fact that the latent constructs generate the variation in the measured or observed variable.

In order to test whether adding the correlated residuals disturbed the fundamental associations among the latent constructs, the factor intercorrelations between the initial and final confirmatory factor models (Table 6.1) were correlated. This correlation was .99, indicating that the model modifications did not alter the basic pattern of factor intercorrelations.

Structural Model Analyses

The final stage in data analyses for a particular model is the creation of a structural or path model, which includes regression effects representing unidirectional influences of one variable upon another. As a rule, we do not include regression paths within time, because their causal interpretation may be ambiguous. Within-time associations are captured as correlations among constructs, factor loadings, or correlated residuals. The regression effects in which we are most interested are those across time that may have a plausible "causal" basis.

Because many of the correlated residuals added in the CFA model modifications may simply be another way to account for regression effects across time, the empirically determined (from the modification indices) correlated residuals across time are deleted in the initial structural model. This is done in hopes of capturing these associations as true, across-time causal paths (partial regression effects). All constructs in adolescence are allowed to correlate freely, as are all factor residuals during young adulthood. All young adult constructs are initially predicted from all adolescent constructs.

This beginning model is modified by adding across-time regression paths (based on the Lagrange Multiplier modification indices) and deleting nonsignificant parameters (based on the Wald test). The final model will always include only significant paths. In this instance, the final structural model fit the data quite well (χ^2 = 29.30, d.f. = 34, p = .70, NFI = .99). Associations among the latent factors are graphically displayed in Figure 6.2, whereas the across-time paths that include at least one observed variable are listed in Table 6.2 with their standardized regression weight. The relationships presented in Figure 6.2 and those listed in Table 6.2 are based on the same final structural model, and are presented separately only for reasons of clarity (although this is a rather small model with only 12 variables, the larger models introduced in the following chapters incorporate many more variables than could comfortably be presented in a single figure). Because this is a smaller model that can be presented in one figure, we have done so in Figure 6.3. One may note how the various paths and relationships depicted in Figure 6.3 are mapped to the appropriate parts of Figure 6.2 or Table 6.2. Two-headed arrows represent correlations, and single-headed arrows, especially those relating constructs, reflect causal paths. Correlations among residual variables, including between residual pairs of identical measured variables across time, are not presented because these are not particularly interesting and will not be interpreted. They represent small associations in the model that are necessary to achieve an acceptable fit, but that are not germane to the larger theoretical issues in the model.

It can be seen that Figures 6.1 and 6.2 represent a rather standard combination of factor analytic and simultaneous equation models. The effects described in Table 6.2, on the other hand, represent types of influence that have not previously been reported in the literature. As can be seen in Figure 6.3, the resulting model is not a standard LISREL model, because LISREL was not designed to permit such effects as those shown in Table 6.2.

7

Impact on Family Formation and Stability

One critical task of postadolescent development is establishing the role of marriage and parenthood in one's life (e.g., Havighurst, 1952, 1972; Hogan, 1981). Marital and family processes and interactions are quite complex issues (e.g., Burgess, 1981; Nye, 1976, 1982), and it is a challenging task to determine how drug use relates to these pivotal personal institutions. Data from cross-sectional samples indicate that drug use tends to be negatively associated with being married and having children, but positively related to marital separation and divorce (e.g., Kandel, 1984; Newcomb & Bentler, 1986d). The role of drug use in the occurrence of these life events is not clear. For instance, even though drug abuse and alcoholism have been cited as marital problems more often by divorced than married couples (e.g., Bentler & Newcomb, 1978), it is difficult to establish whether the drug problems preceded the marital problems (perhaps causing them) or whether the drugs were used to relieve marital or family tension (e.g., Kandel, Davies, & Raveis, 1985; Orford & O'Reilly, 1981). Yamaguchi and Kandel (1985a) hypothesized and found in retrospective data that marijuana use was associated with postponement of marriage and parenthood and increased risk of marital dissolution. Robins et al. (1970) reported that, with retrospective data, Black adults who used marijuana as adolescents reported greater infidelity and fathering of illegitimate children than adolescent nonusers. In a different vein, Newcomb and Bentler (1985) found that high school drug use (particularly cigarettes, alcohol, and hard drugs, but not cannabis) predicted early involvement in marriage.

Similarly, the impact of adolescent drug use on family formation (getting married and having children), happiness in an intimate relationship, the level of relationship importance in one's life, and the choice to engage in marital alternatives (i.e., cohabitation) is not well understood. Little research has examined the influence of teenage drug use on timing of marriage and parenthood or has determined the impact of early drug use on the performance of these roles.

The choice to get married and perhaps have children represents a significant decision for young adults, implying a radical change in life-style and responsibility. The increase in responsibility and extent of life-style change accompanying family formation may not be well appreciated by those who marry early in life, because they have little life experience and perhaps are not fully mature enough to handle the strains of marital roles (e.g., Booth & Edwards, 1985; Kandel et al., 1985). Research has consistently demonstrated that early marriage has a poorer chance of success (higher divorce rates and greater marital dissatisfaction) than marriage at a later point in life, presumably when the individual has had the opportunity to gain greater life experience, maturity, and self-awareness (e.g., Bahr & Galligan, 1984; see Newcomb & Bentler, 1981, for a review). Relationship satisfaction also seems to be negatively related to early marriage (e.g., Bentler & Newcomb, 1978). It seems clear that some process implicit in marriage at an early age works against a successful relationship.

Cohabitation has received a great deal of research attention in the past 15 years, with many concerned about how living together will influence marriage rates and marital success. Although it was initially hypothesized that cohabitation prior to marriage would enhance the subsequent marriage, such an effect has not been found (Newcomb & Bentler, 1980b). In fact, a significantly higher divorce rate has been found among those who cohabited before marriage compared to marriages that were not preceded by cohabitation among a sample of late adolescents and young adults (e.g., Newcomb, 1986c). Thus those who cohabit and marry at an early age are doubly at risk for marital dissolution.

Another influence on the success of a marriage and family formation is the family of origin. Research has indicated that those people who come from families with conflict, parental disruption (divorce), and poor cohesion have greater difficulty in their own marriages or relationships. It is likely that these people lack a positive example of how to function in a marriage to ensure adjustment and satisfaction, as this was not present in their family of origin (e.g., Newcomb & Bentler, 1981). Similarly, those from unhappy families also tend to be wary of marriage and may prefer cohabitation to matrimony (see Newcomb, 1981, 1983, for reviews).

The critical question addressed in this chapter is how teenage drug use interacts with these converging influences on family development and formation in young adulthood (e.g., Adams, 1985; Lowe & Witt, 1984). Does early drug use perhaps predict premature involvement in family formation possibly leading to the ultimate breakdown of the marriage? Do early drug users prefer to live together rather than get married as another aspect of their lack of traditionalism? Does early drug use affect how satisfied a young adult can feel in a relationship? These questions and others are addressed in the analyses to follow.

Design of the Model

In this model, which assesses the impact of teenage drug use on family formation, four constructs are included from the adolescent data (one is a single-indicator factor) and five constructs are from the young adult data (two of which are single-indicator factors). Two of the adolescent constructs are Drug Use and Social Conformity as included in all of the models. The other two constructs include Family Support (with indicators of good relationship with parents and good relationship with family) and Parental Divorce as a single-indicator factor. Although it would have been desirable to include adolescent measures for marital satisfaction and something like relationship competence, this was not possible because the vast majority of the teenagers had never been married and measures of relationship competence were not assessed at that time. In young adulthood, five constructs were measured including Relationship Satisfaction (with indicators of happy with relationship and trouble with relationship), Family Formation (with indicators of marriage during the past four years and number of children), Relationship Importance (with indicators of current level of involvement and dating importance), Cohabitation History (a single item about whether the subject had lived with someone in a sexual relationship without being married), and Divorce Past 4 Years (a single item). A more thorough description of all of these measures is given in the Appendix.

The statistical and methodological details related to the development of this model are provided in the "Technical Summary" section at the end of this chapter. Figure 7.1 depicts how the latent constructs were identified by the measured variables in the final confirmatory factor analysis (CFA) model. Table 7.1 presents the factor intercorrelations for the initial and final CFA models. The final structural model is depicted in Figure 7.2 and Table 7.2. The figure presents the relationship among latent factors, whereas the table reports the nonstandard effects that include at least one measured variable.

Interpretation

The confirmatory factor analysis provides correlations among the nine factors or constructs that are disattenuated for measurement error (except for those that are defined by only one indicator, where the measurement error has been fixed at zero). As such, these correlations represent the true or error-free association among the constructs. In the final CFA model for drug use and family formation, the adolescent Drug Use factor was significantly correlated with all other factors except Relationship Satisfaction. Teenage Drug Use was significantly related to lowered Social Conformity, lowered Family Support, Parental Divorce, higher Family Formation, greater Relationship Importance, having cohabited, and having a Divorce (see Table 7.1). Adolescent Social Conformity was significantly associated with higher Family Support, an intact

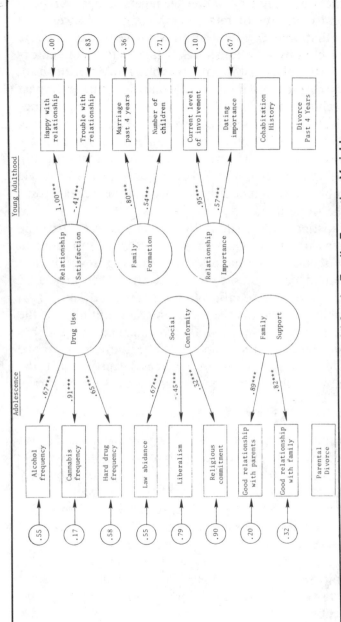

Figure 7.1. Final Confirmatory Factor Analysis Model for the Family Formation Variables

NOTE: Large circles represent latent factors, rectangles are measured variables, and the small circles with numbers are residual variances. Factor loadings are standardized and significance levels were determined by critical ratios ($*p < .05$; $**p < .01$; $***p < .001$). Not depicted in the figure are two-headed arrows (correlations) joining each possible pair of factors. Values for these correlations are provided in Table 7.1.

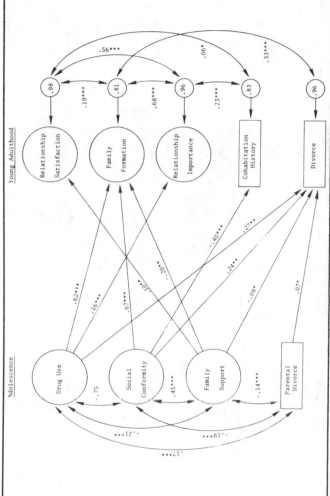

Figure 7.2. Final Structural or Path Model for the Family Formation Variables

NOTE: The measurement portion of this model is not depicted for simplicity. Two-headed arrows reflect correlations and single-headed arrows represent across-time regression effects. Parameter estimates are standardized, residual variables are variances, and significance levels were determined by critical ratios (*p < .05; **p < .01; ***p < .001). Nonstandard effects for this model are given in Table 7.2.

TABLE 7.1
Factor Intercorrelations of the Initial (upper triangle) and Final (lower triangle) Confirmatory Factor Model

Factor	I	II	III	IV	V	VI	VII	VIII	IX
Late Adolescence									
I Drug Use	1.00	−.78***	−.22***	.17***	.05	.19***	.21***	.36***	.12***
II Social Conformity	−.70***	1.00	.46***	−.19***	.05	.07	−.14**	−.37***	.01
III Family Support	−.21***	.43***	1.00	−.14***	.11**	−.06	−.01	−.19***	−.04
IV Parental Divorce	.16***	−.19***	−.14***	1.00	−.05	.05	.06	.10***	.08**
Young Adulthood									
V Relationship Satisfaction	.04	.05	.10**	−.04	1.00	.13***	.55***	.04	−.05
VI Family Formation	.18***	.09	−.04	.05	.17***	1.00	.65***	.05	.39***
VII Relationship Importance	.19***	−.11***	−.01	.06	.55***	.64***	1.00	.28***	.05
VIII Cohabitation History	.34***	−.34***	−.18***	.09**	.05	.01	.27***	1.00	.06*
IX Divorce	.12**	.01	−.04	.08**	−.05	.39***	.05	.07*	1.00

*p < .05; **p < .01; ***p < .001.

TABLE 7.2
Direct Across-Time Causal Paths
Not Depicted in Figure

Adolescent Predictor Variable		Young Adult Consequent Variable		Standardized
Observed Variable	Latent Variable	Observed Variable	Latent Variable	Parameter Estimate[a]
hard drug frequency		trouble with relationship		.08**
liberalism		trouble with relationship		.08**
liberalism		number of children		.08**
religious commitment		dating importance		.07*
good relationship with parents		number of children		.09**

a. Significance level determined by a critical ratio of the unstandardized parameter estimate divided by its standard error.
*p < .05; **p < .01.

family of origin, lowered Relationship Importance, and not
having cohabited. Family Support was significantly related to
an intact family of origin, relationship satisfaction, and
choosing not to cohabit. Finally, parental divorce was significantly associated with choosing to cohabit and getting
divorced. Among the young adult constructs, Relationship
Importance was highly correlated with Relationship Satisfaction, Family Formation, and having cohabited. There were
several other significant correlations among the young adult
constructs and these can be seen in Table 7.1.

In the final structural model, several interesting significant
relationships emerged. General Drug Use during the teenage
years significantly predicted involvement in Family Formation,
Relationship Importance, and Divorce. Use of hard drugs was
significantly related to having trouble with relationships. From
this pattern of effects, it is clear that early drug involvement
leads to early marriage and having children, which then often
results in divorce. Use of hard drugs in particular seems to

affect the amount of trouble experienced in a relationship (as does having liberal attitudes; see Table 7.2). On the other hand, adolescent Social Conformity also led to early Family Formation, a rejection of cohabitation, and an increase in divorce. It is interesting that both Drug Use and Social Conformity, themselves highly inversely correlated, should both influence Family Formation and Divorce in the same direction. In other words, both Social Conformity and Drug Use lead to early involvement with marriage and children and also to divorce.

This finding of teenage drug involvement leading to early family formation at first appears at odds with Kandel's (1980) observation that "married persons show the lowest rates of [drug] use" (p. 249). Her comment, however, is based largely on cross-sectional analyses and does not consider the possible socializing influence of the marital role, which she introduced in later research (e.g., Yamaguchi & Kandel, 1985a, 1985b). Thus it remains possible that early drug use leads to early family involvement, as hypothesized in precocious development theory and supported in our present and earlier findings (Newcomb & Bentler, 1985). Yet this family involvement may lead to role socialization by reduction of drug use or role transition by divorcing if the drug use is maintained (e.g., Newcomb & Bentler, 1987a; Yamaguchi & Kandel, 1985a). In either case, current drug use would be associated with not being married and being divorced as noted by Kandel (1980) and other analyses of ours (Newcomb & Bentler, 1986d).

Socially conforming individuals may be highly motivated to do the "traditional thing" of getting married and having children (while also avoiding the marriage alternative of cohabitation). As a result, this desire to be conforming and traditional may propel them into family responsibilities before they have acquired the necessary level of maturity and life experience to handle these adult obligations in an efficient manner. Consequently, they may divorce. Similarly, early drug use may lead a precociously mature adolescent to seek out other trappings of adulthood (i.e., marriage and children) without the requisite maturity to succeed with these roles. In fact, use of drugs may have prevented or inhibited the development of relationship competence and maturity necessary to succeed in an intimate relationship. It is also possible that the drug use itself, which preceded matrimony, may have continued into the marriage and damaged it as a consequence. Although there is some evidence to suggest that getting married decreases drug use for some (Newcomb & Bentler, 1987a; Yamaguchi & Kandel, 1985a), if this does not occur for various personal or relationship reasons, the marriage may suffer as a result of the drug involvement. Also in support of the precocious development theory is the significant effect of early drug use increasing Relationship Importance as young adults.

Aside from the drug use consequences effects in this model are other interesting developmental patterns regarding family formation. Family Support, but not Parental Divorce, was significantly associated with increased Relationship Satisfaction and lowered involvement in Family Formation. Thus a good relationship with one's family of origin delays formation of one's own family and encourages positive intimate relationships. The adolescent may not need to escape from a bad home life to create a family of his or her own prematurely. Finally, both a lack of Family Support and a disrupted family of origin (Parental Divorce) increased the chance of being divorced in young adulthood. This corroborates other research that has demonstrated that a poor relationship with one's family and having parents who divorced often are themes that get replayed in the offspring's life when they marry (e.g., Mott & Moore, 1979; Pope & Mueller, 1979). Thus marital and family disharmony is passed along from generation to generation. Fortunately, these effects, although significant, were relatively small, indicating that numerous other forces are at work at generating marital disruption for the young adult. The whole problem certainly cannot be placed on the parents. In the present model, other factors such as early Drug Use and Social Conformity had greater influence on divorcing as a young adult. On the other hand, a positive relationship with one's parents during adolescence increases the likelihood of having children as young adults (see Table 7.2).

Technical Summary

Confirmatory Factor Analyses

The first step in our data analyses is to assess the adequacy of our hypothesized measurement model using confirmatory factor analysis. An initial CFA model was run that (a) fixed all factor variances at unity and (b) allowed all constructs (latent factors and single-indicator factors representing constructs) to correlate freely. Because there were no repeatedly measured variables included in this model, no a priori across-time correlated residual variables were included. This initial model did not adequately reflect the data (χ^2 = 196.12, d.f. = 86, p < .001), although the Normed Fit Index (NFI) was sufficiently large (.93) to suggest that minor modifications to the model should yield an acceptable fit. Factor intercorrelations for this initial model are presented in the upper triangle of Table 7.1.

By examining the Lagrange Multiplier modification indices (Bentler, 1986c; Bentler & Chou, 1986), correlations among 14 pairs of residuals were added to the model. No additional factor loadings were necessary. These modifications resulted in a model that adequately reflected the data (χ^2 = 86.44, d.f. = 72, p = .12, NFI = .97), or that could not be rejected as a plausible explanation of the data. Factor intercorrelations for this final confirmatory factor analysis model are presented in the lower triangle of Table 7.1. All hypothesized factor loadings were significant. Standardized factor loadings and residual variables (variances) of the observed variables in this final CFA (confirmatory factor analysis) model are graphically depicted in Figure 7.1.

In order to test whether adding the correlated residuals disturbed the fundamental associations among the latent constructs, the factor intercorrelations between the initial and final confirmatory factor models were correlated. This correlation was higher than .99, indicating that the model modifications did not alter the basic pattern of factor intercorrelations.

Structural Model Analyses

The final stage in data analyses for this model is the creation of a structural or path model, which includes regression effects representing unidirectional influences of one variable upon another. As mentioned previously, we do not include regression paths within time, as the causal interpretation of these may be ambiguous. Within-time associations are captured as correlations among constructs, factor loadings, or correlated residuals. The regression effects in which we are most interested are those across time that may be plausibly interpreted in a causal manner.

Because many of the correlated residuals added in the model modifications to create the final CFA may represent across-time regression effects, these empirically determined across-time correlated residuals were deleted in the initial structural model. This is done in hopes of capturing these associations as across-time causal paths. All constructs in adolescence are allowed to correlate freely, as are all factor residuals during young adulthood. All young adult constructs are initially predicted from all adolescent constructs.

This beginning model was modified by adding across-time regression paths (based on the modification indices) and deleting nonsignificant parameters. The final model includes only significant paths. In this instance, the final structural model fit the data quite well (χ^2 = 100.33, d.f. = 72, p = .16, NFI = .97). Associations among the latent factors are graphically displayed in Figure 7.2, whereas the across-time paths that include at least one observed variable are listed in Table 7.2 with their standardized regression weight. As in all presentations of the final structural model, the relationships presented in Figure 7.2 and those listed in Table 7.2 are based on the same final model, and are presented separately only for reasons of clarity. It would require an extremely busy and overly complicated figure to depict graphically all of the significant relationships in the final model.

8

Impact on
Criminality and
Deviant Behavior

The relationship between drug use and deviant attitudes and behavior has often been noted. Deviance or rebelliousness is often the most salient predictor of increased drug use among adolescents (e.g., Huba & Bentler, 1982, 1983a, 1984; Smith & Fogg, 1978). Others consider deviance and drug use to be indicators of general problem behavior during adolescence (e.g., Donovan & Jessor, 1985; Jessor & Jessor, 1977). It is less clear, however, whether drug use itself somehow causes or generates deviant attitudes and behavior, or vice versa. Much of the research demonstrates that although drug use and deviance are significantly correlated at one occasion, they do not affect each other over time. Although Robins et al. (1970) had reported significantly greater violent behavior and nondrug adult police involvement among Black adult males who were marijuana users in adolescence, as compared to controls, Johnston, O'Malley, and Eveland (1978) concluded in their study of adolescent drug use and delinquency that "the hypothesis that the association (between drug use and delinquency) exists because such drug use somehow causes other kinds of delinquency has suffered a substantial, if not mortal, blow" (p. 56). Similarly, Speckart and Anglin (1985) found no cross-lagged effects between narcotics use and criminality, although quite significant contemporaneous associations were noted.

Huba and Bentler (1983a) found that alcohol use in early adolescence led to decreased law abidance or social conformity three years later. Cannabis and hard drug use did not have such an impact on law abidance. Similarly, Huba and Bentler (1984) found that early adolescent cannabis use had a direct influence on performing deviant acts four years later, whereas hard drug use predicted deviance negatively (possibly a suppressor effect). Using longitudinal data from middle adolescence to the middle twenties, Kandel, Simcha-Fagan, and Davies (1986) found that for men there was no predictive association between early use of marijuana or other illicit drugs and theft or aggressive behavior. On the other hand, among the women, early marijuana use increased aggressive behavior, whereas early use of other illicit substances increased criminal thefts. Halikas et al. (1983), in a longitudinal study of 147 White subjects over six to seven years, found arrests for nondrug crime was a significant consequence of regular marijuana use.

Bennett and Wright (1984) examined the associations between drinking and burglary using interviews from 21 offenders serving sentences. Most offenders admitted to drinking before at least some of their burglaries; one-third admitted that most of their offenses were committed while under the influence of alcohol. Strong correlations were noted between the frequency of preoffense drinking and their typical rates of drinking. The offenders denied a causal association between their alcohol use and their criminal behavior: Either their offenses were planned in drinking situations, independently of the amount of alcohol consumed, or they drank frequently anyway and saw no reason to alter their drinking patterns because they intended to commit a crime.

Osgood (1985) examined several structural models among adolescents and young adults of the relationship between criminal behavior, problem alcohol use, marijuana use, other illicit drug use, and problem driving. Problem drinking became less associated with other forms of deviance over time (as alcohol became legal and normatively accepted or condoned). Illicit drug use became more associated with other forms of deviance over time. One form of deviance did not have a causal impact upon other types. A general common factor of deviance (or criminality) was fairly stable, however, there were also specific stabilities for the residuals of particular types of deviance. Thus there was a common cause of deviant/problem behavior, that did not tend to be reciprocally generative over time.

Anglin and Speckart (1986) examined the cross-lagged associations between narcotics use, dealing drugs, and crime. Dealing predicted narcotics use. Narcotics use, crime, and dealing were highly associated during periods of elevated narcotics use, and were not related during periods of reduced narcotics involvement.

Clayton and Tuchfeld (1982) criticized much of the research concerning drug use and criminal behavior. Using the Hirschi and Selvin (1973) criteria for causality discussed above, they argued that criminal involvement is indeed causally related to drug use (usually illicit and specifically heroin). They concluded that what others call spurious relationships, they call intervening or mediating variables. Clearly, the debate has not ended.

An important distinction not often drawn in these studies is that between deviant attitudes and engaging in deviant behavior. Although there is a reasonable association between holding an attitude, belief, or intention and performing a behavior related to that attitude (e.g., Bentler & Speckart, 1979), the relationship is certainly not perfect. It is likely that an attitude may be a better predictor or indicator of a general deviance syndrome rather than any particular deviant act. In other words, attitudes may reflect a general personological tendency toward performing deviant behaviors, and may be more closely associated to the behaviors than would be the association between different types of deviant behaviors. If this were true, we would expect to find a stronger association between deviant attitudes and behavior than between different types of deviant behavior. This pattern of relationships has been generally noted in research on deviant attitudes and behaviors (e.g., Huba & Bentler, 1984; Donovan & Jessor, 1985). A corollary of this notion would be that the mechanism or process by which one type of deviant behavior would influence, cause, or generate another type of deviant behavior would be via the intervening attitudinal structure. Thus the psychological makeup of the individual would be the mediating process. The exception to this, however, would be if there were some functional relationship between the types of deviant behaviors. The typical example for this is that heroin addicts must steal in order to maintain their habit. Thus stealing (one type of deviant behavior) is functionally related to narcotic addiction and using hard drugs (a different type of deviant behavior).

In our analyses, we focus largely on deviant behaviors that are generally recognized as such by society and institutionalized in our laws. Deviant attitudes are captured with our Social Conformity construct. Because our goal is to determine the consequences of teenage drug use, we examine the impact of drug use on engaging in various criminal behaviors as young adults, and do not test how early deviant behavior influences drug use over time. Such analyses have been presented elsewhere (e.g., Huba & Bentler, 1983a, 1984; Newcomb, Maddahian, & Bentler, 1986). The reciprocal influence between deviant attitudes and drug use was investigated in Chapter 6.

An important influence on the choice to engage in any behavior during adolescence is peer pressure and imitation of peer models. For instance, peer drug use is one of the strongest predictors of self use (e.g., Akers et al., 1979; Elliott et al., 1985; Huba & Bentler, 1982; Jessor et al., 1980; Kandel, 1973; Newcomb, Maddahian, & Bentler, 1986; Newman, 1984; Penning & Barnes, 1982) and there is a high association between peer and self sexual involvement in the teenage years (e.g., Newcomb, Huba, & Bentler, 1986c; Schultz, Bohrnstedt, Borgatta, & Evans, 1977). It seems likely that one of the precipitating influences for committing criminal activities may be one's peers or friendship network. Thus having a deviant friendship network may be a confounding influence when testing the association between early drug use and performing various criminal activities later. For this reason, it is vital to include peer influence in analyses that examine the drug/crime relationship; this has not been regularly done in other research of this type (e.g., Speckart & Anglin, 1986). This important factor is incorporated in our model described below.

Design of the Model

In the model for this chapter, which assesses the impact of teenage drug use on performing deviant and criminal behaviors, four constructs are included from the adolescent data and four constructs are from the young adult data. Two of the adolescent constructs are Drug Use and Social Conformity as included in all of the models. The other two constructs include Criminal Activities (with indicators of confrontational acts, stealing episodes, and property damage) and Deviant Friendship Network (with measured indicators of confrontational friends, friends deviant at school, and friends who steal). Although it would have been ideal to include adolescent measures for arrest history and involvement with the criminal justice system, these variables were not assessed when our subjects were teenagers. One can reasonably assume, however, that there is at least a moderate association between performing criminal acts and getting caught and held responsible for such behavior. In young adulthood, four constructs were measured including Drug Crime Involvement (with indicators of arrests and convictions for driving while intoxicated and selling or possessing drugs), Violent Crime Involvement (with indicators for the number of arrests and convictions for vandalism, carrying a deadly weapon, and assault), Property Crime Involvement (with indicators for the number of arrests and convictions for theft and other infractions), and Criminal Activities (with indicators identical to those from the adolescent period). A more thorough description of these variables is given in Chapter 4 and in the Appendix.

The statistical and methodological details related to the development of this model are provided in the "Technical Summary" at the end of this chapter. Two sets of analyses were performed for these data: The first using the standard ML estimator and the second using a method (AGLS) to account for the extreme nonnormality of these data (see the Appendix). The first analyses are presented in the typical manner in Tables 8.1 and 8.2 and Figures 8.1 and 8.2. Figure 8.1 depicts how the latent constructs were identified by the measured variables in the final confirmatory factor analysis (CFA) model. Table 8.1 presents the factor intercorrelations for the initial and final

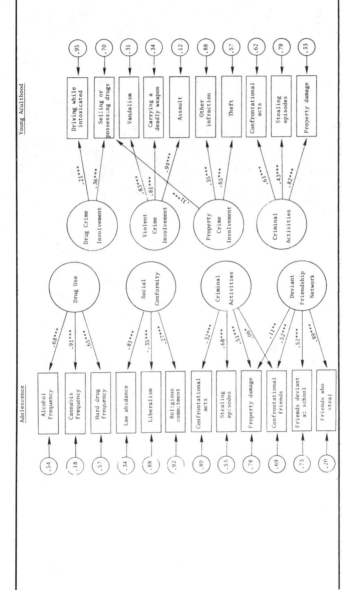

Figure 8.1. Final Confirmatory Factor Analysis Model for the Deviant Behavior Variables

NOTE: Large circles represent latent factors, rectangles are measured variables, and the small circles with numbers are residual variances. Factor loadings are standardized and significance levels were determined by critical ratios (*p < .05; **p < .01; ***p < .001). Not depicted in the figure are two-headed arrows (correlations) joining each possible pair of factors. Values for these correlations are provided in Table 8.1.

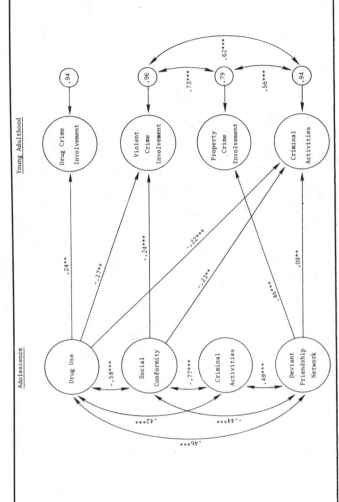

Figure 8.2. Final Structural or Path Model for the Deviant Behavior Variable

NOTE: The measurement portion of this model is not depicted for simplicity. Two-headed arrows reflect correlations and single-headed arrows represent across-time regression effects. Parameter estimates are standardized, residual variables are variances, and significance levels were determined by critical ratios (*p < .05; **p < .01; ***p < .001). Nonstandard effects for this model are given in Table 8.2.

108

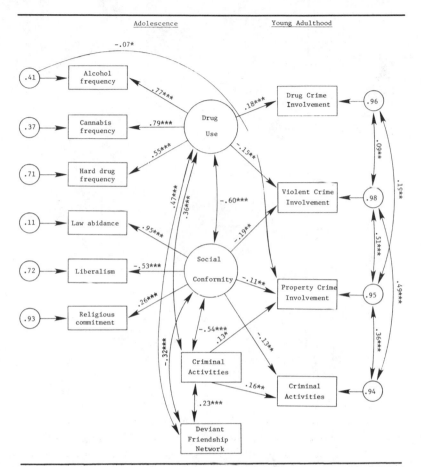

Figure 8.3. Final Structural Model Including Measurement Model for the Distribution-Free Estimates (AGLS) of the Deviant Behavior Variables

NOTE: Large circles reflect latent factors, rectangles represent measured variables, and small circles with numbers are residual variances. Two-headed arrows are correlations and single-headed arrows represent regression effects. Parameter estimates are standardized and significance levels were determined by critical ratios (*p < .05; **p < .01; ***p < .001).

CFA models. The final structural model is depicted in Figure 8.2 and Table 8.2. The figure presents the relationship among latent factors, whereas the table reports the nonstandard effects that include at least one measured variable. Figure 8.3 summarizes the results for the second set of analyses.

TABLE 8.1
Factor Intercorrelations for the Initial (upper triangle) and Final (lower triangle) Confirmatory Factor Analysis Models

Factor	I	II	III	IV	V	VI	VII	VIII
Late Adolescence								
I Drug Use	1.00	−.72***	.41***	.50***	.26***	−.05	.23***	.01
II Social Conformity	−.60***	1.00	−.83***	−.49***	−.27***	−.13**	−.39***	−.21***
III Criminal Activities	.43***	−.82***	1.00	.46***	.27***	.06	.49***	.15**
IV Deviant Friendship Network	.52***	−.51***	.55***	1.00	.14*	.04	.25***	.14**
Young Adulthood								
V Drug Crime Involvement	.28***	−.24***	.13**	.04	1.00	−.23***	.67***	.02
VI Violent Crime Involvement	−.01	−.16***	.08*	.05	−.15**	1.00	.74***	.60***
VII Property Crime Involvement	.22***	−.37***	.49***	.23***	.63***	.64***	1.00	.67***
VIII Criminal Activities	−.03	−.18***	.11**	.13**	−.13**	.64***	.60***	1.00

*p < .05; **p < .01; ***p < .001.

TABLE 8.2
Direct Across-Time Causal Paths
Not Depicted in Figure

Adolescent Predictor Variable		Young Adult Consequent Variable		Standardized Parameter Estimate[a]
Observed Variable	*Latent Variable*	*Observed Variable*	*Latent Variable*	
	Drug Use	confrontational acts		.19**
	Drug Use	stealing episodes		.11**
alcohol frequency (R)[b]		theft		−.11**
hard drug frequency (R)		assault		.05**
liberalism (R)		property damage		−.06*
religious commitment (R)		vandalism		−.06*
confrontational friends (R)		confrontational acts		.09**
stealing episodes (R)		carry deadly weapon		.09**
	Deviant Friendship Network	stealing episodes		.17**
friends who steal		selling or possessing drugs		.18**
friends deviant at school (R)		vandalism		.08**

a. Significance level determined by a critical ratio of the unstandardized parameter estimate divided by its standard error.
b. (R) denotes variable residual.
*p < .05; **p < .01; ***p < .001.

Interpretation

The CFA estimates correlations among the eight factors or constructs that are disattenuated for measurement error. As such, these correlations represent the true or error-free associations among the constructs and provide valuable data regarding how the constructs are related. In the final CFA model for drug use and deviant behavior, the adolescent Drug Use factor was significantly correlated with all other adolescent factors and two of the four young adult factors. Teenage Drug Use was significantly related to lowered Social Conformity, more Criminal Activities (during adolescence, but not young adulthood), having a Deviant Friendship Network, Drug Crime Involvement, and Property Crime Involvement (see Table 8.1). Adolescent Social Conformity was significantly associated with lowered criminal or deviant behavior on all factors. Engaging in Criminal Activities as an adolescent was significantly related to all of the young adult constructs, but only substantially so with Property Crime Involvement. Having a very Deviant Friendship Network was associated with performing Criminal Activities (at both age levels), but was not correlated with Drug Crime Involvement and Violent Crime Involvement in the final CFA model. Among the young adulthood constructs, Criminal Activities, Violent Crime Involvement, and Property Crime Involvement were all highly intercorrelated in a positive direction. Drug Crime Involvement was to a small degree negatively correlated with both Criminal Activities and Violent Crime Involvement, but was highly positively correlated with Property Crime Involvement.

Three additional factor loadings were necessary to include in the measurement portion of the models. These indicated that the general tendency toward performing Criminal Activities during adolescence was also predictive of having confrontational friends, that the tendency to have a Deviant Friendship Network also influenced doing things that created property damage, and that arrests and convictions for Property Crime Involvement during young adulthood also predicted selling or possessing drugs. Thus, during adolescence, the overlap between self and peer behavior appears to be associated with damaging property and having aggressive and confrontational friends. In young adulthood, selling or possessing drugs aside from reflecting a general inclination toward Drug Crime Involvement was also reflected in Property Crime Involvement.

In the final structural model, several interesting and significant relationships were found between the latent constructs (see Figures 8.2 and 8.3). General Drug Use during adolescence significantly influenced getting arrested or convicted for Drug Crime Involvement in young adulthood, after controlling for all other adolescent constructs. Interestingly, however, teenage Drug Use negatively predicted arrests and/or convictions for Violent Crime Involvement during young adulthood, and had no direct impact on later Property Crime Involvement. In the ML model (Figure 8.2), adolescent Drug Use predicted decreased young adult Criminal Activities, although this effect was not apparent in the CFA factor correlations nor as a path in the more appropriate AGLS model (Figure 8.3). Early Social Conformity predicted decreased Criminal Activities, decreased Violent Crime Involvement, and, in the AGLS solution, decreased Property Crime Involvement. Adolescent Deviant Friendship Network had no direct effect on any of the young adult constructs in the AGLS model (there were two effects in the ML model): Its influence was mediated through the other adolescent constructs via its high correlations with them. Early Criminal Activities significantly increased the chances of engaging in Criminal Activities and Property Crime Involvement as young adults, but did not directly affect Drug Crime Involvement and Violent Crime Involvement. These last effects were only noted in the AGLS model (Figure 8.3), while the predictor constructs were reversed in the ML model (Figure 8.2).

These paths among latent constructs indicate that deviant attitudes (as reflected in lack of Social Conformity) were as strong, if not stronger predictors of later deviant behavior, as reflected in Criminal Activities, Violent Crime Involvement, and Property Crime Involvement, than were early deviant acts (adolescent Criminal Activities). On the other hand, immersion in a Deviant Friendship Network during adolescence did not have a direct impact on increasing later deviant behavior, such as Criminal Activities and arrests and/or convictions for Property Crime Involvement (in the AGLS model, Figure 8.3). Early Drug Use significantly affected the frequency of arrests and convictions for Drug Crime Involvement, but did not generalize in a positive direction to other types of crimes. In fact, teenage Drug Use significantly decreased Violent Crime Involvement as young adults, after controlling for the influences of teenage deviant attitudes and behavior. This inverse relationship (and a similar one also noted in the ML model) between early Drug Use and later deviant behavior is not a suppressor effect: the zero-order correlation between the constructs is also negative. Thus we must conclude that early Drug Use seems to decrease this specific type of later criminal behavior (Violent Crime Involvement), from adolescence to young adulthood.

This last point is a fascinating one, because it suggests that drug use may become less associated with general deviancy (as reflected in all types of criminal activities) over time. This is corroborated by the fact that there was no residual factor correlation between Drug Crime Involvement and the other deviant behavior factors during young adulthood in the ML model (Figure 8.2), and quite small correlation in the AGLS model (Figure 8.3), as well as by the pattern of correlations in the final CFA model (Table 8.1). On the other hand, the residuals of all three nondrug crime variables or factors were in both models quite highly positively correlated, indicating that they share great commonality in young adulthood. Thus drug use and the problems associated with drug use (i.e., driving while intoxicated and selling and possessing drugs) become disassociated with other forms of deviance as the teenager grows to adulthood. None of the deviant attitude or behavior constructs during adolescence, except for Drug Use, predicted Drug Crime Involvement. Thus deviant attitudes (lack of Social Conformity) and non-drug-related deviant behaviors as a teenager did not directly influence Drug Crime Involvement as a young adult. This suggests that the syndrome of problem behaviors identified among an adolescent population (e.g., Donovan & Jessor, 1985) does not remain a unified construct as the teenager matures, but rather differentiates into at least two types of deviant behavior: drug-use-related problems and other forms of deviance. Greater diversity in clusters of problem behaviors and deviant involvement apparently characterizes this period of development.

When we look beyond the relationships between general tendencies or latent factors, a greater degree of cross-fertilization between Drug Use and other specific types of deviant behavior is apparent (see Table 8.2). The residual variable of hard drug frequency was associated with later assault violation. This indicates that the specific use of hard drugs (separate from general drug involvement) increased the frequency of assault violations as a young adult. Thus we may guardedly conclude that specific use of hard drugs as a teenager increases aggressive and assaultive behavior as a young adult. This is clearly a very negative consequence of early drug use. On the other hand, the specific use of alcohol during adolescence decreased arrests and/or convictions for theft during young adulthood (or Property Crime Involvement in the AGLS model, Figure 8.3). Again, this supports the divergence or differentiation of deviant behaviors as the teenager develops into an adult. In fact, this suggests that heavy involvement with alcohol to the exclusion of illicit drugs (possibly reflecting a resistance to progressing to harder and strictly illegal substances) may inhibit or decrease certain types of criminal behavior (theft) over time. The general factor of teenage Drug Use (reflecting heavy involvement with both licit and illicit substances), however, was associated with increased confrontational acts and stealing episodes during young adulthood. At least for these specific types of deviant behaviors, there is a cross-fertilization over time. Several other small associations were noted between early deviant attitudes and behavior and later specific types of deviant behavior, suggesting a certain degree of synergism over time regarding various types of non-drug-related deviance. For instance, having a Deviant Friendship Network during adolescence increased the number of stealing episodes as young adults. Similarly, the number of teenage stealing episodes increased arrests and/or convictions for carrying a deadly weapon. Clearly, a life-style of deviant and criminal involvement is progressing and solidifying during this critical maturational period from adolescence to young adulthood.

Technical Summary

Confirmatory Factor Analyses

The first step in our data analyses is to assess the adequacy of our hypothesized measurement model, as outlined above.

An initial confirmatory factor model was run that (a) fixed all factor variances at unity, (b) allowed all constructs to correlate freely, and (c) included correlations between the residuals of the three indicators of the Criminal Activities construct (because these three variables were measured repeatedly). This initial CFA model did not adequately reflect the data (χ^2 = 559.18, d.f. = 178, p < .001), although the Normed Fit Index (NFI) was sufficiently large (.88) to suggest that minor modifications to the model should yield an acceptable fit. Factor intercorrelations for this initial model are presented in the upper triangle of Table 8.1.

By examining the modification indices (Bentler, 1986c; Bentler & Chou, 1986), correlations among 47 pairs of residuals were added to the model. In addition, three nonhypothesized factor loadings were necessary. These modifications resulted in a model that adequately reflected the data (χ^2 = 149.16, d.f. = 128, p = .10, NFI = .97). This model could not be rejected as a plausible explanation of the data. Factor intercorrelations for this final confirmatory factor analysis model are presented in the lower triangle of Table 8.1. All hypothesized factor loadings were significant. Standardized factor loadings and variances of residuals of the observed variables for this final CFA model are graphically depicted in Figure 8.1.

In order to test whether adding the correlated residuals disturbed the fundamental associations among the latent constructs, the factor intercorrelations between the initial and final confirmatory factor analysis models were correlated. This correlation was higher than .97, indicating that the model modifications did not alter the basic pattern of factor intercorrelations.

Structural Model Analyses

The next stage in data analyses was the creation of a structural or path model, which includes regression effects representing unidirectional influences of one variable upon another. As mentioned previously, we do not include regression paths within time. Within-time associations are captured as correlations among constructs, factor loadings, or correlated residuals. The regression effects in which we are most interested are those across time that may have a plausible causal inference. The empirically determined across-time correlated residuals were deleted in the initial structural model. All young adult constructs were initially predicted from all adolescent constructs.

This beginning model was modified by adding across-time regression paths (based on the modification indices) and deleting nonsignificant parameters. The final model includes only significant paths. In this instance, the final structural model fit the data quite well (χ^2 = 140.50, d.f. = 145, p = .59, NFI = .97). Associations among the latent factors are graphically displayed in Figure 8.2, whereas the across-time paths that include at least one observed variable are listed in Table 8.2 with their standardized regression weights. As in all presentations of the final structural model, the relationships presented in Figure 8.2 and those listed in Table 8.2 are based on the same final model, and are presented separately only for reasons of clarity.

Additional Analyses

Many of the variables included in this deviant behavior model are extremely nonnormally distributed. As a result, the model presented above, which is based on the maximum likelihood (ML) estimator (that includes an assumption of multivariate normality), may be inaccurate because of this normality violation. A distribution-free estimator (AGLS-arbitrary distribution generalized least squares: Bentler, 1983; Browne, 1984) does not require multivariate normality in the data. Unfortunately, this procedure is difficult to use in models with over 20 observed variables (e.g., Bentler & Newcomb, 1986a).

The final structural model presented above was tested with the AGLS estimator and was not able to reach a solution due to technical difficulties that we were not able to rectify. One aspect of the problem was the large number of variables. To reduce the number of variables, summed scores were created for all latent factors except Drug Use and Social Conformity. We then tested a model that included two latent factors (Drug Use and Social Conformity) and two summed, observed variables (Criminal Activities and Deviant Friendship Network) from the adolescent age period, and four summed, observed variables from the young adult data. Thus this model is parallel to the initial structural model developed above, except that six of the constructs are now measured (summated) variables rather than latent factors.

An initial structural model was tested and then refined for the variables and factors described above using the AGLS estimator. The final model that fit the data quite well, $\chi^2(37, N = 654) = 35.72$, p = .53, NFI = .94, is presented in Figure 8.3. Nonsignificant paths were deleted and parameter estimates are standardized. In this model, which was not distorted by the nonnormality of the data, young adult Drug Crime Involvement was significantly predicted only from adolescent Drug Use, which corroborates the earlier results. Similarly, young adult Violent Crime Involvement was significantly predicted from less adolescent Drug Use and less adolescent Social Conformity, as in the previous model. Thus there is some consistency of results across methods, but it is not as much as has been reported (Huba & Harlow, 1987). The main discrepancy between the current model and the previous one above is in the prediction of Property Crime Involvement and Criminal Activities. In the AGLS solution, Property Crime Involvement was predicted from lowered earlier alcohol use (residual), low Social Conformity, and high Criminal Activities. On the other hand, Criminal Activities was predicted from lowered adolescent Social Conformity and earlier Criminal Activities. The critical distinction between results from these two methods for drug use consequences is the lack of a direct effect from early Drug Use to decreased Criminal Activities, which is included in the maximum likelihood model but not in the AGLS model. Thus this effect must be considered guardedly, although most other critical effects were corroborated using this more appropriate method. Unfortunately, due to the necessity of using summed scores rather than latent factors, we were unable to verify the more specific effects of particular types of drugs on specific types of deviant behavior, as given in Table 8.2.

Although not directly related to drug use effects, the other critical differences between the ML and AGLS models are in the influences of adolescent Criminal Activities and Deviant Friendship Network. In the AGLS model, the Deviant Friendship Network variable had no direct impact on any young adult variable, whereas in the ML model this variable (latent factor, in this case) predicted young adult Property Crime Involvement and Criminal Activities. The reverse situation occurs on the impact of adolescent Criminal Activities. In this situation, we would favor the AGLS solution, because it is not distorted due to the normality violations, and it captures the stability effect for Criminal Activities (which was not found in the ML solution). It makes more intuitive sense that later self-behaviors are predicted more accurately from earlier self-behaviors rather than peer behaviors.

9

Impact on Sexual
Behavior and
Involvement

One of the overriding concerns and preoccupations of most adolescents is dating and sexual involvement. Folk wisdom suggests that drugs often pave the way for initiating sexual behavior ("Candy is dandy, but likker is quicker"), and Bentler and Newcomb (1986a) found that extent of general drug use and sexual involvement were correlated higher than .70. Donovan and Jessor (1985) suggest that this strong association is caused by an underlying tendency toward deviance or problem behavior. In other words, drug use and sexual activity may not causally affect each other, because they are themselves predicted by a more general tendency; the apparent association is spurious. This hypothesis would predict very little across-time influence between early drug use and later sexual behavior (controlling, of course, for early sexual behavior), even though the within-time or contemporaneous associations between these activities may be quite high.

At low dose levels, drugs may facilitate sexual interaction, perhaps by reducing inhibitions (e.g., Nicholi, 1984). Chronic and excessive drug use, however, may result in various types of sexual dysfunction (e.g., Smith, Wesson, & Apter-Marsh, 1984). These effects are largely the result of the acute or chronic pharmacological effects of the drugs. It is less clear whether teenage drug use affects general attitudes and approaches to dating and sexual involvement.

For instance, Yamaguchi and Kandel (1985b) found that marijuana apparently increased the probability of cohabiting, a clear indication of premarital sexual permissiveness. Similar patterns have been reported by Newcomb (1986c; Newcomb & Bentler, 1985) for other drugs as well. It is most likely, however, that drug use and cohabitation (or sexual permissiveness) are both generated by the same general underlying cause (unobserved), such as deviancy or lack of social conformity. Yamaguchi and Kandel (1985b) also found that separation from a cohabital partner was related to illicit drug use other than marijuana.

Very little research has examined the association between drug use and sexual behaviors among adolescents, aside from testing hypotheses related to a general deviance syndrome. On the other hand, a great deal of energy has been devoted to studying sexual activities and practices of teenagers. Historically, these studies have typically been directed toward determining the incidence (e.g., Barrett, 1980), age of onset, and changes over time of various types of sexual activities (e.g., Downey, 1980; Raboch & Bartak, 1980). For instance, Diepold and Young (1979) reviewed data that indicated that teenage women have been steadily increasing their level of dating and sexual behavior and are converging with males who have previously reported much higher levels of involvement and incidence of sexual activities than women. They further claim that although there has not been a sexual revolution per se, as frequently depicted in the popular press, there has been a steady evolution in the sexual behavior of adolescents. Specific types of behavior that have been examined in this manner include dating, kissing, petting, masturbation, premarital intercourse, homosexual contact, and birth control (e.g., Clayton & Bokemeier, 1980; Diepold & Young, 1979; Freeman, Rickels, Huggins, Mudd, Garcia, & Dickens, 1980; Jorgensen & Sontegard, 1984). Studies of college student samples reveal that about 75% of the women and 83% of the men have engaged in premarital intercourse (e.g., Murstein & Holden, 1979). It is important to understand in a developmental manner the processes by which most college students have chosen to engage in premarital sexual intercourse, contrary to prevailing ideology (Reiss, 1981), and whether drug use plays a significant role in the variations in emerging sexual behavior. Simply observing the incidence and prevalence levels of various sexual activities cannot provide a clear explanation of how these developmental patterns emerge nor how drug use may have influenced them. Of course, changing and evolving patterns of sexuality, partner choice, and consequent cultural milieu shifts all have important theoretical and practical implications for the institutions of marriage and family, as well as larger patterns of societal evolution (e.g., Downey, 1980; Udry, 1980; White, 1982; and see Chapter 7).

One simple approach commonly taken to study the developmental antecedents or concomitants of teenage sexual involvement has been to test for various correlates of sexual behavior (e.g., Newcomb, 1985) or differences between virgins and nonvirgins. For example, Dornbusch et al. (1981) examined the relative influence of biological preparedness and social influences upon the onset of teenage dating activities. They concluded that psychological readiness was not as crucial in determining when dating behavior will commence as were the social influences of parents and friendship networks. Murstein and Holden (1979) found few differences between virginal and nonvirginal men, whereas women reported many differences depending upon their history of sexual experience. Sexually inexperienced women reported being closer to both parents, felt that they were less attractive, and came from a more religious home than women who had engaged in premarital sexual intercourse. Jessor and Jessor (1975) compared virgins and nonvirgins in high school and college in regard to a variety of psychosocial factors and concluded that nonvirgins were more deviance-prone, less conventional, perceived their environment as more conducive to problem behavior, and had engaged in more deviant and less conforming behavior than virgins. Some contradictory findings also have been reported regarding drug use and sexual behavior. Jessor and Jessor (1977) note that drug use and sexual experience are positively associated, while Murstein and Holden (1979) found higher drug use among sexually inexperienced adolescents.

Although these correlates of teenage sexual activity move

the field a step closer to understanding adolescent influences on sexual behavior—certainly more than simple incidence and attitude cataloging (e.g., Hass, 1981)—many studies have received criticism on methodological and theoretical grounds (Diepold & Young, 1979). The limited use of adequate statistical procedures and appropriate methodologies has hampered understanding the more complex, developmental patterns and processes of adolescent sexual behavior. For example, Jurich (1979) emphasized the necessity of examining interdependent influences on the development of premarital sexual standards and behavior, because such attitudes and behavior are multiply determined. Data analyses that do not consider numerous influences in a simultaneous manner lack the ability to study complex configural patterns of development.

A fruitful beginning to using a more multicausal approach that provides a richer and more realistic understanding of the processes of sexual socialization has been offered in more recent studies. For instance, several researchers have used multiple regression analysis or path analytic methods to evaluate simultaneously various theories regarding teenage sexual involvement (e.g., Bentler & Peeler, 1979; D'Augelli & Cross, 1975; DeLamater & MacCorquodale, 1979; Hornick, 1978; Jessor & Jessor, 1977; Libby, Gray, & White, 1978), while others have used the newer latent-variable causal modeling methodologies as incorporated in the present set of analyses (e.g., Bentler & Huba, 1979; Newcomb & Bentler, 1983; Newcomb et al., 1986c).

Multiple regression analyses have occasionally been used to examine several different influences on particular criterion measures such as the transition to nonvirginity (Jessor & Jessor, 1975), timing of first intercourse (Jessor, Costa, Jessor, & Donovan, 1983), attitudes toward premarital sexual relations (Singh, 1980), couples' sexual experience (D'Augelli & Cross, 1975), and sexual ideology and current behavior (DeLamater & MacCorquodale, 1979). Multiple classification analysis has been used to study teenage pregnancy and contraceptive use (Zelnik, Kantner, & Ford, 1981).

Path analytic methods have also been used to examine

simultaneously the multiple influences on sexual attitudes and behavior. For instance, Schultz, Bohrnstedt, Borgatta, and Evans (1977) examined a system of six variables in order to develop a model of college students' premarital sex experience. They found that factors such as friends' sex behavior had a major influence on the student's sex behavior both directly and as a mediator for attitudes and other structural factors (i.e., off-campus residence). Hornick (1978) also used path analysis to examine a large system of observed variables that were reflected in five more broadly defined areas. In general, the results of these analyses indicated that social background characteristics influenced an individual's sexual attitudes and behavior through the mediation of reference group (e.g., parental and peer attitudes) and individual psychological orientation (e.g., religiosity) variables. Bentler and Peeler (1979) found in a simultaneous path analysis design that personality measures (neuroticism, extroversion, and attitudes toward masturbation) predicted actual behavior (heterosexual and monosexual behaviors), which in turn predicted orgasmic responsiveness (during coitus and masturbation).

Finally, in a large model that included eight latent constructs (reflected in 26 observed variables), Newcomb et al. (1986c) found that importance of dating was the single most powerful influence on sexual and dating involvement among teenagers. Importance of dating mediated various other influences on sexual activity, such as self-acceptance, heterosexual competence, and stressful life events. Interestingly, dating and sexual involvement appeared to influence the selection of deviant and sexually active social networks, rather than the reverse. Of course, longitudinal data that were not available in this study must be consulted to confirm this conclusion.

Numerous other studies have examined other important but more specific aspects of adolescent and young adult sexual development and behavior. One area that has received a great deal of attention is contraceptive use. A wide range of factors have been studied to account for the use of contraception and choice of a reliable method. Such significant influences have included attitudes and intentions (Jorgensen & Sontegard, 1984), friends' use of contraception and length of time the partners knew each other (Sack, Billingham, & Howard, 1985), and several other behavioral, attitudinal, and demographic qualities (e.g., Geis & Gerrard, 1984). One consistent finding is that men are less informed about contraception, are less likely to recognize the risk of pregnancy, and have fewer attitudes supportive of birth control than women (e.g., Freeman et al., 1980). Interestingly, in another study, the use of effective birth control was predicted more accurately from male variables than female variables (Geis & Gerrard, 1984). More effective contraception was used by men who were not dogmatic, were in a committed and stable relationship, became involved sexually at an older age, and were knowledgeable about birth control methods. The authors point out, however, that such men employ types of effective contraception (i.e., the pill, IUD) that are typically the responsibility of the woman. Thus these qualities in the men may attract women who use more reliable birth control. Many of these factors appear to be similar to those of a socially conforming individual who is disinclined toward problem or deviant behavior. It is possible that a disinterest in drug use may be related to this characterological pattern. For example, Robins et al. (1970) reported that adult Black males who had used marijuana in adolescence were significantly more likely to have fathered illegitimate children than those who had been nonusers. Similarly, it has been found that female heroin addicts use contraception significantly less frequently than a national sample of women (Ralph & Spigner, 1986). And, among teenage girls, the frequency of smoking cigarettes was negatively related to age at first intercourse and use of effective birth control (Zabin, 1984). Thus lack of sexual responsibility (use of none or ineffective birth control) may be related to problem behavior, deviance, and drug use. Many of these factors are included in the models of drug use and sexual behavior that we report below.

Design of the Model

A great deal of the literature reviewed above has found different patterns and processes of teenage sexual development for men compared to women. As a result, we will depart from our standard approach of combining the sexes for the analyses and create separate models for men and women. The variables and latent constructs are essentially identical in both models, with the exception of one additional young adult construct in the women's model (Abortion Occurrence).

In the two models for this chapter—which assess the impact of teenage drug use on dating attitudes, sexual behavior, and contraceptive use—six constructs are included from the adolescent data (three latent factors and three single-variable factors that are treated as constructs) and seven constructs are from the young adult data for the women, whereas six constructs are from the young adult data for the men (one young adult construct for the men and women is a single-variable factor). Two of the adolescent constructs, Drug Use and Social Conformity, are included in all of the models. The other four constructs include Early Sexual Involvement (with measured indicators for age of first sexual contact and age of first sexual intercourse), Frequency of Sexual Events (a single-indicator factor), Number of Sexually Active Friends (a single-indicator factor), and Satisfaction with Opposite-Sex Relationships (a single-indicator factor). Our assessment of sexual behavior and activity was less detailed in the teenage years than we were able to assess in young adulthood. As a result, the young adult measures provide greater detail than those in adolescence. Fortunately, those measures obtained during adolescence are of a general nature, while targeting critical information (e.g., Sexually Active Friends). Thus the teenage variables should provide an adequate baseline to gauge the influence of drug use on the more detailed young adult assessments. In young adulthood, six constructs were included for both men and women. These included Birth Control Effectiveness (with measured-variable indicators of effectiveness of current birth control and effectiveness of future birth control), Dating Competence (reflected by three scales of dating competence 1, 2, and 3), Satisfaction with Intimacy (with indicators of happy with sex life, happy being close with someone, and satisfaction with sexual intercourse), Number of Relationships (reflected in the number of steady partners and the number of sexual partners), Frequency of Intercourse (with measured-variable indicators for intercourse frequency per week and intercourse frequency per month), and Contracted Venereal Disease (a single-variable factor). For the women only, an additional young adult construct was included in the model. This latent construct was Abortion Occurrence (with indicators of ever had an abortion and number of abortions). A more thorough description of these measures is given in Chapter 4 and in the Appendix.

Separate "Interpretation" sections are devoted to the women's and men's models in this chapter, as are separate "Technical Summary" sections. A final "Summary Interpretation" contrasts the results from the two models.

The statistical and methodological details related to the development of these models are provided in the "Technical Summary" sections at the end of this chapter. Figure 9.1 depicts how the measured variables were generated by the latent constructs in the final confirmatory factor analysis (CFA) model for the women, whereas analogous results for the men are given in Figure 9.3. Table 9.1 presents the factor intercorrelations for the initial and final CFA models of the women's data (Table 9.3 for the men's data). The final structural model for the women is depicted in Figure 9.2 and Table 9.2, and in Figure 9.4 and Table 9.4 for the men. The figure presents the relationship among latent factors, whereas the table reports the nonstandard effects that include at least one measured variable.

Interpretation of the
Women's Model

In the final CFA model for drug use and sexual behavior for the women, the adolescent Drug Use factor was significantly correlated with all other adolescent factors except Satisfaction with Opposite-Sex Relationships and all young adult constructs except for Birth Control Effectiveness and Satisfaction with Intimacy. Teenage Drug Use was significantly related to lowered Social Conformity, Early Sexual Involvement, high Frequency of Sexual Events, a large Number of Sexually Active Friends, more Dating Competence, a greater Number of Relationships, a high Frequency of Intercourse, higher Abortion Occurrence, and having Contracted Venereal Disease

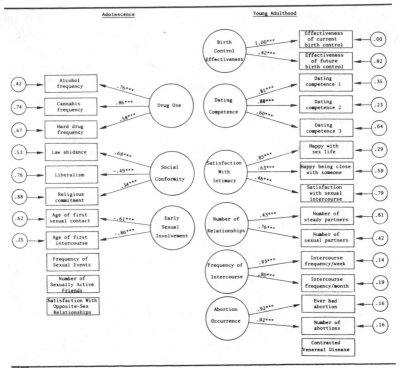

Figure 9.1.   Final Confirmatory Factor Analysis Model for the Women's Sexual Behavior Variables

NOTE: Large circles represent latent factors, rectangles are measured variables, and the small circles with numbers are residual variances. Factor loadings are standardized and significance levels were determined by critical ratios (*p < .05; **p < .01; ***p < .001). Not depicted in the figure are two-headed arrows (correlations) joining each possible pair of factors. Values for these correlations are provided in Table 9.1.

(see Table 9.1). Adolescent Social Conformity was correlated significantly with eight of the nine same constructs with which Drug Use was correlated, except in a consistently reversed direction. Social Conformity was not significantly associated with Dating Competence. Early Sexual Involvement was significantly associated with higher Drug Use, lower Social Conformity, higher Frequency of Sexual Events, a greater Number of Sexually Active Friends, increased Dating Competence, greater Number of Relationships, a higher Frequency of Intercourse, a greater likelihood of Abortion Occurrence, and a higher possibility that she had Contracted Venereal Disease.

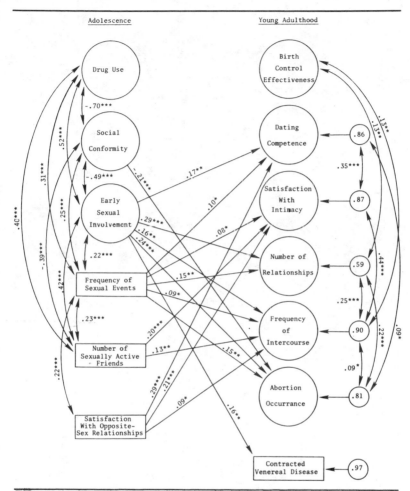

Figure 9.2. Final Structural or Path Model for the Women's Sexual Behavior Variables

NOTE: The measurement portion of this model is not depicted for simplicity. Two-headed arrows reflect correlations and single-headed arrows represent across-time regression effects. Parameter estimates are standardized, residual variables are variances, and significance levels were determined by critical ratios (*p < .05; **p < .01; ***p < .001). Nonstandard effects for this model are given in Table 9.2.

Most of the remaining sexual behavior and activity constructs were correlated in expected directions (greater involvement, more activity, more abortions, and more venereal disease). The two satisfaction factors were correlated somewhat less with the

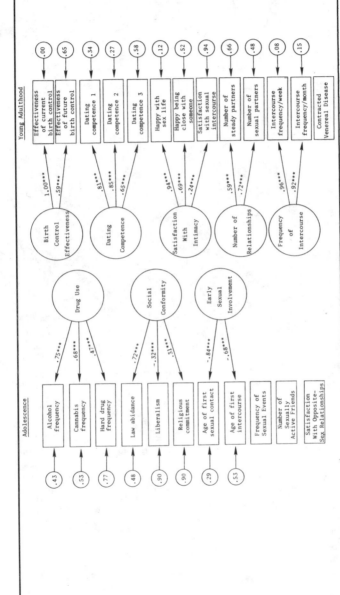

Figure 9.3. Final Confirmatory Factor Analysis Model for the Men's Sexual Behavior Variables

NOTE: Large circles represent latent factors, rectangles are measured variables, and the small circles with numbers are residual variances. Factor loadings are standardized and significance levels were determined by critical ratios (*p < .05; **p < .01; ***p < .001). Not depicted in the figure are two-headed arrows (correlations) joining each possible pair of factors. Values for these correlations are provided in Table 9.3.

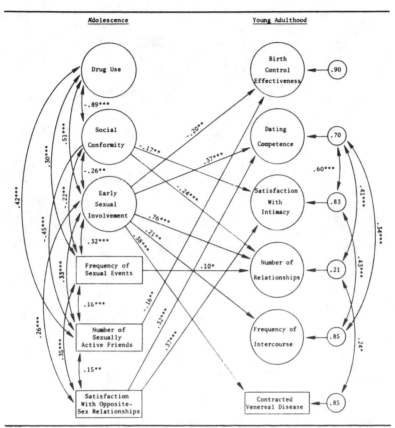

Figure 9.4. Final Structural or Path Model for the Men's Sexual Behavior Variables

NOTE: The measurement portion of this model is not depicted for simplicity. Two-headed arrows reflect correlations and single-headed arrows represent across-time regression effects. Parameter estimates are standardized, residual variables are variances, and significance levels were determined by critical ratios (*p < .05; **p < .01; ***p < .001). Nonstandard effects for this model are given in Table 9.4.

activity and behavior factors, whereas the Birth Control Effectiveness construct was significantly correlated only with a decrease on Contracted Venereal Disease.

In the final structural model, several interesting and significant effects were found between the adolescent and young adult latent constructs (see Figure 9.2). Within the context of the controls used, these represent causal influences over time. Interestingly, there was no direct effect of teenage

TABLE 9.1
Analyses of the Women's Data: Factor Intercorrelations for the Initial (upper triangle) and Final (lower triangle) Confirmatory Factor Analysis Models

Factor	I	II	III	IV	V	VI	VII	VIII	IX	X	XI	XII	XIII
Late Adolescence													
I Drug Use	1.00	-.74***	.48***	.23***	.38***	.02	.01	.14**	.07	.54***	.20***	.30***	.13**
II Social Conformity	-.71***	1.00	-.47***	-.26***	-.43***	-.04	-.06	-.08	-.03	-.46***	-.14***	-.37***	-.10*
III Early Sexual Involvement	.48***	-.45***	1.00	.23***	.39***	.04	-.05	.19***	.06	.59***	.19***	.35***	.12**
IV Frequency of Sexual Events	.24***	-.22***	.22***	1.00	.23***	.23***	-.05	.26***	.19***	.26***	.17***	.25***	.04
V Number of Sexually Active Friends	.40***	-.41***	.38***	.23***	1.00	.05	-.04	.15**	.21***	.35***	.23***	.22***	.12**
VI Satisfaction with Opposite-Sex Relationships	.02	-.05	.04	.23***	.05	1.00	-.05	.28***	.25***	.08	.13**	.10*	-.06
Young Adulthood													
VII Birth Control Effectiveness	.01	-.08	-.05	-.04	-.04	-.05	1.00	-.03	.04	.02	.10*	.03	-.07*
VIII Dating Competence	.15**	-.03	.19***	.26***	.15**	.28***	-.04	1.00	.47***	.23***	.26***	.21***	-.07
IX Satisfaction with Intimacy	.08	-.06	.05	.18***	.23***	.24***	.01	.46***	1.00	.15**	.53***	.11*	-.09*
X Number of Relationships	.52***	-.48***	.57***	.26***	.37***	.08	.05	.24***	.17***	1.00	.31***	.39***	.18***
XI Frequency of Intercourse	.20***	-.17**	.19***	.17***	.23***	.13**	.05	.26***	.53***	.34***	1.00	.21***	.01
XII Abortion Occurrence	.32***	-.34***	.33***	.26***	.23***	.10*	.03	.21***	.12*	.42***	.22***	1.00	.11**
XIII Contracted Veneral Disease	.13**	-.10*	.12**	.04	.12**	-.06	-.07*	-.06	-.09*	.16**	.01	.10*	1.00

*p < .05; **p < .01; ***p < .001.

132

TABLE 9.2
Analyses of the Women's Data: Direct Across-Time Causal Paths Not Depicted in Figure 9.2

Adolescent Predictor Variable		Young Adult Consequent Variable		Standardized Parameter Estimate[a]
Observed Variable	Latent Variable	Observed Variable	Latent Variable	
alcohol frequency (R)[b]		number of steady partners		.10*
hard drug frequency (R)		happy being close with someone		−.09**
hard drug frequency			Number of Relationships	.42***
	Social Conformity	dating competence 3		.08*
	Social Conformity	happy with sex life		−.12**
	Social Conformity	number of steady partners		.17**
law abidance (R)		dating competence 2		−.09**
religious commitment (R)		effectiveness of future birth control		.09**
religious commitment			Satisfaction with Intimacy	.21***
	Early Sexual Involvement	number of steady partners		.28**
age of first sexual contact (R)		dating competence 3		.10**
number of sexually active friends		effectiveness of future birth control		.09**
number of sexually active friends		dating competence 2		.06*
frequency of sexual events		dating competence 2		.09**
satisfaction with opposite-sex relationships		dating competence 2		.10**

a. Significance level determined by a critical ratio of the unstandardized parameter estimate divided by its standard error.
b. (R) denotes variable residual.
*p < .05; **p < .01; ***p < .001.

TABLE 9.3

Analyses of the Men's Data: Factor Intercorrelations for the Initial (upper triangle) and Final (lower triangle) Confirmatory Factor Analysis Models

Factor	I	II	III	IV	V	VI	VII	VIII	IX	X	XI	XII
Late Adolescence												
I Drug Use	1.00	-.81***	.47***	.32***	.39***	.17**	-.15*	.20**	.11	.69***	.23**	.26***
II Social Conformity	-.84***	1.00	-.30***	-.25***	-.48***	-.08	.07	-.08	-.13	-.55***	-.41***	-.08
III Early Sexual Involvement	.53***	-.29***	1.00	.32***	.33***	.28***	-.23***	.44***	.21**	.74***	.32***	.36***
IV Frequency of Sexual Events	.34***	-.24***	.31***	1.00	.18**	.38***	-.17**	.22**	.11	.46***	.06	.20**
V Number of Sexually Active Friends	.44***	-.48***	.31***	.18**	1.00	.20**	-.23***	.21**	.15*	.39***	.16*	.13*
VI Satisfaction with Opposite-Sex Relationships	.19**	-.07	.29***	.38***	.20**	1.00	-.18**	.46***	.41***	.38***	.18**	.15*
Young Adulthood												
VII Birth Control Effectiveness	-.18*	.05	-.23**	-.17**	-.23**	-.18**	1.00	-.25***	-.16*	-.18*	-.14*	-.06
VIII Dating Competence	.27**	-.12	.48***	.24**	.22**	.47***	-.27***	1.00	.68***	.63***	.38***	.25***
IX Satisfaction with Intimacy	.02	-.18	.22**	.12	.17**	.41***	-.16*	.68***	1.00	.34***	.49***	.15*
X Number of Relationships	.66***	-.54***	.67***	.45***	.37***	.37***	-.20**	.67***	.33***	1.00	.28**	.47***
XI Frequency of Intercourse	.27**	-.40***	.32***	.06	.16*	.18**	-.14*	.42***	.47***	.27**	1.00	.08
XII Contracted Veneral Disease	.29***	-.09	.36***	.20**	.13*	.15*	-.06	.27***	.14*	.46***	.08	1.00

*p < .05; **p < .01; ***p < .001.

TABLE 9.4
Analyses of the Men's Data: Direct Across-Time
Causal Paths Not Depicted in Figure 9.4

Adolescent Predictor Variable		Young Adult Consequent Variable		Standardized
Observed Variable	*Latent Variable*	*Observed Variable*	*Latent Variable*	*Parameter Estimate*[a]
cannabis frequency (R)[b]		number of steady partners		.23***
	Social Conformity	happy being close with someone		.23***
law abidance			frequency of intercourse	−.29***
	Early Sexual Involvement	number of steady partners		.17*

a. Significance level determined by a critical ratio of the unstandardized parameter estimate divided by its standard error.
b. (R) denotes variable residual.
*p < .05; **p < .01; ***p < .001.

Drug Use on any of the young adult constructs or measured variables. All effects of general adolescent Drug Use on later sexual behavior, satisfaction, and activity were mediated through the contemporaneous associations between teenage Drug Use and the teenage sexual behavior constructs and Social Conformity (which were quite substantial). This indicates that teenage Drug Use does not directly affect changes in sexual behavior or attitudes from adolescence to young adulthood. This does not say that drug use may not be related to specific incidents of sexual behavior (i.e., choosing to have intercourse while intoxicated or high), although general drug use of many different substances does not have any long-standing impact on patterns of sexual functioning.

There were three significant across-time effects for specific types of drug substances on the young adult variables, however (see Table 9.2). A high frequency of hard drug use increased the Number of Relationships, the specific use of hard drugs decreased reported happiness with being close to someone, and the specific use of alcohol increased the number of steady partners. These represent the only direct effects of drug use on sexual functioning from adolescence to young adulthood for this sample of women. Use of hard drugs appears to expand the range of intimate partners, while at the same time limiting happiness with being close to someone. If having a wide range of sexual partners can be inferred as a degree of promiscuity or indiscriminate sexual behavior, then hard drug use appears to be one causal influence for these types of sexual functioning. Specific use of alcohol increased the number of steady partners (not necessarily sexual partners) and may be the result of the socially disinhibiting effects of alcohol.

Looking at the pattern of factor correlations within the adolescent age period, it is clear that Drug Use is highly associated with Early Sexual Involvement, Frequency of Sexual Events, and Number of Sexually Active Friends, but is not associated with Satisfaction with Opposite-Sex Relationships. In other words, teenage drug use is related correlationally with heightened sexual behavior and a sexually active friendship network, but is unrelated to happiness or satisfaction with romantic partners. Thus a distinction can be made between behaviors and environments, and affective or emotional aspects of sexual involvement. Consequently, the high correlations within time between Drug Use and sexual behaviors, coupled with the blatant lack of a direct impact of general Drug Use on sexual behavior over time, supports the syndrome notion of problem or deviant behavior (e.g., Donovan & Jessor, 1985). Thus the high association between substance use and sexual behavior among adolescents (e.g., Bentler & Newcomb, 1986a) does not represent a causal relationship, but is spurious and is probably generated by an underlying construct of general deviance. We must conclude that there is no direct impact of general teenage Drug Use on sexual behavior and functioning from adolescence to young adulthood for this sample of women (except for the three specific effects of alcohol and hard drugs noted above).

On the other hand, the final structural model for the women's data provides important new information for understanding female sexual development into young adulthood.

Birth Control Effectiveness was not predicted from any adolescent variable and was significantly correlated with only two young adult constructs (lowered Contracted Venereal Disease and increased Number of Relationships). This supports previous research that found that prediction of contraceptive behavior for women was more difficult than for men (Geis & Gerrard, 1984). Two small effects across time were found that indicated that the Number of Sexually Active Friends and the residual of religious commitment increased the effectiveness of future birth control.

Early Sexual Involvement was a strong predictor of most young adult constructs, suggesting that an early age of sexual initiation and involvement sets a life-style pattern characterized by greater and more frequent sexual behavior. Interestingly, Early Sexual Involvement did not predict later Satisfaction with Intimacy. This again points out the distinction between a high level of sexual sophistication and involvement (i.e., many partners, frequent intercourse, sexual competence) and happiness or satisfaction in an intimate relationship. These are apparently independent processes, although some research suggests that they may be inversely related, such that those with high levels of sexual involvement and numerous partners become callous and jaded, resulting in decreased satisfaction, liking, and loving for their partner(s), and less romanticism (Cunningham & Antill, 1981).

Many other interesting relationships are apparent in Figure 9.2 and Table 9.3, which will not be expanded upon here because they are more specific to female sexual development than to the impact of drug use on sexual behavior. Some of these other patterns include the fact that Social Conformity only directly affected one young adult construct (decreased Abortion Occurrence), while inhibiting happiness with sex life. Although, as noted above, sexual behavior (i.e., Early Sexual Involvement) does not seem to change feelings or satisfaction with sexual relationships, Satisfaction with Opposite-Sex Relationships (an affectively oriented adolescent variable) does increase certain types of behavior (i.e., Frequency of Intercourse), as well as being related to increased Satisfaction with Relationships and Dating Competence.

Interpretation of the
Men's Model

In the final CFA model for drug use and sexual behavior for the men, the adolescent Drug Use factor was significantly correlated with all other adolescent factors and all young adult constructs except for Satisfaction with Intimacy. For the men, teenage Drug Use was significantly related to lowered Social Conformity, Early Sexual Involvement, high Frequency of Sexual Events, a large Number of Sexually Active Friends, increased Satisfaction with Opposite-Sex Relationships, less Birth Control Effectiveness, more Dating Competence, a greater Number of Relationships, a higher Frequency of Intercourse, and having Contracted Venereal Disease (see Table 9.3). Adolescent Social Conformity was correlated significantly with an older age of Sexual Involvement, a low Frequency of Sexual Events, a low Number of Sexually Active Friends, a low Number of Relationships, and a low Frequency of Intercourse. Early Sexual Involvement was significantly correlated with all factors in the direction of greater sexual involvement, higher frequencies of sexual behavior, and more competency and satisfaction with intimacy situations. The remaining correlations among the other sexual behavior, attitude, and satisfaction constructs were all in the expected direction and most were significant (see Table 9.3 for details).

The final structural model for the men's data revealed a similar lack of direct and significant impact of early Drug Use on any young adult construct, as was found in the women's data. All effects of teenage Drug Use on later sexual activity, attitudes, and satisfaction were mediated through the high associations between adolescent Drug Use and adolescent Social Conformity and the sexual activity and environment constructs. The one minor exception to this general pattern is that the specific use of cannabis directly increased the number of steady partners as young adults. This is the only direct effect of drug use on sexual functioning in the men's model, and we must conclude that, in general, there is no effect of teenage Drug Use on male sexual development from adolescence to young adulthood.

The pattern of within-time correlations between Drug Use and the other adolescent constructs were very similar to those found for the women. In other words, Drug Use was correlated with behavioral and environmental aspects of sexual functioning, but was not correlated with Satisfaction with Opposite-Sex Relationships. This supports the syndrome notion of deviant or problem behaviors, which is distinct from happiness or affective components of sexual activity, at least in regard to drug use.

As in the women's model, Early Sexual Involvement was an important predictor for most young adult constructs, except for Satisfaction with Intimacy. In this model, however, Birth Control Effectiveness was predicted significantly from two adolescent constructs: Later sexual involvement and a low Number of Sexually Active Friends predicted increased Birth Control Effectiveness. In other words, sexually precocious men with many sexually active friends do not use effective birth control as young adults. Because these adolescent qualities or characteristics are also correlated with a lack of Social Conformity and increased Drug Use, effective use of birth control is inversely related to deviance, problem behavior, or precocious development. This confirms our earlier speculation based on the Geis and Gerrard (1984) study that men who are more traditional, in a committed relationship, and became involved sexually at an older age also used more effective birth control. Thus deviance-prone men are less sexually responsible in terms of using effective birth control. This conclusion relates to deviance-prone indicators of sexual behavior and does not represent a cross-influence of one type of deviance (i.e., drug use) to the sexual area of functioning.

Adolescent Social Conformity decreased young adult Satisfaction with Intimacy and Number of Relationships. Thus males committed to conforming to societal expectations will not become involved with many different women, but will also be less happy with intimacy in their lives. This may result from a conflict between a desire to conform and be traditional and to engage pleasurably in sexual and intimate behavior. It may also reflect the notion that too much traditionalism or social conformity is detrimental to a close intimate relationship, as noted by Newcomb and Bentler (1980b).

Numerous other interesting relationships are apparent in Figure 9.4 and Table 9.4. The bulk of these focus, however, on patterns of male sexual development rather than the impact of drug use on sexual functioning. Consequently, these will not be elaborated upon further.

Summary Interpretation

Despite the fact that we had expected rather different patterns of drug use on sexual behavior and functioning for men compared to women, such big differences were not found in our separate models. Certainly, some different patterns emerged, but the general conclusion that teenage drug use does not directly affect sexual behavior, attitudes, or happiness in young adulthood was confirmed for both the men and the women. This result, of course, was for the general Drug Use factor representing use of many different substances. There were a few specific effects for certain substances. Most notably, hard drug use increased the Number of Relationships and decreased happiness being close with someone for the women, and cannabis increased the number of steady partners for the men. In other words, these substances for men and women, respectively, increased the number of intimate relationships experienced by young adulthood.

The general patterns of sexual development also appeared similar for men and women. Early Sexual Involvement was a critical factor for increasing many aspects of sexual activity and behavior for both male and female young adults. Although it could be argued that early or young sexual initiation simply increases the number of years at risk for certain behaviors (i.e., Contracting Venereal Disease) or the increased opportunity to have more sexual partners, this does not account for its effect on such outcomes as Frequency of Intercourse. Thus we must conclude that Early Sexual Involvement is a portent of a life-style characterized by increased sexual involvement and activity for both men and women. It is unrelated, however, to amount of sexual enjoyment or satisfaction. It is possible, of course—but not testable in the current data—that early sexual involvement in part stems from sex hormone differences between individuals, with earlier involvement implying higher sex drive. The consequent higher level of sexuality in young adulthood would be a natural consequence if such an individual difference were maintained across time. On the other hand, adolescent Drug Use was moderately to highly related to Early Sexual Involvement, Frequency of Sexual Events, and Number of Sexually Active Friends. Thus, although Drug Use had little impact on generating changes in sexual involvement or satisfaction over time (with the exception of the number of sexual partners), Drug Use was highly associated with several sexual behaviors and events. This provides support for the precocious development theory, which predicts that early sexual involvement (a premature sign of adult behavior) would be related to drug use. Teenage drug use and early sexual involvement (age at first intercourse and sexual contact) appear to be aspects of an adolescent life-style characterized by precocious acquisition of adult roles. Effects of this early sexual involvement are both positive and negative. On the positive side, those heavily involved in sexual behavior as a teenager have higher dating competence as young adults, perhaps as a result of their greater sexual experience. On the negative side, however, these individuals are more likely to contract venereal disease, have abortions (among the women), and use ineffective birth control (among the men). In other words, precocious development provides some positive aspects of adult roles, but perhaps without the necessary maturity and responsibility to perform adequately in these roles.

The men's and women's models diverge in some important aspects as well. For instance, Early Sexual Involvement had a much greater impact on subsequent Number of Relationships in males (.76) as compared to females (.29). This result portends a sex difference that is still quite common. Another interesting finding was that Birth Control Effectiveness could not be predicted from any adolescent constructs for the females, whereas sexually precocious and perhaps deviant-prone males used less effective birth control as young adults. Because the consequences of ineffective birth control are largely the women's, it is possible that sexually precocious males have a disregard for their partners' well-being, and that a component of a deviance-prone life-style may include a lack of sensitivity and empathy for at least their intimate partners, if not other members of society. On the other hand, the inability to predict Birth Control Effectiveness for the women indicates that effective use of contraception may be related to nonsexual aspects of the women's life, such as attitudes and intentions (e.g., Jorgensen & Sontegard, 1984) and other more general coping and protective mechanisms.

Many other intriguing aspects of male and female sexual development from adolescence to young adulthood are captured in the two models developed in this chapter. Most of this is beyond our specific task of determining the impact of teenage drug use, and must be left to the readers' interpretation of the tables and figures.

Although it would have been possible to create a multiple-group model that would directly contrast parameter estimates obtained for the men's and women's data, this was not done for two reasons. First, there were very few sexual behavior consequences of teenage drug use, and the direct comparison of men and women on these would probably be uninteresting. The second reason is that such a model would be quite sensitive to invariance across groups (due to the power of the sample size), much of which would be unrelated to drug use. For these reasons, and considerations of space, we did not perform these multiple-group analyses.

Technical Summary for the Women

Confirmatory Factor Analyses

An initial confirmatory factor model was run for the women's data that (a) fixed all factor variances at unity, and (b) allowed all constructs (or single-variable factors, which are treated like constructs) to correlate freely. There were no identical repeated measures in this model, so there were no across-time correlated residuals included on an a priori basis. This initial CFA model did not adequately reflect the data (χ^2 = 389.60, d.f. = 225, p < .001), although the Normed Fit Index (NFI) was sufficiently large (.90) to suggest that minor modifications to the model should yield an acceptable fit.

Factor intercorrelations for this initial CFA model are presented in the upper triangle of Table 9.1.

By examining the modification indices (Bentler, 1986c; Bentler & Chou, 1986), correlations among 20 pairs of residuals were added to the model. In addition, one residual variance was fixed at zero to prevent it from being estimated at a negative value, which would be an improper solution. This residual was on the effectiveness of current birth control variable. These modifications resulted in a model that adequately reflected the data ($\chi^2 = 215.75$, d.f. = 206, p = .31, NFI = .95). This model could not be rejected as a plausible explanation of the data. Factor intercorrelations for this final CFA model are presented in the lower triangle of Table 9.1. All hypothesized factor loadings were significant and no additional ones were necessary. Standardized factor loadings and residual variables (variances) of the observed variables for this final CFA model are graphically depicted in Figure 9.1.

In order to test whether adding the correlated residuals and fixing the one residual at zero disturbed the fundamental associations among the latent constructs (or single-variable factors), the factor intercorrelations between the initial and final confirmatory factor analysis models were correlated. This correlation was higher than .99, indicating that the model modifications did not alter the basic pattern of factor intercorrelations and that the final CFA model can be accepted as a plausible representation of the data.

Structural Model Analyses

The final stage in data analyses for this model was the creation of a structural or path model, which included regression effects representing unidirectional influences of one variable upon another within the context of our normal model setup (described previously). All empirically determined across-time correlated residuals were deleted in this model.

This beginning model was modified by adding across-time regression paths (based on the modification indices) and deleting nonsignificant parameters. The final model includes only significant paths. In this instance, the final structural model fit the data quite well ($\chi^2 = 238.07$, d.f. = 244, p = .60, NFI

= .94). Associations among the latent factors are graphically displayed in Figure 9.2, whereas the across-time paths that include at least one observed variable are listed in Table 9.2 with their standardized regression weights. As in all presentations of the final structural model, the relationships presented in Figure 9.2 and those listed in Table 9.2 are based on the same final model, and are presented separately only for reasons of clarity.

Technical Summary for the Men

Confirmatory Factor Analyses

The first step in our analyses of the men's data was to use CFA in the usual way, to assess the adequacy of our hypothesized measurement model, as done for the women's data. As before, there were no identical repeated measures in this model, so there were no across-time correlated residuals included on an a priori basis. This initial CFA model did not adequately reflect the data (χ^2 = 253.31, d.f. = 190, p < .001), although the Normed Fit Index (NFI) was sufficiently large (.86) to suggest that minor modifications to the model should yield an acceptable fit. Factor intercorrelations for this initial CFA model are presented in the upper triangle of Table 9.3.

By examining the modification indices, correlations among 13 pairs of residuals were added to the model. In addition, one residual variance was fixed at zero to prevent it from being estimated at a negative value, which would be an improper solution. This residual was on the effectiveness of current birth control variable, as in the women's model. These modifications resulted in a model that adequately reflected the data (χ^2 = 151.11, d.f. = 178, p = .93, NFI = .92). This model could not be rejected as a plausible explanation of the data. Factor intercorrelations for this final CFA model are presented in the lower triangle of Table 9.3. All hypothesized factor loadings were significant and no additional ones were necessary. Standardized factor loadings and residual variables (variances) of the observed variables for this final CFA model are graphically depicted in Figure 9.3.

In order to test whether adding the correlated residuals and fixing the one residual at zero disturbed the magnitude of the associations among the latent constructs (or single-variable factors), the factor intercorrelations between the initial and final CFA models were correlated. This correlation was higher than .99, indicating that the model modifications did not alter the basic pattern of factor intercorrelations and that the final CFA can be accepted as a plausible representation of the data for the men.

Structural Model Analyses

The final stage in data analyses for this model of the men's data was the creation of a structural or path model, using the procedures specified several times previously, for example, the empirically determined across-time correlated residuals were deleted from the initial structural model, and all constructs in adolescence and factor residuals during young adulthood were allowed to correlate freely.

This beginning model was modified by adding across-time regression paths (based on the modification indices) between measured variables and/or latent factors and by deleting nonsignificant paths and correlations. The final model includes only significant paths and correlations. In this instance, the final structural model fit the data quite well (χ^2 = 190.87, d.f. = 228, p = .91, NFI = .90). Associations among the latent factors are graphically displayed in Figure 9.4, whereas the across-time paths that include at least one observed variable are listed in Table 9.4 with their standardized regression weights. As usual, the relationships presented in Figure 9.4 and those listed in Table 9.4 are based on the same final model.

10

Impact on
Educational Pursuits

Obtaining an education is one of the primary tasks of the teenage years, and often continues into young adulthood if a college education and professional career are sought. It is quite possible that drug use may interfere with these learning experiences, and thus jeopardize future goals that may require an academic background (e.g., Friedman, Glickman, & Utada, 1985). A defining feature of adolescent problem drinking (Jessor et al., 1980) is the experience of negative consequences at school and a disinterest in academic achievement (Jessor & Jessor, 1977). Newcomb and Bentler (1986a) found that use of cigarettes and hard drugs in high school was directly related to dropping out of school before completion, even after controlling for academic achievement and educational aspirations. Drug use did not decrease educational aspirations beyond initial levels, but was associated with decreased college involvement. This corroborates Kandel's (1978) conclusion that drug use does not create an amotivational syndrome (i.e., little interest in school), but it may reinforce and consolidate an existing lack of educational direction. On the other hand, Newcomb & Bentler (1986a) found that poor academic achievement in high school was unrelated to changes in drug use levels into young adulthood.

These patterns are somewhat different among college students. For instance, Mellinger, Somers, Bazell, and Manheimer (1978) found that drug use was not related to dropping out of college for most students. The exception was for those who had begun multiple drug use in high school, whose parents did not have college degrees, and who expressed ambivalence about attending college. Students with these types of background and attitudes did leave college prematurely. Similarly, Hendin and Haas (1985) studied a college sample of chronic marijuana users. They reported that marijuana use was not directly responsible for poor school performance. They did find that heavy marijuana use consolidated regressive coping behavior, which permitted the avoidance of critical life decisions and tasks, and as a result produced negative consequences. Consistent with earlier reports (e.g., Miranue, 1979), they did not, however, find that drug use interfered directly with the learning process.

Although the high school data and the college data seem to be at odds, it must be remembered that a substantial self-screening process has occurred before an individual will attend college. For example, drug use is heavier among students in an alternative high school (Beauvais & Oetting, 1986), whose students tend to be less likely to go on to college. More specifically, Newcomb and Bentler (1985) found that those who were heavier drug users in high school were significantly less likely to go on to college. As a result, drug use consequences for those in college may be quite distinct from those in high school. The drug use consequences studies that are focused solely on college students are examining a different period of life (young adulthood) from the teenage consequences studies, where different maturational tasks and developmental goals are confronted. It is possible that the greater maturity of college-age drug users (and the fact they used drugs less frequently in high school) may help obviate the negative effects of use, which would not be possible among younger, less mature, and less experienced high school students. Similarly, studies of college students represent a restricted and highly selected group of individuals whose consequences of drug use cannot be generalized to those not choosing to go to college. In our analyses for this chapter, our sample includes those who have and have not chosen to pursue a college education, and as a result our findings should have a wider range of generalizability than those from more restricted samples.

Various studies have found a strong association between numerous types of drug use and decreased scholastic performance (e.g., grade point average) and less interest in going to college (e.g., Bachman, Johnston, & O'Malley, 1981; Bry et al., 1982; Mills & Noyes, 1984; Newcomb, Maddahian, & Bentler, 1986). Previous research has attempted to test theories regarding the causal relationship between drug use and scholastic performance among adolescents. Three distinct theories have been offered to explain this often noted relationship (e.g., Brunswick & Messeri, 1984a). The first hypothesis suggests that drug use is a result of poor academic achievement and can be seen as a way to cope or self-medicate the frustration and distress resulting from poor school performance. This theory has been called a psychogenic interpretation (e.g., Brunswick & Messeri, 1984a; Gossett, Lewis, & Phillips, 1972; Reeder, 1977). A second explanation, implying an opposite causal sequence, posits that academic failure is the result of drug use, which presumably interferes with the learning process. This we call the impaired ability interpretation. A third distinct hypothesis suggests that both drug use and poor school performance are manifestations of rejecting traditional values and are associated with more general psychological tendencies toward deviance, problem behavior, and nonconventionality (e.g., Bachman et al., 1981; Huba & Bentler, 1983a, 1984; Jessor & Jessor, 1977), and is called the general deviance hypothesis. This general deviance hypothesis would predict a high association between drug use and a lack of interest in education within occasions, although they would not be expected to be mutually generative over time.

When longitudinal data have been consulted, the impaired ability interpretation is typically not supported, while general support has been found for the psychogenic and general deviance theories (e.g., Brunswick & Messeri, 1984a, 1984b; Bachman et al., 1984). The majority of these findings are based on students while in high school, however. It is quite possible that different mechanisms are at work and thus different results may emerge when the transition from adolescent to young adult is examined. Different processes may be more prevalent at different points during adolescence, and in fact may occur in a sequence. For instance, perhaps the psychogenic process occurs early among young adolescents, and is superseded by either the impaired abilities or the general deviance influences in later adolescence or young adulthood, as noted by Newcomb and Bentler (1986a), who found support for the impaired abilities and general deviance hypothesis for post-adolescent development.

A contributing force to the denigration of traditional educational pursuits may be the allure of earning one's own money and the freedom this permits the adolescent. Being self-supporting is an attractive adult goal for many adolescents, who may forsake the financially insecure prospect of college in order to begin earning their own money at an early age. Thus a drive toward precocious development may contribute to the abandonment of the traditional goals of a college, or even high school, education for the adult trappings of self-support and independence. Although, unfortunately, we did not have a measure of work or job involvement during adolescence, we do have a measure of amount earned during several months as teenagers, which we use as a proxy for high school work force involvement.

Although it is likely that college involvement and holding a steady job may be mutually exclusive activities for some people, other people face the task of finding some balance between work and obtaining a college education. For this reason, our model for this chapter includes a construct for work force involvement, as well as college involvement, which should provide a more detailed accounting of how people integrate these activities in their lives, should they be pursuing both.

Design of the Model

In the model for this chapter, which assesses the impact of teenage drug use on educational pursuits, four constructs are included from the adolescent data and four constructs are from the young adult data (one is a single-variable factor). Two of the adolescent constructs are Drug Use and Social Conformity as included in all of the models. The other two constructs include Academic Potential (with manifest indicators of grade point average and educational plans) and Income (with indicators of Salary 1, 2, and 3 representing earned income from three different months). In young adulthood, three constructs were measured including Educational Aspirations (with manifest-variable indicators for educational plans and educational expectations), College Involvement (reflected in measures of college attendance, part-time job and college, and part-time employment), Work Force Involvement (with observed indicators of full-time job or military, full-time employment, income, and months worked), and Graduated from High School (a single-variable factor). Based on earlier analyses of these data, four additional factor loadings were added on an a priori basis to the initial confirmatory factor analysis model (Newcomb & Bentler, 1986a). College Involvement had additional indicators of decreased full-time employment, decreased full-time job or military pursuits, and decreased months worked, whereas Work Force Involvement had one additional indicator of decreased college attendance. A more thorough description of the variables is given in Chapter 4 and in the Appendix.

The statistical and methodological details related to the development of this model are provided in the "Technical Summary" at the end of this chapter. Figure 10.1 depicts how the latent constructs were identified by the measured variables in the final confirmatory factor analysis (CFA) model. Table 10.1 presents the factor intercorrelations for the initial and final CFA models. The final structural model is depicted in Figure 10.2 and Table 10.2. The figure presents the relationship among latent factors, whereas the table reports the nonstandard effects that include at least one measured variable.

Interpretation

In the final CFA model for drug use and educational pursuits, the adolescent Drug Use factor was significantly correlated with all other adolescent factors and all of the four young adult factors. Teenage Drug Use was significantly related to lowered Social Conformity, lowered Academic Potential, increased Income, decreased young adult Educational Aspirations, decreased College Involvement, increased

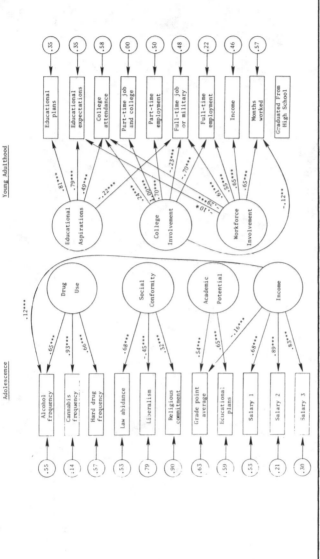

Figure 10.1. Final Confirmatory Factor Analysis Model for the Educational Pursuits Variables

NOTE: Large circles represent latent factors, rectangles are measured variables, and the small circles with numbers are residual variances. Factor loadings are standardized and significance levels were determined by critical ratios (*p < .05; **p < .01; ***p < .001). Not depicted in the figure are two-headed arrows (correlations) joining each possible pair of factors. Values for these correlations are provided in Table 10.1.

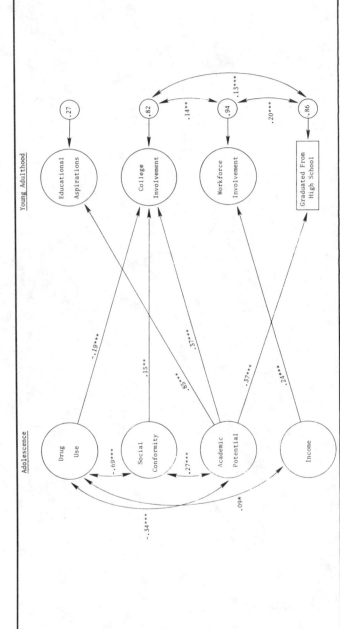

Figure 10.2. Final Structural or Path Model for the Educational Pursuits Variables

NOTE: The measurement portion of this model is not depicted for simplicity. Two-headed arrows reflect correlations and single-headed arrows represent across-time regression effects. Parameter estimates are standardized, residual variables are variances, and significance levels were determined by critical ratios (*p < .05; **p < .01; ***p < .001). Nonstandard effects for this model are given in Table 10.2.

TABLE 10.1

Factor Intercorrelations for the Initial (upper triangle) and Final (lower triangle) Confirmatory Factor Analyses

Factor	I	II	III	IV	V	VI	VII	VIII
Late Adolescence								
I Drug Use	1.00	−.76***	−.33***	.10**	−.29***	−.20***	.16***	−.18***
II Social Conformity	−.68***	1.00	.32***	−.04	.21***	.04	−.17**	.08
III Academic Potential	−.31***	.23***	1.00	−.06	.79***	.44***	−.17**	.36***
IV Income	.08*	−.07	−.01	1.00	−.06	.00	.25***	−.04
Young Adulthood								
V Educational Aspirations	−.29***	.25***	.88***	−.06	1.00	.37***	−.23***	.31***
VI College Involvement	−.19***	.05	.44***	.02	.33***	1.00	.08	.27***
VII Work Force Involvement	.13**	−.13**	−.14**	.25***	−.11*	.08	1.00	.09*
VIII Graduated from High School	−.17***	.09*	.37***	−.03	.31***	.25***	.13**	1.00

*p < .05; **p < .01; ***p < .001.

TABLE 10.2
Direct Across-Time Causal Paths
Not Depicted in Figure

Adolescent Predictor Variable		Young Adult Consequent Variable		Standardized Parameter Estimate[a]
Observed Variable	Latent Variable	Observed Variable	Latent Variable	
	Drug Use	income		.11***
alcohol frequency		full-time job or military		.06*
alcohol frequency (R)[b]		college attendance		.08**
hard drug frequency (R)			Graduated from High School	−.09**
religious commitment (R)		college attendance		−.07*
	Academic Potential	college attendance		.39***
grade point average (R)			Educational Aspirations	.09**
grade point average (R)			College Involvement	.07*
	Income	full-time employment		.11***
	Income	income		.20***

a. Significance level determined by a critical ratio of the unstandardized parameter estimate divided by its standard error.
b. (R) denotes variable residual.
*p < .05; **p < .01; ***p < .001.

Work Force Involvement, and lowered Graduated from High
School (see Table 10.1). Adolescent Social Conformity was
significantly associated with increased Academic Potential,
increased young adult Educational Aspirations, decreased
Work Force Involvement, and higher Graduated from High
School. Adolescent Academic Potential was significantly
related to increased young adult Educational Aspirations,
increased College Involvement, decreased Work Force Involvement, and increased likelihood of Graduated from High

School. Adolescent Income level was significantly associated with only young adult Work Force Involvement. Among the young adulthood constructs, Educational Aspirations, College Involvement, and Graduated from High School were all positively and significantly correlated. Work Force Involvement was negatively associated with Educational Aspirations and positively related with Graduated from High School.

Five additional factor loadings were necessary to include in the measurement portion of the model (see Figure 10.1). Among the adolescent measures, two additional factor loadings indicated that the general tendency toward having a high earned Income also predicted increased frequency of alcohol use and lowered grade point average. Among the young adulthood constructs, the general tendency toward having high Educational Aspirations also predicted increased college attendance and decreased full-time job or military pursuits, whereas the general tendency toward increased Work Force Involvement also predicted decreased college attendance and educational expectations.

These correlations and additional factor loadings indicate that college pursuits are typically inversely related to work or job pursuits to a small to moderate degree. They are not mutually exclusive, however, and it is certainly possible that some individuals pursue both activities simultaneously. Nevertheless, the general tendency is for a high involvement in one to preclude the other. There was a small but significant positive correlation between Income and Drug Use. It is possible that involvement in work pursuits, resulting in high salary or income, during adolescence is a nontraditional pursuit or activity. Thus high Income during adolescence may be a feature of precocious development that is not problem-oriented or deviance-prone in nature. It may be related to a premature desire for independence and autonomy, however, which is associated with deviant behavior (Newcomb et al., 1981).

The final structural model for drug use and educational pursuits indicates that teenage Drug Use decreased College Involvement as young adults, while controlling for Social Conformity and Academic Potential. In other words, using drugs as a teenager had a direct influence on decreasing activities related to traditional academic pursuits (i.e., a college education). Similarly, the specific use of hard drugs as an adolescent increased the likelihood of dropping out of high school before completion. These results can be interpreted in at least two ways. One way of understanding these results is that drug use somehow interfered with the learning process and thus reduced academic and educational pursuits. This would support the impaired abilities hypothesis discussed earlier. On the other hand, it is possible that teenage drug use predicts a nontraditional life-style that does not include traditional educational activities. In other words, drug use is only associated with decreased educational involvement due to the generally deviant or nonconforming characteristics of the individual. Although this process may partially be true, it is less likely the sole interpretation because the impact of teenage Drug Use on decreased College Involvement was evident even while controlling for adolescent Social Conformity. Thus, although the general deviance hypothesis may partially account for the findings, the impaired abilities process appears to be the strongest interpretation of the findings.

Teenage Drug Use did not have a direct effect on young adult Work Force Involvement, although it was positively correlated with adolescent Income and significantly increased young adult income (one aspect of Work Force Involvement). So, although adolescent Drug Use did not directly increase the degree of Work Force Involvement in young adulthood, it was already associated with increased employment activities as an adolescent, as reflected in the adolescent Income construct. Thus a certain degree of precocious development was already evident in this sample during adolescence regarding amount of Drug Use (in particular, the effect of Income on alcohol use as reflected in the additional factor loading) and amount of earned Income. Drug Use as a teenager increased amount of money earned between adolescence and young adulthood, suggesting greater commitment and involvement in the labor force, with the concomitant rejection of traditional educational pursuits of college (or even high school). This also supports the notion that early or young job involvement is an aspect of precocious development that is not generally seen to have problem or deviance-prone consequences.

Interestingly, the specific use of alcohol as a teenager, apart from general Drug Use, predicted increased College Involvement as a young adult, whereas the general use of alcohol during adolescence, and indirectly the general use of all drugs, predicted full-time job or military activities as a young adult. These results imply that teenagers who only use alcohol and do not make the transition to illicit drugs tend to be more conforming and follow traditional pursuits of a college education, compared to those teenagers who use high levels of alcohol, in addition to other illicit substances, who reject traditional activities of College Involvement and prefer full-time employment or joining the military.

The other non-drug-related patterns of results from this model indicate that Academic Potential and grade point average synergistically generated increased Educational Aspirations and increased College Involvement as young adults. Teenage Social Conformity also predicted College Involvement over and above the effect of Academic Potential. This clearly supports the speculation that, in the 1980s, college attendance is a traditional and conforming pursuit. As a result, studies of drug use consequences that focus only on college students are by the process of self-selection examining a highly restricted sample, who are most conforming and whose drug use was less involved as a teenager compared to those who did not choose to pursue a college program or even complete high school.

Technical Summary

Confirmatory Factor Analyses

The usual first step in our analyses is to assess the adequacy of our hypothesized measurement model. The standard initial CFA model did not adequately reflect the data (χ^2 = 556.47, d.f. = 154, p < .001), although the Normed Fit Index (NFI) was sufficiently large (.88) to suggest that minor modifications to the model should yield an acceptable fit. Factor intercorrelations for this initial CFA model are presented in the upper triangle of Table 10.1.

By examining the modification indices (Bentler, 1986c; Bentler & Chou, 1986), correlations among 22 pairs of residuals were added to the model. In addition, five nonhypothesized factor loadings were necessary. These modifications resulted in a model that adequately reflected the data (χ^2 = 134.64, d.f. = 128, p = .33, NFI = .97). This model could not be rejected as a plausible explanation of the data as represented in the final CFA model. Factor intercorrelations for this final CFA model are presented in the lower triangle of Table 10.1. All hypothesized factor loadings were significant. Standardized factor loadings and residual variables (variances) of the observed variables for this final CFA model are graphically depicted in Figure 10.1.

The factor intercorrelations between the initial and final CFA models were correlated higher than .99, indicating that the model modifications did not alter the basic pattern of factor intercorrelations.

Structural Model Analyses

The usual initial structural model was created, and was then modified by adding across-time regression paths (based on the modification indices) and deleting nonsignificant parameters. The final model fit the data quite well (χ^2 = 162.97, d.f. = 147, p = .17, NFI = .97). Associations among the latent factors are graphically displayed in Figure 10.2, whereas the across-time paths that include at least one observed variable are listed in Table 10.2 with their standardized regression weight.

11

Impact on
Livelihood Pursuits

Another defining feature of the adolescent years is entry into the job market. Many teenagers have part-time jobs while in high school. Upon leaving school, some may delay full-time employment in favor of further education, while others may enter the work force immediately.

Drug use may affect livelihood pursuits in several ways. As teenagers, drug use may influence the timing of employment initiation, the type of jobs pursued, the stability of employment situations, job performance, and work satisfaction. Very few of these potential consequences have been examined empirically. Certainly current substance abuse or alcoholism will affect job performance and stability, as evidenced in the rise of employee assistance programs and loss of productivity due to substance use (e.g., Quayle, 1983). Drug users tend to have less stable job histories than nonusers (e.g., Kandel, Murphy, & Karus, 1985; Newcomb & Bentler, 1986d). It is not clear, however, whether drug use is the cause of these problems, or whether those who use drugs are more likely to have difficulty maintaining a job due to the type of person they are (as somehow reflected in their drug use). Or, perhaps, the stress and frustration of a particular job generate the drug use (e.g., Gupta & Jenkins, 1984).

Drug use on the job has become a recent concern to the National Institute on Drug Abuse and other governmental agencies. Use of drugs at the work site may reduce productivity, create significant safety hazards, and affect the psychological climate of the work setting. It needs to be determined whether such behavior is the result of job stresses (e.g., Seeman & Anderson, 1983), or whether it is the result of long-standing patterns of drug involvement that may have begun during adolescence.

If there is a true association between teenage drug use and any facet of adult livelihood pursuits, it needs to be defined. Donovan et al. (1983) have begun to trace these patterns from adolescence to young adulthood in regard to consequences of problem drinking. Other drugs must be considered as well and the range of work-related consequences expanded (such as satisfaction). Crucial to this task is the separation of drug consumption from adverse consequences. Preliminary work in this area regarding alcohol has been offered by Sadava (1985). Again, this needs to be expanded to encompass other drugs and a wider range of negative consequences as related to work force involvement and other critical areas of life.

Kandel (1980) concluded from her review of the drug literature that the "Findings pertaining to labor force participation are among the most consistent. The unemployed have the highest rates of use of most drugs" (p. 249). The majority of research reviewed by Kandel (1980) was cross-sectional in design, leaving the question of causal direction ambiguous. It is possible that drug use creates employment difficulties in a similar fashion as suggested by the impaired ability theory. On the other hand, those who are without jobs may use drugs to cope with the stress and frustration of unemployment, as in a psychogenic or self-medication interpretation. One recent longitudinal study found that there was no clear causal connection between the experience of being unemployed and increased drug use (Bachman et al., 1984). In contrast, another study reported that, among women (but not men), marijuana involvement in adolescence predicted an increased number of employment and unemployment spells (Kandel et al., 1986).

Another form of livelihood or income resource that does not involve a job or employment is that of government compensation or assistance. Many people subsist on welfare, food stamps, or other types of support provided by the government. It is certainly possible that drug use may be related to or influence the use of public assistance. Such a connection could be hypothesized on several grounds. Early and chronic drug abuse may have impaired the emotional and physical functioning of a person to such an extent as to prohibit gainful employment in the workplace, placing the burden for their survival on public funds. On the other hand, excessive drug use may reflect a life-style of irresponsibility, laziness, and lassitude that does not place a high value on financial self-support and maintenance of a steady job. These speculations would suggest that high levels of teenage drug use may lead to a greater reliance on public assistance for food and shelter. Similarly, early drug use may be related or lead to a decrease in the general amount of time spent in regular employment later in life, via the processes discussed above.

Implicit in each of these types of livelihood pursuits is a level of monetary income. A final question concerns whether early drug use influences the amount of income earned later in life. At least two hypotheses can be suggested that predict different outcomes. The precocious development notion would predict that drug use is associated with earlier involvement in work activities, which would lead to greater work experience and seniority, which in turn would predict higher salaries compared to those who do not use drugs and enter the work force at an older age. On the other hand, those who enter the job market at a young age do so at the expense of further education, resulting in a limitation of the upward mobility of their career. Thus those who use fewer drugs as a teenager, go on to college, and pursue a skilled or professional career may ultimately achieve a higher salary than their teenage drug-using peers. This later effect may not be apparent in young adulthood, however, when many of the more conforming and less drug-using individuals are in college and furthering their education.

Design of the Model

In the model for this chapter, which assesses the impact of teenage drug use on livelihood pursuits, four constructs are included from the adolescent data and five constructs are from the young adult data (one is a single-variable factor). Two of the adolescent constructs are Drug Use and Social Conformity as included in all of the models. The other two constructs include Academic Potential (with manifest indicators of grade point average and educational plans) and Income (with indicators of Salary 1, 2, and 3 representing earned income from three different months). As mentioned in Chapter 10, we do not have any adolescent measures for job or work involvement. As a result, amount of money earned, as reflected in our Income construct, is used as a proxy for degree of work force involvement for adolescents. In young adulthood, five constructs were measured including Income (with manifest-variable indicators of Salary 1, 2, and 3 representing earned income from three different months during the year preceding assessment), Job Instability (reflected in measures of times fired past four years, times lost job past four years, and times collected unemployment past four years), Job Satisfaction (with observed measures of happy with work and trouble with work), Collected Public Assistance (with observed indicators of collected welfare past four years and collected food stamps past four years), and Amount Worked Past Year (a single-variable factor). Although Salary 1, 2, and 3 appear to be identical measures at both time points, they were assessed for different months during the preceding years, and thus were not strictly identical. A further description of the various indicators is given in Chapter 4 and in the Appendix.

The statistical and methodological details related to the development of this model are provided in the "Technical Summary" at the end of this chapter. Figure 11.1 depicts how the latent constructs were identified by the measured variables in the final confirmatory factor analysis (CFA) model. Table 11.1 presents the factor intercorrelations for the initial and final CFA models. The final structural model is depicted in Figure 11.2 and Table 11.2. The figure presents the relationship among latent factors, whereas the table reports the nonstandard effects that include at least one measured variable.

Interpretation

In the final CFA model for drug use and livelihood pursuits, the adolescent Drug Use factor was significantly correlated with all other adolescent factors and two of the five young adult factors. Teenage Drug Use was significantly related to

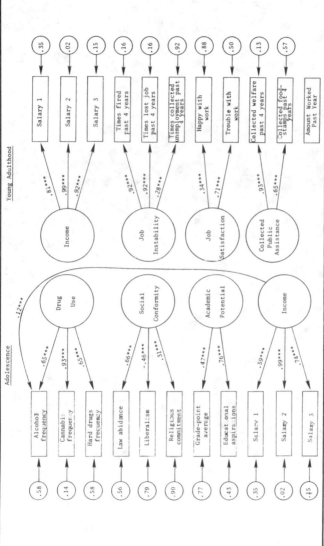

Figure 11.1. Final Confirmatory Factor Analysis Model for the Livelihood Pursuits Variables

NOTE: Large circles represent latent factors, rectangles are measured variables, and the small circles with numbers are residual variables. Factor loadings are standardized and significance levels were determined by critical ratios (*p < .05; **p < .01; ***p < .001). Not depicted in the figure are two-headed arrows (correlations) joining each possible pair of factors. Values for these correlations are provided in Table 11.1.

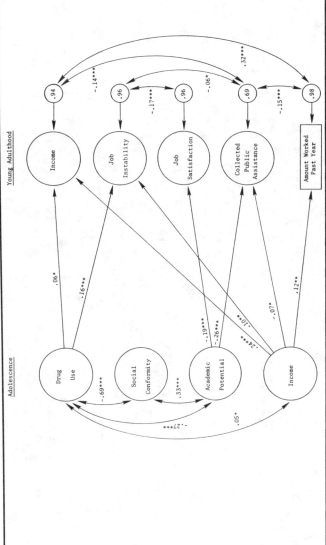

Figure 11.2. Final Structural or Path Model for the Livelihood Pursuits Variables

NOTE: The measurement portion of this model is not depicted for simplicity. Two-headed arrows reflect correlations and single-headed arrows represent across-time regression effects. Parameter estimates are standardized, residual variables are variances, and significance levels were determined by critical ratios (*p < .05; **p < .01; ***p < .001). Nonstandard effects for this model are given in Table 11.2.

TABLE 11.1
Factor Intercorrelations for the Initial (upper triangle) and Final (lower triangle) Confirmatory Factor Models

Factor	I	II	III	IV	V	VI	VII	VIII	IX
Late Adolescence									
I Drug Use	1.00	−.77***	−.35***	.10**	.09*	.17***	.05	.05	.03
II Social Conformity	−.69***	1.00	.32***	−.04	.01	−.18***	−.03	−.04	−.02
III Academic Potential	−.28***	.36***	1.00	−.08	−.06	−.11*	−.19***	−.25***	−.09*
IV Income	.06*	−.03	−.01	1.00	.25***	.09**	.06	−.11**	.14***
Young Adulthood									
V Income	.08*	.02	−.05	.25***	1.00	.02	.01	−.17***	.34***
VI Job Instability	.17***	−.18***	−.09*	.09**	.02	1.00	−.15***	−.06	.05
VII Job Satisfaction	.04	−.04	−.23***	.12*	.03	−.22***	1.00	.07*	−.03
VIII Collected Public Assistance	.05	−.01	−.25***	−.09**	−.16***	−.06	.07	1.00	−.17***
IX Amount Worked Past Year	.03	−.02	−.08*	.12**	.34***	.06	−.03	−.15***	1.00

*p < .05; **p < .01; ***p < .001.

165

TABLE 11.2
Direct Across-Time Causal Paths
Not Depicted in Figure

Adolescent Predictor Variable		Young Adult Consequent Variable		Standardized Parameter Estimate[a]
Observed Variable	Latent Variable	Observed Variable	Latent Variable	
hard drug frequency (R)[b]		happy with work		.09**
	Social Conformity	happy with work		.13**
liberalism			Collect Public Assistance	.09*
	Academic Potential	salary 2		.05**
	Academic Potential	times collected unemployment past 4 years		−.11**

a. Significance level determined by a critical ratio of the unstandardized parameter estimate divided by its standard error.
b. (R) denotes variable residual.
*p < .05; **p < .01; ***p < .001.

lowered Social Conformity, lowered Academic Potential, increased Income during both adolescence and young adulthood, and increased Job Instability (see Table 11.1). Adolescent Social Conformity was significantly associated with increased Academic Potential and decreased Job Instability in young adulthood. Adolescent Academic Potential was significantly related to decreased young adult Job Instability, decreased Job Satisfaction, decreased Collection of Public Assistance, and decreased Amount Worked Past Year. Adolescent Income was significantly related to all young adult constructs, positively to all except Collected Public Assistance. Among the young adulthood constructs, Income was significantly associated with lower Collected Public Assistance and higher Amount Worked Past Year. Job Instability was negatively related to Job Satisfaction, while Collected Public Assistance was positively related with Job Satisfaction and negatively correlated with Amount Worked Past Year.

One unexpected factor loading was necessary to include in the measurement portion of the model (see Figure 11.1). This reflected the fact that the general tendency to have a high earned income in adolescence was also related to increased alcohol use. This effect was also noted in our analyses of Educational Pursuits and indicates that young involvement in the job market, as reflected in high earned income, is marginally associated with general Drug Use (the significant but low positive correlation between factors) and alcohol in particular (as evident in the additional factor loading).

The final structural model provides some fairly clear answers to questions posed at the beginning of this chapter. The most important effects of teenage Drug Use on later livelihood pursuits is on Job Instability. Adolescent Drug Use had a direct and positive influence on increasing Job Instability in young adulthood, as reflected in collecting unemployment and being fired from jobs. This is evident while controlling for Academic Potential and general deviance via our Social Conformity construct. The mechanism of this influence is still unclear, however. It is possible that because early drug use predicts later drug use that the job instability may have resulted from using drugs on the job. On the other hand, early drug use may have impaired the development or learning process of responsible employment behaviors, such as conscientiousness, thoroughness, reliability, and so on, resulting in job instability.

Teenage Drug Use also increased Income to a small but significant extent from adolescence to young adulthood. This is probably due to the hypothesis presented earlier suggesting that drug use, as a feature of precocious development, propels a teenager into the work force at a younger age and thus this person has gained more work experience and seniority at a job, compared to more conforming and less drug-using youngsters who furthered their education in college. It is an interesting paradox that teenage drug use predicts both increased income and increased job instability in young adulthood. We are obviously capturing a frame in the sequence of development whose future course we cannot predict accurately—the coefficients, for example, are very small. It seems quite likely, however, that once the college-prepared adults enter the job market, their higher salaries as a result of their education will change the current picture. We might expect that over a greater length of time teenage Drug Use may predict a decrease in income later in adulthood. More lengthy follow-ups are necessary to test such a theory. In the present analyses, however, we can certainly observe a modest short-term reward for precocious development, that being increased income. Yet, the long-term rewards may not be as attractive, if our theories are accurate.

Turning next to job satisfaction, this was significantly decreased by teenage Academic Potential and was totally unrelated to general teenage Drug Use. There was a small effect for the residual of hard drug use to increase happiness with work, however. Thus job satisfaction as a young adult is predicted from a lack of teenage interest and ability in academic pursuits and the use of hard drugs. In some sense, being happy with a job as a young adult, a job that obviously could not require a great deal of academic preparation, is a slightly deviant occurrence. On the other hand, unhappiness with such a job is predicted from an early interest and ability with academic endeavors and an avoidance of hard drug use. Thus those who are academically inclined in adolescence, but may not have been able to pursue their educational interests as they grew older, feel unhappy and frustrated with their current job or work situation. We must conclude, however, that general teenage Drug Use does not affect Job Satisfaction in young adulthood, despite the fact that it does increase Job Instability.

Collecting Public Assistance as a young adult was significantly predicted from a lack of Academic Potential and decreased Income as Adolescents. Collecting Public Assistance was not directly or indirectly related to drug use during the teenage years, refuting our hypotheses of such a linkage presented above. Based on these results, it appears that teenage drug use, in the amounts reported by these individuals, does not generate a life-style of irresponsibility and laziness, nor does it generally impair physical and emotional functioning to the extent that public assistance is needed for survival. Of course, these results are based on a period of four years, and it is certainly possible that more pronounced negative effects may require a substantially greater period of time to appear. Teenage liberalism was a significant predictor of Collecting Public Assistance as young adults. Combining this fact with Academic Potential and Income as negative predictors of Collecting Public Assistance, it appears that reliance upon public support occurs for those who do not have the intellectual interest or abilities for college pursuits, did not enter the work force as teenagers, and have somewhat liberal, nonsocially conforming attitudes. In such a personological interpretation of the regression results, these type of people seem to fall between conforming teenagers (who may likely pursue a college education and the jobs this would afford) and precociously developing teenagers (who shunned traditional education, but entered the job market early), leaving them somewhat ineffectual in providing self-support. These are people who may not have acquired the life skills and maturity to be self-sufficient, but not because of drug use. Other factors such as family background and upbringing must be considered in understanding those who Collect Public Assistance.

Finally, Amount Worked Past Year was predicted only from teenage Income. Amount Worked as a young adult was neither directly nor indirectly related to Drug Use, Social Conformity, or Academic Potential as a teenager. As with the results for Collected Public Assistance, early Drug Use did not generate a pattern of irresponsibility, laziness, and work avoidance, despite the fact that it increases Job Instability. In fact, via the process of precocious development, early drug use may increase interest in self-sufficiency and independence, as afforded by a job.

Technical Summary

Confirmatory Factor Analyses

As always, our first step in the data analyses is to determine the adequacy of our hypothesized measurement model using confirmatory factor analysis. The standard model setup was used. This initial CFA model did not adequately reflect the data ($\chi^2 = 360.07$, d.f. = 174, p < .001), although the Normed Fit

Index (NFI) was sufficiently large (.93) to suggest that minor modifications to the model should yield an acceptable fit. Factor intercorrelations for this initial CFA model are presented in the upper triangle of Table 11.1.

By examining the modification indices (Bentler, 1986c; Bentler & Chou, 1986), correlations among 23 pairs of residuals were added to the model. In addition, one nonhypothesized factor loading was necessary. These modifications resulted in a model that adequately reflected the data (χ^2 = 164.74, d.f.= 148, p = .16, NFI = .97). This model could not be rejected as a plausible explanation of the data as represented in the final CFA model. Factor intercorrelations for this final CFA model are presented in the lower triangle of Table 11.1. All hypothesized factor loadings were significant. Standardized factor loadings and residual variables (variances) of the observed variables for this final CFA model are graphically depicted in Figure 11.1.

In order to test whether adding the correlated residuals disturbed the fundamental associations among the latent constructs, the factor intercorrelations between the initial and final confirmatory factor analysis models were correlated. This correlation was higher than .98, indicating that the model modifications did not alter the basic pattern of factor intercorrelations to any noticeable or substantial extent.

Structural Model Analyses

The final stage in our data analyses for this model was the creation of a structural or path model, using the general model setup described several times previously. This beginning model was modified by adding across-time regression paths and deleting nonsignificant parameters. The final structural model fit the data quite well (χ^2 = 165.14, d.f. = 148, p = .59, NFI = .97). Associations among the latent factors are graphically displayed in Figure 11.2, whereas the across-time paths that include at least one observed variable are listed in Table 11.2 with their standardized regression weights.

12

Impact on Mental Health

There has been frequent debate regarding the relationship between drug use and mental health or emotional distress. Little doubt exists that drug use is often preceded by some type of emotional discomfort (e.g., Huba, Newcomb, & Bentler, 1986; Kaplan, 1985; Newcomb & Harlow, 1986; Paton, Kessler, & Kandel, 1977). This effect appears to occur over a relatively short period of time (i.e., one year or less) and is more difficult to observe over longer periods of time (e.g., Newcomb & Bentler, 1986d). It is not clear, however, what impact drug use has on changes in long-term psychological status.

In general, the findings seem to be mixed depending upon the specific drug substance under examination and the duration of time studied. For instance, using a random sample of adults, Aneshensel and Huba (1983) found that alcohol use (but not cigarette use) led to a short-term (four-month) decrease in depression (possibly a suppressor effect) and a longer-term (one-year) increase in depression. No effects of drug use on changes in emotional distress or adverse reactions to drugs were observed over a one-year or three-year period during adolescence (Huba et al., 1986; Newcomb & Bentler, in press).

There are certainly immediate unpleasant effects possible from use of drugs (e.g., Huba et al., 1986; Naditch, 1974, 1975; Naditch, Alker, & Joffe, 1975; Smart & Adlaf, 1982). Yet it is not apparent whether these effects generalize into long-term and enduring consequences to emotional makeup or whether

they represent time-limited periods of discomfort and dys-
phoria. Drugs are also often sought to relieve emotional
distress (e.g., Labouvie, 1986), as well as prescribed for the
same purpose, and thus it would not be surprising if nonpre-
scribed use of certain drugs did reduce emotional discomfort in
certain circumstances. Khantzian and Khantzian (1984) believe
that cocaine users somehow select that substance to self-
medicate or treat a preexisting affective disorder, typically
dysthymia. Perhaps use of such mood-altering substances can
relieve, on a temporary basis, emotional distress. Whether such
positive effects can be maintained is an important question.
Huba and Bentler (1982) and Bentler (1987b) found that early
cannabis use increased positive self-concept over time, suggesting some positive long-term benefits. Such benefits may
also depend upon the stage in the life cycle and other
conditions. For example, Bentler (1987b) found no effect of
late adolescent cannabis use on changes in self-acceptance into
young adulthood. It is quite probable that the longer-term
effects also may be more damaging. For instance, Newcomb,
Bentler, and Collins (1986) found that alcohol use decreased
self-derogation, but increased dissatisfaction with peer relationships and perceived environment from late adolescence to
young adulthood. Similarly, Washton and Gold (1984) consider cocaine use to be the cause of the emotional deterioration
they have observed among cocaine abusers (who themselves
often associate cocaine use with their problems).

The mental health consequences of teenage drug use are
certainly far from clear. Continued research will help separate
the influences of specific types of substances, from specific
outcomes, over varying lengths of time. This chapter will
contribute to this accumulating knowledge by studying the
impact of teenage drug use on mental health or emotional
distress four years later as young adults.

The construct of emotional or psychological distress has
been discussed by Dohrenwend, Shrout, Egri, and Mendelsohn
(1980) as a set of nonspecific symptoms and distress signals
that are not exclusively diagnostic of a particular syndrome.
These symptoms might either accompany an acute or chronic
condition of disturbed psychological functioning or represent

a strong reaction to environmental stressors. In this conception, psychological distress consists of such possible facets as dysphoric feelings, self-devaluation, anxiety, irritability, confusion, and inability to concentrate. Tanaka and Huba (1984) explored empirically the construct of psychological distress and concluded that it was a stable second-order factor related to a range of lower-order variables.

Although the research efforts of Dohrenwend et al. (1980) and Tanaka and Huba (1984) suggest that a single factor or construct may adequately represent the notion of emotional or psychological distress at a high order of abstraction, lower-order differentiation is also justified because the primary-order constructs tested by Tanaka and Huba (1984) were not perfectly correlated. Although in our analyses for this chapter we use a general factor of Emotional Distress as a control or baseline condition during adolescence, we have provided a greater degree of specificity for the young adult consequent constructs.

Coming together to create emotional well-being are various interrelated processes and qualities that may be differentially influenced by prior drug use. For instance, suicide is a major problem among teenagers and young adults (e.g., Simons & Murphy, 1985), and it is important to determine whether drug use somehow contributes to feelings or tendencies toward self-destruction. It is possible that high levels of chronic drug use may create permanent changes in thought patterns and reality testing, which may lead to bizarre or psychotic thinking. Certainly acute episodes of drug intoxication or drug toxicity can generate unusual thought processes. These generally subside rapidly following the drug high. It is not clear whether chronic repetition of such events may have an accumulating effect and result in permanent impairment of the thought processes.

Affective and emotional dispositions, as well as outlook on life, may also be influenced by drug use. Drugs are often used to relieve depression or dysphoric feelings and may have that immediate effect. The long-term effects, however, may be the opposite, as suggested by Aneshensel and Huba (1983). Outlook, direction, or purpose in life may also be affected by drug use. Although we have seen that drug use does not directly lead to an amotivational syndrome as related to educational pursuits nor to laziness or lassitude regarding employment pursuits, it may well influence one's outlook on life over time.

Design of the Model

In the model for this chapter, which assesses the impact of teenage drug use on mental health, three constructs are included from the adolescent data and five constructs are from the young adult data. Two of the adolescent constructs are Drug Use and Social Conformity. The other adolescent construct is Emotional Distress (with observed indicators of [lack of] deliberateness, [lack of] diligence, [lack of] self-acceptance, and depression). In young adulthood, five latent constructs were incorporated into the model including Psychoticism (with indicators of magic ideation 1, 2, and 3), Depression (with measured-scale indicators of [lack of] positive affect, negative affect, impaired motivation, and impaired relationships), Emotional Distress (with the same four indicators as in adolescence), Purpose in Life (with indicators of PIL 1, 2, and 3), and Suicide Ideation (reflected in items measuring think about killing self, told someone kill self, and life end with suicide). A more thorough description of these variables is given in Chapter 4 and in the Appendix.

The statistical and methodological details related to the development of this model are provided in the "Technical Summary" at the end of this chapter. Figure 12.1 depicts how the measured variables were generated by the latent constructs in the final confirmatory factor analysis (CFA) model. Table 12.1 presents the factor intercorrelations for the initial and final CFA models. The final structural model is depicted in Figure 12.2 and Table 12.2. The figure presents the relationship among latent factors, whereas the table reports the nonstandard effects that include at least one measured variable.

Interpretation

In the final CFA model for drug use and mental health, the adolescent Drug Use factor was significantly correlated with

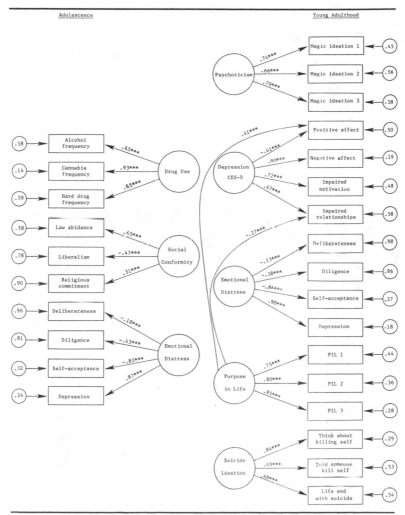

Figure 12.1. Final Confirmatory Factor Analysis Model for the Mental Health Variables

NOTE: Large circles represent latent factors, rectangles are measured variables, and the small circles with numbers are residual variances. Factor loadings are standardized and significance levels were determined by critical ratios (*$p < .05$; **$p < .01$; ***$p < .001$). Not depicted in the figure are two-headed arrows (correlations) joining each possible pair of factors. Values for these correlations are provided in Table 12.1.

all other adolescent factors and three of the five young adult factors. Teenage Drug Use was significantly related to lowered Social Conformity, higher Emotional Distress in both adolescence and young adulthood, increased Psychoticism, and

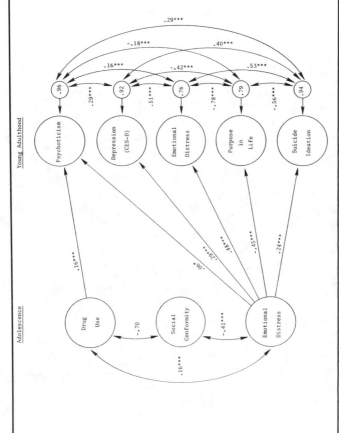

Figure 12.2. Final Structural or Path Model for the Mental Health Variables

NOTE: The measurement portion of this model is not depicted for simplicity. Two-headed arrows reflect correlations and single-headed arrows represent across-time regression effects. Parameter estimates are standardized, residual variables are variances, and significance levels were determined by critical ratios (*p < .05; **p < .01; ***p < .001). Nonstandard effects are given in Table 12.2.

176

TABLE 12.1
Factor Intercorrelations for the Initial (upper triangle) and Final (lower triangle) Confirmatory Factor Model

Factor	I	II	III	IV	V	VI	VII	VIII
Late Adolescence								
I Drug Use	1.00	-.77***	.18***	.17***	.05	.08*	-.07*	.01
II Social Conformity	-.70***	1.00	-.38***	-.17**	-.06	-.21***	.21***	-.07
III Emotional Distress	.15***	-.41***	1.00	.06*	.35***	.48***	-.45***	.24***
Young Adulthood								
IV Psychoticism	.16***	-.19***	.06*	1.00	.34***	.16***	-.21***	.28***
V Depression (CES-D)	.06	-.06	.29***	.30***	1.00	.72***	-.64***	.53***
VI Emotional Distress	.07*	-.19***	.49***	.16***	.57***	1.00	-.83***	.56***
VII Purpose in Life	-.07*	.17***	-.45***	-.18***	-.49***	-.83***	1.00	-.56***
VIII Suicide Ideation	.00	-.08*	.24***	.29***	.44***	.57***	-.59***	1.00

*$p < .05$; **$p < .01$; ***$p < .001$.

TABLE 12.2
Direct Across-Time Causal Paths Not Depicted in Figure

Adolescent Predictor Variable		Young Adult Consequent Variable		Standardized Parameter Estimate[a]
Observed Variable	Latent Variable	Observed Variable	Latent Variable	
	Drug Use	deliberateness		−.09**
alcohol frequency (R)[b]		positive affect		.08**
alcohol frequency (R)		impaired relationship		−.08**
hard drug frequency (R)			Suicide Ideation	.08**
law abidance (R)		diligence		.07*
liberalism (R)		depression		.07**
liberalism (R)			Purpose in Life	−.05*
	Emotional Distress	self-acceptance		−.10**
	Emotional Distress	told someone kill self		.08**
diligence (R)		negative affect		−.05**
diligence (R)		self-acceptance		.10***
diligence (R)		life end with suicide		.08**
diligence (R)			Purpose in Life	.08**

a. Significance level determined by a critical ratio of the unstandardized parameter estimate divided by its standard error.
b. (R) denotes variable residual.
*p < .05; **p < .01; ***p < .001.

decreased Purpose in Life in adulthood (see Table 12.1). Adolescent Social Conformity was significantly associated with decreased Emotional Distress in both adolescence and young adulthood, decreased Psychoticism, increased Purpose in Life, and decreased Suicide Ideation. Adolescent Emotional Distress was significantly related to all young adult constructs in expected directions (i.e., more Psychoticism, more Depression, more Emotional Distress, less Purpose in Life, and more Suicide Ideation).

Two additional factor loadings were necessary to include in the measurement portion of the model (see Figure 12.1). These were among the young adult measures and reflected the fact that the general tendency toward having a high Purpose in Life was also related to increased positive affect and decreased impaired relationships.

As is apparent in the final structural model (Figure 12.2 and Table 12.2), Social Conformity in adolescence had no direct influence on any of the constructs assessed in young adulthood. The impact of Social Conformity was mediated through the high negative correlations with Drug Use or Emotional Distress. Emotional Distress was significantly predictive of all young adult constructs in the expected directions, representing stability effects across time. Young adult Drug Use was significantly predictive of increased young adult Psychoticism and decreased young adult deliberateness. Adolescent specific use of alcohol (residual) was significantly predictive of increased positive affect and decreased impaired relationship aspects of Depression in young adulthood. Finally, adolescent specific use of hard drugs (residual) was significantly predictive of increased Suicidal Ideation in young adulthood, after controlling for earlier Emotional Distress.

The results indicate that general Drug Use and involvement with specific substances in adolescence influenced, in a small to moderate extent, emotional and psychological status during young adulthood. These effects were apparent while controlling for adolescent Emotional Distress levels and degree of Social Conformity. Thus it can be concluded that there are psychological health consequences to adolescent drug use, and emotional distress can be seen as both a cause and an outcome of youthful drug involvement. These effects were not observed for the general Emotional Distress factor (except for Drug Use decreasing deliberateness), however, but were apparent on more specialized types of psychological or emotional functioning.

Specifically, general Drug Use during adolescence was related to increased psychotic thinking in young adulthood, and thus could be seen as interfering with important cognitive processes, perhaps to the detriment of other life areas. The effect is small, but still quite significant. It appears that high levels of drug use during the teenager years increase unusual or bizarre thoughts, beliefs, or behaviors in young adulthood, as reflected in the Psychoticism construct (measured by the magic ideation scale). Such a deterioration in thought processes might be expected to increase with time and continued drug use, and can adversely affect other life areas where clear and unimpeded cognitive functioning is required. Similarly, teenage Drug Use decreased deliberateness in young adulthood. This suggests that early drug use has a long-term impact on planning, organization, and directed behavior as reflected in a decrease in deliberateness. This effect, combined with the increased Psychoticism, indicates that teenage Drug Use interferes with organized cognitive functioning and increases thought disorganization into young adulthood.

On the other hand, adolescent hard drug use was associated with increased Suicide Ideation in young adulthood, beyond levels of Emotional Distress already experienced in adolescence. This is an important consequence of hard drug use and warrants careful attention and consideration. Thus use of hard drugs as a teenager, implying a high degree of drug involvement, appears to increase self-destructive thoughts and tendencies. The mechanism of this effect, however, is unclear. It is possible that heavy use of hard drugs may undermine a will to live, decrease survival skills or motivation, increase negative feedback by others, or degrade one's perception of life to the point where suicide becomes an option.

Interestingly, not all adolescent drug use consequences were negative. Alcohol use was related to decreased depression as reflected in more positive feelings and improved social relationships. Alcohol seems helpful in alleviating certain types of depression, and may reflect the general, social acceptability of alcohol use and its apparent facilitating impact on social interactions. This effect is evident during a critical period of development from adolescence to young adulthood, when true adult relationships are begun, emerging social skills must be brought to fruition, and the use of alcohol becomes legal. This apparent positive effect of alcohol may not occur for different periods of life, when other developmental tasks are faced, and the meaning of alcohol may not be the same.

The specific effects noted for hard drug use and alcohol use are for the non-factor-determined portion of these substances. They do not reflect general drug use, but in fact represent specific use of these substances independent of general use of many substances. Thus these results reflect effects of the specific drug and not a general tendency to use drugs as tapped in the Drug Use construct.

It is noteworthy that aside from the effect of alcohol on decreasing certain aspects of depression, in this essentially normal sample, teenage Drug Use was unrelated to other affective aspects of mental health functioning during young adulthood. Drug Use did not generate changes in general amounts of Emotional Distress, Purpose in Life, or Depression. Thus the impact of Drug Use appears to be only on specific types of emotional functioning, such as Psychoticism, deliberateness, and Suicide Ideation.

Technical Summary

Confirmatory Factor Analyses

As always, our first step in the data analyses is to determine the adequacy of our hypothesized measurement model, using confirmatory factor analysis with the standard specification, which, of course, included four a priori correlations between the residual variables of the four repeated measures of the Emotional Distress construct. This initial CFA model did not adequately reflect the data (χ^2 = 755.77, d.f. = 292, p < .001), although the Normed Fit Index (NFI) was sufficiently large (.90) to suggest that minor modifications to the model should yield an acceptable fit. Factor intercorrelations for this model are presented in the upper triangle of Table 12.1.

By examining the Lagrange Multiplier indices (Bentler, 1986c; Bentler & Chou, 1986), correlations among 47 pairs of residuals and two nonhypothesized factor loadings were added to the model. These modifications resulted in a model that adequately reflected the data (χ^2 = 258.79, d.f. = 243, p = .23, NFI = .96). Factor intercorrelations for this final CFA model are presented in the lower triangle of Table 12.1. All hypothesized factor loadings were significant. Standardized factor loadings and residual variables (variances) for this final CFA model are graphically depicted in Figure 12.1.

The factor intercorrelations between the initial and final confirmatory factor analysis models were correlated higher than .99, indicating that the model modifications did not alter the basic pattern of factor intercorrelations to any noticeable or substantial extent.

Structural Model Analyses

The final stage in our data analyses for this model was the creation of a structural or path model using the standard specification discussed several times previously. This beginning model was modified by adding across-time regression paths (based on the modification indices) and deleting nonsignificant parameters. The final structural model fit the data quite well (χ^2 = 262.08, d.f. = 252, p = .32, NFI = .96). Associations among the latent factors are graphically displayed in Figure 12.2, whereas the across-time paths that include at least one observed variable are listed in Table 12.2 with their standardized regression weights.

13

Impact on
Social Integration

Very little conclusive research has been done regarding the impact of drug use on aspects of social relatedness, including social support, loneliness, assertiveness, or social competencies. Many drug users appear to have problems with social relationships (Spotts & Shontz, 1983); however, it is not clear whether the difficulties have emerged as a result of their drug use, or whether drug use is used to handle their social inabilities (e.g., Beckman, 1980). For instance, past drinkers as compared to lifelong abstainers were found to be significantly less sociable (Eward, Wolfe, Moll, & Harburg, 1986). Similarly, Sadava and Thompson (in press) found that loneliness was significantly related to alcohol use problems and adverse consequences.

The direction of association between social integration and drug use in these studies is quite unclear. In a longitudinal study, Pentz (1985) found that drug use decreased social skills as mediated by a decrease in self-efficacy. On the other hand, Bentler and Newcomb (1986b) found that adolescent alcohol use increased perceived social support as young adults.

Further research is necessary to determine the relationship and causal direction between drug use and various aspects of social functioning, including social skills, social support, loneliness, and social network. Drugs are often used to facilitate social interaction, for example, the cocktail party as an illustration. The logical questions—about whether this works in a longer time frame and what other impact drug use may have on social exchange and social integration—remain unanswered.

Loneliness has been defined as a deficiency in one's social relationships that is subjectively experienced as unpleasant (Peplau & Pearlman, 1982). Loneliness has been associated with a variety of psychological difficulties including depression (e.g., Young, 1982); suicide ideation (e.g., Diamant & Windholz, 1981); psychosomatic symptoms such as headaches, fatigue, and poor appetite (e.g., Rubenstein & Shaver, 1980); anxiety (e.g., Russell, Peplau, & Cutrona, 1980); neuroticism and general maladjustment (e.g., Goswick & Jones, 1981); aggression and rape (e.g., Check, Perlman, & Malamuth, 1983; Sermat, 1980); and problem behavior among adolescents such as poor grades, running away from home, and illegal behavior (e.g., Brennan & Auslander, 1979). These findings suggest that painful deficits in one's social attachments have severe implications for psychological functioning and adjustment that may require professional intervention (e.g., Rook, 1984).

Social support has been defined as "the existence or availability of people on whom we can rely, people who let us know that they care about, value, and love us" (Sarason, Levine, Basham, & Sarason, 1983). Thus social support is an interwoven network of personal relationships that provides companionship, assistance, attachment, and emotional nourishment to the individual. Social support has been found to have a variety of positive influences both as a direct effect on healthy adjustment and growth, and as a buffer against the disorienting effects of stressful life events (e.g., Cohen & Wills, 1985; Sarason et al., 1983). Specifically, social support has been linked with decreased morbidity and mortality (e.g., Berkman, 1985), increased mental health and positive psychological functioning (e.g., Kessler & McLeod, 1985; Leavy, 1983), and physically healthy status (e.g., Broadhead et al., 1983; Mitchell, Billings, & Moos, 1982; Wortman & Conway, 1985). Thus the presence of supportive people in one's life enhances both physical and emotional well-being.

Recent research has found that different measures of loneliness and social support are generated by a single general construct of attachment to social networks (Newcomb & Bentler, 1986e), although at a lower level of abstraction the concepts retain their uniqueness. In this chapter, we examine the impact of teenage Drug Use on young adult Social Support and Loneliness, while controlling for adolescent Social Support and Social Conformity. Unfortunately, we do not have an adolescent loneliness measure, and thus must rely on the adolescent Social Support measure as a proxy for a missing adolescent loneliness measure. Such a substitution is justified based on the research cited above, which found that a single underlying construct generated both loneliness and social support.

Design of the Model

In the model for this chapter, which assesses the impact of teenage drug use on social integration, three constructs are included from the adolescent data and two constructs are from the young adult data. Two of the adolescent constructs are Drug Use and Social Conformity as included in all of the models. The other adolescent construct is Social Support (with observed indicators of good relationship with parents, good relationship with family, good relationship with adults, and good relationship with peers). In young adulthood, two latent constructs were incorporated into the model including Loneliness (with indicators of Lonely 1, 2, and 3) and Social Support (with the same four indicators as in adolescence). A more thorough description of these variables is given in Chapter 4 and in the Appendix.

The statistical and methodological details related to the development of this model are provided in the "Technical Summary" at the end of this chapter. Figure 13.1 depicts how the measured variables were generated by the latent constructs in the final confirmatory factor analysis (CFA) model. Table 13.1 presents the factor intercorrelations for the initial and final CFA models. The final structural model is depicted in Figure 13.2 and Table 13.2. The figure presents the relationship among latent factors, whereas the table reports the nonstandard effects that include at least one measured variable.

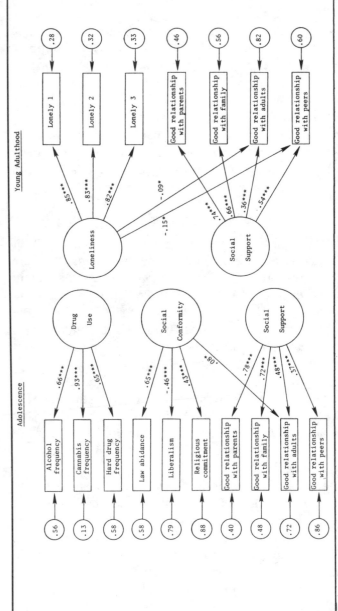

Figure 13.1. Final Confirmatory Factor Analysis Model for the Social Integration Variables

NOTE: Large circles represent latent factors, rectangles are measured variables, and the small circles with numbers are residual variances. Factor loadings are standardized and significance levels were determined by critical ratios (*p < .05; **p < .01; ***p < .001). Not depicted in the figure are two-headed arrows (correlations) joining each possible pair of factors. Values for these correlations are provided in Table 13.1.

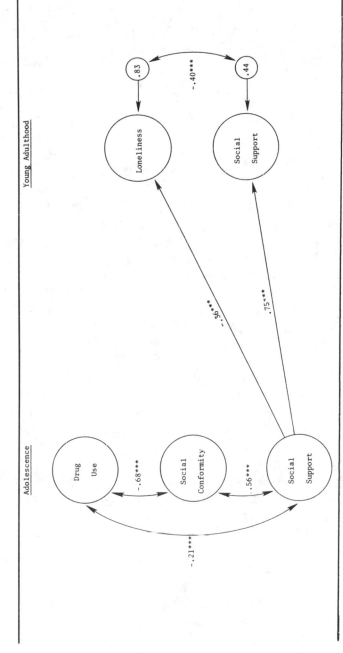

Adolescence | Young Adulthood

Figure 13.2. Final Structural or Path Model for the Social Integration Variables

NOTE: The measurement portion of this model is not depicted for simplicity. Two-headed arrows reflect correlations and single-headed arrows represent across-time regression effects. Parameter estimates are standardized, residual variables are variances, and significance levels were determined by critical ratios (*p < .05; **p < .01; ***p < .001). Nonstandard effects are given in Table 13.2.

TABLE 13.1

Factor Intercorrelations for the Initial (upper triangle)
and Final (lower triangle) Confirmatory Factor Analyses

Factor		I	II	III	IV	V
Late Adolescence						
I	Drug Use	1.00	−.78***	−.21***	−.04	.05
II	Social Conformity	−.69***	1.00	.47***	.27***	−.24**
III	Social Support	−.22***	.52***	1.00	.61***	−.38***
Young Adulthood						
IV	Social Support	−.05	.36***	.78***	1.00	−.49***
V	Loneliness	.06	−.21***	−.47***	−.57***	1.00

*p < .05; **p < .01; ***p < .001.

Interpretation

In the final CFA model for drug use and social integration, the adolescent Drug Use factor was significantly correlated with all other adolescent factors and none of the young adult factors. Teenage Drug Use was significantly related to lowered Social Conformity and lower Social Support during adolescence (see Table 13.1). Adolescent Social Conformity was significantly associated with increased Social Support in both adolescence and young adulthood and decreased Loneliness in young adulthood. Adolescent Social Support was significantly related to both young adult constructs in expected directions, that is, more Social Support and less Loneliness. In young adulthood, Loneliness and Social Support were negatively correlated as expected.

Three additional factor loadings were necessary to include in the measurement portion of the model (see Figure 13.1). One involved the adolescent measures, indicating that the general tendency toward Social Conformity was associated (slightly) with good relationships with adults. Two additional factor loadings were needed among the young adult measures and reflected the fact that the general tendency toward Loneliness was also minimally, but significantly, related to decreased good relationships with adults and decreased good relationships with peers.

The final structural model (Figure 13.2 and Table 13.2) indicates that general teenage Drug Use did not directly

TABLE 13.2
Direct Across-Time Causal Paths Not Depicted in Figure

Adolescent Predictor Variable		Young Adult Consequent Variable		Standardized Parameter Estimate[a]
Observed Variable	Latent Variable	Observed Variable	Latent Variable	
alcohol frequency			Social Support	.09**
alcohol frequency (R)[b]		good relationship with parents		.05*
alcohol frequency (R)			Loneliness	−.09**
hard drug frequency (R)		lonely 2		.05*
hard drug frequency (R)			Social Support	−.10**
liberalism (R)		good relationship with adults		−.08**
religious commitment (R)		good relationship with adults		.08**
good relationship with family (R)			Loneliness	−.11**
good relationship with adults (R)			Loneliness	−.16***
good relationship with peers (R)			Social Support	.09**

a. Significance level determined by a critical ratio of the unstandardized parameter estimate divided by its standard error.
b. (R) denotes variable residual.
*p < .05; **p < .01; ***p < .001.

influence either Loneliness or Social Support in young adulthood. There was an indirect effect of early Drug Use on these two consequent factors, via the relevant correlations with Social Conformity and Social Support, but Drug Use was nonsignificantly correlated with young adult Social Support and Loneliness in the CFA models (see Table 13.1). Similarly, there was no direct effect of adolescent Social Conformity on young adult Loneliness or Social Support. There was, however, an indirect effect via the high correlation between Social Support and Social Conformity during adolescence. Finally, adolescent Social Support predicted both a lack of Loneliness and increased Social Support (a stability effect) in young adulthood.

Despite this apparent lack of impact of general Drug Use on social integration, there were several interesting effects for specific types of drugs (see Table 13.2). Alcohol use during adolescence increased Social Support (and specifically increased good relationship with parents) and decreased Loneliness in young adulthood. This corroborates, with different measures, our findings from the previous chapter on Mental Health, regarding the effect of alcohol on improving social relationships. We must conclude that alcohol use during adolescence appears to increase social integration, decrease loneliness, and increase good relationships with other important people as the individual matures into adulthood. It must be remembered that this is a special time in life that places a strong emphasis on personal relationships and social interactions, during which alcohol becomes legal and socially condoned. Most of the findings for teenage alcohol use are based on the residual of the measure, indicating that it represents the specific use of alcohol, independent of cannabis and hard drugs. These findings may apply to those who use alcohol, perhaps even heavily, but who do not make the transition on to illicit substances, and thus may be more conforming or traditional than those who use all types of drugs. Specific use of alcohol may be an indicator of gregariousness that would be expected to be positively related to social supports and good relationships with adults and inversely related to loneliness.

On the other hand, the specific use of hard drugs (residual component) during the teenage years led to decreased Social Support and some increased loneliness (on one of the three indicators of the Loneliness factor) in young adulthood. Hard drug use appears to have a negative or disruptive impact on social integration. There were no specific effects for cannabis use.

It appears that the type of drug use is the critical factor when considering the impact of teenage drug use on young adult social integration. The specific use of a societally legalized substance—alcohol—seems to enhance social functioning and integration, whereas the use of illegal hard drugs has the opposite effect. Because high levels of alcohol use tend to generate use of illicit substances (e.g., Newcomb & Bentler, 1986c), those who do not make the transition to cannabis and hard drugs display a resistance to this general pattern. This resistance may be social conformity, a negative reaction to illicit drugs, peer pressure away from illicit drugs, or other important characteristics that make these teenagers unique and that may help explain the positive influence of alcohol use. On the other hand, the positive effect of alcohol may represent a true benefit to the awkward and perhaps socially conscious teenager, who may be overcoming shyness and social uncertainty. Alcohol may provide the disinhibition necessary for some to perform in a social situation, which should then enhance aspects of social integration.

On the other hand, use of hard drugs as a teenager appears to interfere with social functioning and integration, resulting in greater isolation and alienation as a young adult. Hard drug use may have disturbed the normal maturational development whereby the teenager acquires essential social skills and relationship competency. It is also possible that hard drug use somehow deteriorates previously acquired social skills and competence resulting in greater detachment from critical social networks.

Combining these results with those from the Mental Health model, it is clear that the specific use of alcohol as a teenager may provide some helpful impact on social functioning, the enhancement of positive affect, improving relationships, decreasing loneliness, and increasing social support. Conversely, the specific use of hard drugs as a teenager appears to generate a deterioration in social relationships, increased loneliness, decreased social support, and a resultant increase in suicidal ideation.

Technical Summary

Confirmatory Factor Analyses

As always, our first step in the data analyses is to determine the adequacy of our hypothesized measurement model using the standard approach to model specification, including the four a priori correlations between the residual variables of the four repeated measures of the Social Support construct. This initial CFA model did not adequately reflect the data (χ^2 = 565.48, d.f. = 105, p < .001), although the Normed Fit Index was sufficiently large (.88) to suggest that minor modifications to the model should yield an acceptable fit. Factor intercorrelations for this initial CFA model are presented in the upper triangle of Table 13.1.

By examining the Lagrange Multiplier indices (Bentler & Chou, 1986; Bentler, 1986c), correlations among 29 pairs of residuals were added to the model. In addition, three nonhypothesized factor loadings were necessary. These modifications resulted in a model that adequately reflected the data (χ^2 = 79.77, d.f. = 74, p = .30, NFI = .98). This model could not be rejected as a plausible explanation of the data as represented in the final CFA model. Factor intercorrelations for this final CFA model are presented in the lower triangle of Table 13.1. All hypothesized factor loadings were significant. Standardized factor loadings and residual variables (variances) of the observed variables for this final CFA model are graphically depicted in Figure 13.1. Adding the correlated residuals did not disturb the fundamental associations among the latent constructs, because the factor intercorrelations between the initial and final confirmatory factor analysis models were very similar, having a correlation higher than .99.

Structural Model Analyses

The initial complete structural model, based upon our standard approach to model specification, was modified by adding needed across-time regression paths and deleting nonsignificant parameters. The final structural model fit the data quite well (χ^2 = 64.18, d.f. = 77, p = .85, NFI = .99). Associations among the latent factors are graphically displayed in Figure 13.2, whereas the across-time paths that include at least one observed variable are listed in Table 13.2 with their standardized regression weights.

14

Impact of
Specific Drugs in a
Large Integrated
Model

In the preceding chapters, models were developed that established some important consequences of teenage drug use on young adult functioning. Although it would have been ideal to study all types of effects in one large model, this was not possible due to several natural limits encountered when creating a large model with many variables. These limits are that theoretical knowledge is often sufficiently incomplete to permit specification of the geometrically increased number of possible effects, computational resources are inadequate due to the expense of running large models, and sample size is inadequate to produce very stable estimates and tests. Thus it was not possible to study a wide range of drug use consequences in the context of a large model that also included a wide range of drug substances (i.e., different types of alcohol, cannabis, or hard drugs), because these would have had to be included at the expense of the more important control variables that are necessary for holding constant antecedent conditions. As a compromise, we have focused on specific areas of life functioning, while testing for the impact of general drug use and the specific impact of alcohol, cannabis, and hard drugs. The previous chapters, therefore, do not capture simultaneously a complete ecology of variables that may be influenced by drug use, while controlling for antecedent or baseline conditions. Yet, such a complete ecology is necessary to evaluate complex, interactional theories of drug use (e.g., Huba et al., 1980; Jessor & Jessor, 1977; Kaplan, 1985; Zucker & Gomberg, 1986).

In this chapter, we develop a large model that is built upon information gathered from the previous analyses. From each of the seven preceding chapters, we selected one or two young adult latent constructs that were best predicted from teenage drug use. At the same time, we have included a wider range of specific drug substances, in order to determine whether the effects noted earlier were due to general drug use, a specific category of substance (alcohol, cannabis, or hard drugs), or a specific type of drug (e.g., beer, hashish, cocaine). In this way, we achieve a broader perspective for understanding the consequences of teenage drug use. In order to conserve the number of variables simultaneously studied in the model, we do not include adolescent baseline and control conditions or factors directly in the model. These influences are statistically controlled by being partialed multivariately from the entire data under analysis (Lee, 1986). Thus all direct effects between early drug use and later functioning that are found in the model are partialed effects in which baseline and control variables have already been accounted for. In this way, of course, the antecedent control factors are partialed as manifest variables that contain measurement error.

Design of the Model

From the adolescent data, we have created 12 substance use measures that are used to reflect three latent constructs (see Chapter 4 and the Appendix for a more complete description of all measures). The constructs are Alcohol Use (with indicators of frequency of use of beer, wine, and liquor), Cannabis Use (with observed measures of frequency of use of marijuana and hashish), and Hard Drug Use (reflected in measured-variable indicators of frequency of use of hypnotics, cocaine, stimulants, psychedelics, inhalants, narcotics, and PCP). In order to capture the sizable correlations that we know exist among these three latent factors (e.g., Huba, Wingard, & Bentler, 1981; Newcomb & Bentler, 1986c), a second-order latent construct was included in the structural models to account for this common factor of General Drug Use (e.g., Bentler & Newcomb, 1986a). Thus, in the analyses to follow, we can test for the influence of General Drug Use (as the second-order latent factor), Alcohol Use, Cannabis Use, or Hard Drug Use (as first-order latent constructs), and any of the 12 individual substances (as measured variables) on outcomes in young adulthood (Bentler & Newcomb, in preparation; Newcomb & Bentler, 1987b). In addition, the consequences of use as reflected in the three first-order factors and the 12 observed measures can be obtained as effects of a drug itself or from the residual of the drug, reflecting the specific and unique use of that substance.

To control for baseline levels that could influence the young adult outcome constructs, 21 variables from the adolescent data were used. These variables were not included as actual constructs in the model, because this would have increased the size of the model beyond manageable limits. Instead, their influence on the entire system of adolescent and young adult variables was partialed out using multiple partial regression. These 21 variables were selected on the basis of being identical or similar to those incorporated as young adult outcome factors, or else, they were good predictors of the young adult constructs. Several control variables were selected from each chapter (i.e., from each substantive model described above). The partialed variables included law abidance, liberalism, religious commitment (the Social Conformity construct from all chapters), good relationship with parents, good relationship with family, good relationship with adults, good relationship with peers (the Family Support construct from Chapter 7 and the Social Support construct from Chapter 13), confrontational acts, stealing episodes, property damage (the Criminal Activities construct from Chapter 8), age of first sexual contact, age of first sexual intercourse (the Early Sexual Involvement factor from Chapter 9), grade point average, educational plans (the Academic Potential construct from Chapters 10 and 11), salary 1, salary 2, salary 3 (the Income factor from Chapters 10 and 11), and diligence, deliberateness, depression, and self-acceptance (the Emotional Distress factor from Chapter 12).

Twelve latent factors and one measured-variable construct (treated as a factor) were selected as outcome constructs from the young adult data. These factors were chosen from the smaller models in each chapter in which they had been shown to be influenced by teenage drug use. At least one construct reflecting each specific life area was chosen from each of the chapters. The constructs assessed in young adulthood included Family Formation (with indicators of marriage past four years and number of children from Chapter 7), Relationship Satisfaction (with indicators of happy with relationship and trouble with relationship from Chapter 7), Divorce (a single variable from Chapter 7), Drug Crime Involvement (with indicators of driving while intoxicated and selling or possessing drugs from Chapter 8), Criminal Activities (with indicators of confrontational acts, stealing episodes, and property damage from Chapter 8), Satisfaction with Intimacy (with indicators of happy with sex life, happy being close with someone, and satisfaction with sexual intercourse from Chapter 9), Number of Relationships (with indicators of number of steady partners and number of sexual partners from Chapter 9), College Involvement (with indicators of college attendance, part-time job and college, and part-time employment from Chapter 10), Job Instability (with indicators of times fired past four years, times lost job past four years, and times collected unemployment past four years from Chapter 11), Income (with indicators of salary 1, 2, and 3 from Chapter 11), Suicide Ideation (with indicators of think about killing self, told someone kill self, and life end with suicide from Chapter 12), Psychoticism (with indicators of magic ideation 1, 2, and 3 from Chapter 12), and Loneliness (with indicators of Lonely 1, 2, and 3 from Chapter 13).

The statistical and methodological details related to the development of this model are provided in the "Technical Summary" at the end of this chapter. Figure 14.1 depicts how the three drug use latent constructs in adolescence were indicated by the measured variables, and Figure 14.2 shows

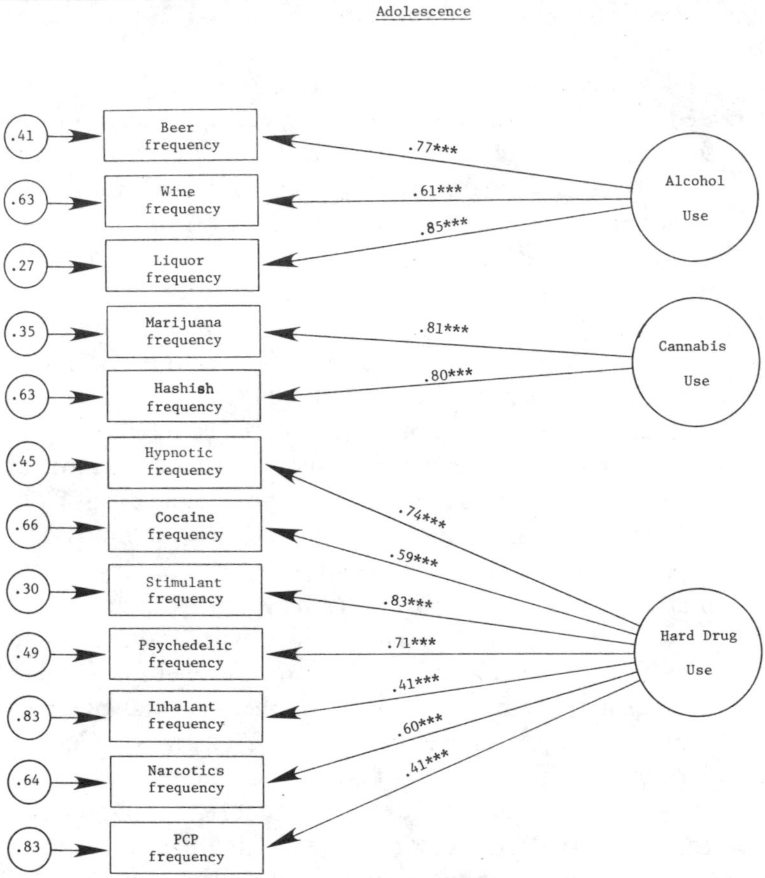

Figure 14.1. Final Confirmatory Factor Analysis Model for the Adolescent Drug Use Variables in the Large Integrated Model

NOTE: The entire CFA model also includes Figure 14.2. Large circles represent latent factors, rectangles are measured variables, and the small circles with numbers are residual variances. Factor loadings are standardized and significance levels were determined by critical ratios (*p < .05; **p < .01; ***p < .001). Not depicted in the figure are two-headed arrows (correlations) joining each possible pair of factors in this figure and Figure 14.2. Values for these correlations are provided in Table 14.1.

how the young adult outcome constructs were defined in the final confirmatory factor analysis (CFA) model. Table 14.1 presents the factor intercorrelations for the initial and final CFA models. The final structural model is depicted in Figure

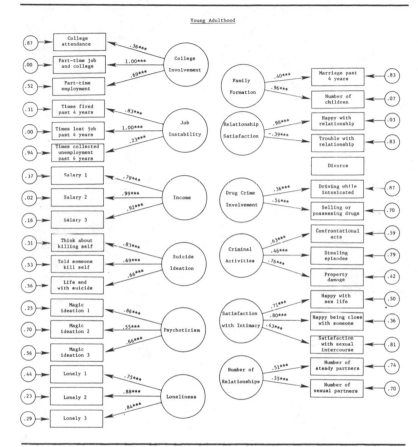

Figure 14.2. Final Confirmatory Factor Analysis Model for the Adolescent Drug Use Variables in the Large Integrated Model

NOTE: The entire CFA model also includes Figure 14.1. Large circles represent latent factors, retangles are measured variables, and the small circles with numbers are residual variances. Factor loadings are standardized and significance levels were determined by critical ratios (*p < .05; **p < .01; ***p < .001). Not depicted. in the figure are two-headed arrows (correlations) joining each possible pair of factors in this figure and Figure 14.1. Values for these correlations are provided in Table 14.1.

14.3, Table 14.2, and Table 14.3. The figure presents the relationship among latent factors, Table 14.2 reports the nonstandard effects that include at least one measured variable, and Table 14.3 provides the correlations among the young adult latent-factor residuals.

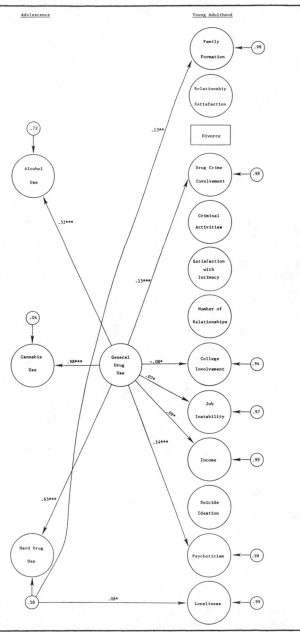

Figure 14.3. Final Structural or Path Model for the Large Integrated Analysis

NOTE: The measurement portion of this model is not depicted for simplicity. Two-headed arrows reflect correlations and single-headed arrows represent across-time regression effects.   Parameter estimates are standardized, residual variables are variances, and significance levels were determined by critical ratios (*p < .05; **p < .01; ***p < .001). Nonstandard effects are listed in Table 14.2.

TABLE 14.1
Factor Intercorrelations for the Initial (upper triangle) and Final (lower triangle) Confirmatory Factor Analysis Models

Factor	I	II	III	IV	V	VI	VII	VIII	IX	X	XI	XII	XIII	XIV	XV	XVI
Late Adolescence																
I Alcohol Use	1.00	.60***	.34***	.13**	.09*	.07*	.03	.12**	.07	.31***	-.12**	.04	.05	.02	.01	-.06
II Cannabis Use	.53***	1.00	.64***	.14**	.04	.10**	.08*	-.07	.02	.35***	-.14***	.08*	.09*	-.05	.10*	-.01
III Hard Drug Use	.34***	.64***	1.00	.18***	.03	.03	.17***	-.05	-.02	.41***	-.08*	.05	.06	.06	.10*	.07
Young Adulthood																
IV Family Formation	.02	.06	.03	1.00	-.02	.40***	-.02	-.12*	.18***	.02	-.30***	-.06	-.08*	-.03	-.06	.13**
V Relationship Satisfaction	.04	.05	.03	-.02	1.00	-.07*	-.04	-.09*	.77***	.07	-.05	-.08*	.06	-.23***	-.09*	-.33***
VI Divorce	.03	.05	.02	.20***	-.09*	1.00	.03	.13**	-.08*	.10*	-.13***	.07*	-.02	.03	-.05	.09*
VII Drug Crime Involvement	.18*	.23**	.31***	-.07	-.04	-.09	1.00	.13**	-.08*	-.05	-.05	.18***	.00	-.01	.05	.05
VIII Criminal Activities	-.08*	-.07	-.04	-.05	-.09*	.04	.14**	1.00	-.09*	.23***	-.10*	-.07*	-.03	.14**	.22***	.06
IX Satisfaction with Intimacy	.05	.01	-.02	.07	.70***	-.04	-.09	.04	1.00	.24***	-.13***	.12**	-.03	-.28***	-.05	-.46***
X Number of Relationships	.27***	.29***	.39***	.12*	.03	.10*	-.09	-.05	.24***	1.00	-.05	.08	-.04	-.02	.19**	-.02
XI College Involvement	-.10**	-.12**	-.08*	-.24***	-.04	-.11**	-.05	.05	.05	-.18***	1.00	.02	.04	.02	.07*	-.07*
XII Job Instability	.05	.08*	-.08*	-.10**	.04	.03	.35***	.11**	.14***	.17***	.02	1.00	.01	.15***	.13**	.08
XIII Income	.05	.08*	.02	-.18***	-.07*	-.05	-.02	-.01	-.03	-.04	.04	-.01	1.00	.01	.07*	.04
XIV Suicide Ideation	.00	-.04	.02	-.03	-.25***	.03	.02	.11*	-.31***	-.06	.02	.17***	.01	1.00	.29***	.36***
XV Psychoticism	.03	.11**	.14**	.03	-.08*	-.05	.04	.24***	-.03	.13*	.05	.14**	.03	.29***	1.00	.20***
XVI Loneliness	-.05	.00	.07	.14**	-.34***	.09*	.19*	.10*	-.47***	-.05	-.08*	.08*	-.07	.36***	.22***	1.00

*p < .05; **p < .01; ***p < .001.

TABLE 14.2
Direct Across-Time Causal Paths Not Depicted in Figure

Adolescent Predictor Variable		Young Adult Consequent Variable		Standardized Parameter Estimate[a]
Observed Variable	Latent Variable	Observed Variable	Latent Variable	
	General Drug Use	stealing episodes		.11***
	Alcohol Use (R)	confrontational acts		−.06*
	Alcohol Use (R)	happy with sex life		.07*
beer frequency			Number of Relationships	.13*
beer frequency (R)[b]			College Involvement	−.22***
beer frequency (R)		salary 1		.05*
beer frequency (R)		told someone kill self		−.10**
beer frequency (R)		lonely 2		−.06*
wine frequency (R)		satisfaction with sexual intercourse		−.10**
liquor frequency (R)		marriage past 4 years		.07*
liquor frequency (R)		selling or possessing drugs		−.08*
liquor frequency (R)		satisfaction with sexual intercourse		−.09**
liquor frequency (R)			College Involvement	−.18**
marijuana frequency (R)		times collected unemployment past 4 years		.11**
hashish frequency (R)			Job Instability	.10**
hashish frequency (R)		stealing episodes		.13**
	Hard Drug Use	trouble with relationship		.07*
	Hard Drug Use (R)	salary 2		.04*
	Hard Drug Use (R)	life end with suicide		.07*

Variable	Outcome	Coefficient
hypnotic frequency (R)	driving while intoxicated	−.09*
hypnotic frequency (R)	property damage	−.07*
hypnotic frequency (R)	satisfaction with sexual intercourse	.09**
hypnotic frequency	Number of Relationships	.35***
hypnotic frequency	Suicide Ideation	.13**
cocaine frequency	Number of Relationships	.20**
cocaine frequency (R)	confrontational acts	.07*
cocaine frequency (R)	stealing episodes	−.10**
cocaine frequency (R)	happy being close with someone	−.06*
cocaine frequency (R)	times fired past 4 years	.11**
stimulant frequency (R)	Divorce	.05*
stimulant frequency (R)	Suicide Ideation	.10**
inhalant frequency (R)	marriage past 4 years	.08*
inhalant frequency (R)	Divorce	.09*
inhalant frequency (R)	part-time employment	.09**
inhalant frequency (R)	Job Instability	.10**
inhalant frequency (R)	Suicide Ideation	.21***
narcotics frequency (R)	think about killing self	.06*
PCP frequency (R)	number of steady partners	−.23***
PCP frequency (R)	times fired past 4 years	.05*
PCP frequency (R)	Family Formation	.08*
PCP frequency (R)	College Involvement	−.12**

a. Significance level determined by a critical ratio of the unstandardized parameter estimate divided by its standard error.
b. (R) denotes variable residual.
*p < .05; **p < .01; ***p < .001.

TABLE 14.3
Correlations Among the Young Adult Factors or Their Residuals

Factor	IV	V	VI	VII	VIII	IX	X	XI	XII	XIII	XIV	XV	XVI
IV Family Formation (R)[a]	1.00												
V Relationship Satisfaction	0[b]	1.00											
VI Divorce (R)	.19***	−.06*	1.00										
VII Drug Crime Involvement (R)	0[b]	0[b]	0[b]	1.00									
VIII Criminal Activities	0[b]	0[b]	0[b]	0[b]	1.00								
IX Satisfaction with Intimacy	0[b]	.68***	0[b]	0[b]	0[b]	1.00							
X Number of Relationships (R)	0[b]	0[b]	0[b]	0[b]	.12**	.32***	1.00						
XI College Involvement (R)	−.23***	0[b]	−.09*	0[b]	.09*	0[b]	−.18**	1.00					
XII Job Instability (R)	−.11**	0[b]	0[b]	0[b]	0[b]	0[b]	0[b]	0[b]	1.00				
XIII Income (R)	−.17***	0[b]	0[b]	0[b]	0[b]	0[b]	0[b]	0[b]	0[b]	1.00			
XIV Suicide Ideation (R)	0[b]	−.25***	0[b]	0[b]	0[b]	−.30***	−.15*	0[b]	.13**	0[b]	1.00		
XV Psychoticism (R)	0[b]	−.06*	0[b]	0[b]	.21***	0[b]	0[b]	0[b]	.13**	0[b]	.31***	1.00	
XVI Loneliness (R)	.14***	−.33***	.07*	0[b]	0[b]	−.48***	−.20**	−.14**	0[b]	−.08*	.36***	.20***	1.00

a. (R) = Factor residual variable.
b. Fixed at zero since correlation was nonsignificant.
*p < .05; **p < .01; ***p < .001.

Interpretation

. In the final CFA model for this large integrated analysis that tested for specific drug effects, the three adolescent drug use constructs were all highly correlated, as expected. These correlations ranged from a low of .34 between Alcohol Use and Hard Drug Use, to a high of .63 between Cannabis Use and Hard Drug Use. Adolescent Alcohol Use was significantly correlated with young adulthood increased Drug Crime Involvement, decreased Criminal Activities, increased Number of Relationships, and decreased College Involvement during young adulthood (see Table 14.1). Adolescent Cannabis Use was significantly correlated with increased drug Crime Involvement, increased Number of Relationships, decreased College Involvement, increased Job Instability, increased Income, and increased Psychoticism in young adulthood. Finally, adolescent Hard Drug Use was significantly correlated with increased Family Formation, increased Drug Crime Involvement, increased Number of Relationships, decreased College Involvement, and increased Psychoticism.

In the final structural model, there were many significant effects of teenage drug use on young adult outcomes. Looking first at the General Drug Use factor, we found that the tendency to use many different drugs as an adolescent led to increased Drug Crime Involvement, decreased College Involvement, increased Job Instability, increased Income, and increased Psychoticism (see Figure 14.3), and to increased stealing episodes as young adults (see Table 14.2). Except for the effect on increased income, General Drug Use as a teenager apparently leads to problems in several areas in life including livelihood, emotional functioning, criminal involvement, and an abandonment of traditional pursuits, such as a college education.

Turning next to the general classes or types of substances, the first-order factor of teenage Alcohol Use had no impacts on young adult factors (see Figure 14.3). The factor residual, however, predicted decreased confrontational acts and increased happiness with sex life (Table 14.2). As noted in the table, use of specific types of alcohol led to decreased interest in College Involvement (for beer and liquor), decreased satisfaction with sexual intercourse (for wine and liquor), decreased loneliness (for beer), and increased Number of Relationships (for beer). Several other influences of teenage alcohol use on young adult outcomes can also be noted in the table. In general, the impact of adolescent alcohol consumption has some positive and some negative effects. Use of alcohol appears to decrease criminal activities and reduce loneliness, while at the same time decreasing traditional pursuits such as College Involvement and increasing early marriage.

There were no direct effects for the Cannabis Use latent construct (Figure 14.3). This is largely due to the fact that Cannabis Use was almost perfectly predicted from the second-order factor of General Drug Use, so that the effects of Cannabis Use are reflected in the influence of General Drug Use. On the other hand, there were a few effects of specific types of cannabis (Table 14.2). Marijuana use as a teenager led to increased times of collecting unemployment, whereas use of hashish increased Job Instability as young adults. Use of hashish also predicted increased stealing episodes. Thus use of cannabis substances is related to work and crime problems. There were no positive effects of cannabis use, as there appeared to be for alcohol use. Because the effects of General Drug Use are substantially ones of Cannabis Use (because of the high loadings noted above), use of cannabis substances as a teenager had a range of negative impacts on the social psychological functioning of the young adult.

Turning finally to the impact of hard drug use, many significant influences were found across time. The general tendency to use all types of hard drugs during adolescence (the Hard Drug Use factor or its residual) significantly generated an increase in young adult Family Formation and increased Loneliness (see the figure), as well as increased trouble with relationship, increased income (reflected in salary 2), and increased belief that life would end with suicide. These findings suggest that use of hard drugs as a teenager is significantly related to interpersonal problems (loneliness and trouble in relationships) and increased feelings of futility, as reflected in the belief that life would end with suicide. If early or young family formation (marriage and having children) reflects a tendency toward precocious development, as we hypothesize, then hard drug use appears to be a contributing factor not only in premature family involvement, but also in the difficulties associated with early marriage and childbearing. Adding more specificity to this interpretation is the fact that PCP use predicted early Family Formation, inhalant use influenced early marriage and subsequent divorce, and early cocaine use led to later divorce. Thus use of various types and all types of hard drugs propels an adolescent into early marriage and children, while at the same time generating marital problems and divorce. This corroborates the detrimental effects of precocious development. Aside from the lack of real maturity reflected in precocious development, early use of inhalants and cocaine may have been carried into the marriage and been a direct source of marital disruption.

Several other effects of specific types of hard drugs were noted. Use of hypnotics as a teenager decreased certain types of criminal behavior (driving while intoxicated and property damage), increased sexual satisfaction and promiscuity (an aspect of precocious development), and increased thoughts of self-destruction (Suicide Ideation). Cocaine use was related to promiscuous sexual conduct (many different partners), aggressiveness (confrontational acts), unhappiness with close relationships, and decreased episodes of theft. Use of stimulants increased Suicide Ideation and frequency of being fired. Use of inhalants as a teenager predicted increased young adult part-time employment, increased Job Instability, and increased Suicide Ideation. Narcotics use was related to increased thoughts about killing oneself. Finally, adolescent use of PCP predicted decreased number of steady partners, increased times being fired, and decreased traditional pursuits, such as College Involvement.

Use of hard drugs as a teenager, both in general and of specific types, predicted a wide range of dysfunctional outcomes as young adults. As a result, we must conclude that adolescent hard drug use is a portent for many difficulties and problems as a young adult, both on a psychoemotional level, as well as on a social and interpersonal level. These problems are quite serious involving suicide ideation, social isolation, divorce, and difficulties maintaining a job.

An examination of the factor intercorrelations for this larger model (Table 14.1) would lead us to expect a direct effect of General Drug Use on young adult Number of Relationships, based on the uniformly moderate correlations between this outcome construct and the Alcohol, Cannabis, and Hard Drug Use factors. This effect was not included in our final model, however. Instead, there were three significant effects over time: teenage use of beer, cocaine, and hypnotics increased Number of Relationships as young adults. These effects were from the drug variable itself and not its residual (R). This implies that there were indirect effects of the latent factors mediated through these substance use variables. Specifically, General Drug Use (itself, almost perfectly defined by Cannabis Use), influenced Alcohol Use and Hard Drug Use, which in turn influenced beer frequency and hypnotic and cocaine frequency, respectively. Thus we can conclude that there are indirect effects of General Drug Use, as well as Alcohol, Cannabis, and Hard Drug Use on Number of Relationships, as mediated through the three specific substances. This accounts for the apparent contradiction between the final CFA and final structural models.

Technical Summary

Confirmatory Factor Analyses

As always, our first step in data analyses is to determine the adequacy of our hypothesized measurement model, as described above. Although each of the young adult constructs was confirmed in the previous analyses, it was critical to reverify them in this different ecology or system of variables. Although unlikely, it is possible that partialing the 21 variables from the data system may have disturbed or tampered with the factor structure. In addition, the drug use measures had not been used in their present form in the previous analyses and needed to be confirmed.

Our typical initial CFA was run, which fixed all factor variances at unity and allowed all constructs to correlate freely (including the single-variable factor of Divorce, which was treated like a construct). The second-order General Drug Use factor was not included in this model. No a priori across-time correlations between residual variables were included, because prior measures had been controlled statistically.

This initial CFA model did not adequately reflect the data (χ^2 = 1503.69, d.f. = 826, p < .001), although the NFI was sufficiently large (.86) to suggest that minor modifications to the model should yield an acceptable fit. Factor intercorrelations for this initial CFA model are presented in the upper triangle of Table 14.1.

By examining the Lagrangian Multiplier modification indices (Bentler & Chou, 1986; Bentler, 1986c), correlations among 89 pairs of residuals were added to the model. In addition, two residual variances were fixed at zero to prevent them from being estimated as negative. No additional factor loadings were necessary. These modifications resulted in a model that adequately reflected the data (χ^2 = 756.47, d.f. = 735, p = .28, NFI = .93). Factor intercorrelations for this final CFA model are presented in the lower triangle of Table 14.1. All hypothesized factor loadings were significant. Standardized factor loadings and residual variables (variances) of the observed variables for this final CFA model are graphically depicted in Figures 14.1 and 14.2. The first figure presents the factor structure of the 12 substance use measures and the second figure presents the factor structure of the young adult constructs. Figures 14.1 and 14.2 are from the same final CFA model, but are presented separately for clarity. The factor intercorrelations from the initial and final CFA models were correlated higher than .95, indicating that the model modifications did not alter the basic pattern of factor intercorrelations to any substantial extent.

Structural Model Analyses

Because many of the correlated residuals added in the model modifications to create the final CFA model may be across-time regression effects, these empirically determined across-time correlated residuals were deleted in the initial structural model. A second-order factor was included, which was hypothesized to generate adolescent Alcohol Use, Cannabis Use, and Hard Drug Use. In the initial structural model, this second-order construct of General Drug Use was allowed to predict all young adult constructs. A series of hierarchical model modifications were conducted to add and delete across-time influences from teenage drug use to the young adult outcome variables. The analyses progressed in a sequence, first looking for the impact of the highest-order factors of drug use, and then testing for lower-order factors, and finally for measured variables of specific types of substance use. This procedure controlled or accounted for the effects of General Drug Use before tests were made for any effects of the first-order factors (Alcohol Use, Cannabis Use, and Hard Drug Use). Similarly, the impact of the first-order factors was established before specific drug effects (e.g., beer, marijuana, cocaine) were considered. In this way, we are able to isolate the effects of General Drug Use (use of all types of substances), from the use of particular types of drugs (alcohol, cannabis, hard drugs), from the impact of specific drug substances (e.g., wine, hashish, hypnotics). We evaluated both the impact of the first-order factors and the measured variables, as well as the impact of their residuals (the second-order factor had no residual because it was an independent variable). Consequences were sought first on the latent factors in young adulthood, and subsequently on the measured-variable indicators of these factors. All factor residuals during young adulthood were allowed to correlate freely.

The final model includes only significant paths and co-variances (correlations), because parameter trimming by the Wald test was also done. No across-time regression path was left in the final model that represented a suppressor effect, that is, an effect in which the coefficient was opposite in sign from the correlation between the factors. There were only a few suppressor effects, and their exclusion did not change the general configuration of the model. Although some researchers prefer to make substantive interpretations of suppressor effects, we have taken a more conservative approach in not considering these effects because their interpretation is open to controversy and ambiguity. Future research will need to address the meaning of suppressor effects and whether they can be substantively interpreted. In this instance, the final structural model fit the data quite well ($\chi^2 = 783.10$, d.f. = 799, p = .65, NFI = .93). Associations among the latent factors are graphically displayed in Figure 14.3, whereas the across-time paths that include at least one observed variable are listed in Table 14.2 with their standardized regression weights. In addition, Table 14.3 includes the correlations among the young adult construct residuals. The relationships presented in Figure 14.3 and those listed in Tables 14.2 and 14.3 are based on the same final structural model, and are presented separately only for reasons of clarity.

15

Integration
and Conclusions

The consequences of teenage drug use are only beginning to be researched in earnest. As a result, there are few solid results and fewer theories to incorporate the existing findings. In this book, we have attempted to summarize those theories that are available, and provide a solid empirical basis relevant to evaluate the theories and to understand the impact of adolescent drug use on young adult development. We have organized these analyses around seven specific areas of life that could be affected by prior drug use, thus helping to identify which aspects of life functioning are influenced by teenage drug use. We have made a special effort to clarify which types of drugs lead to particular outcomes in young adulthood.

The consequences we have observed are effects that manifested themselves over a four-year span from late adolescence to young adulthood. Since the initial drug use measures also included information from early adolescence, the reported effects are bounded by a maximum of an eight-year span from early adolescence to young adulthood. It is quite likely that certain effects of teenage drug use may require a lengthier period of time to become fully apparent. The effects we have noted can be considered quite critical, however, because they occurred over a relatively short duration, and may reflect a life trajectory partially launched by involvement with drugs as a teenager. One might also hypothesize that the trajectories that have been established during this time period will have a propensity to involve some young adults in other situations in the future that will strengthen the negative effects already noted, but also inoculate others against such harmful circumstances. In this chapter, we attempt to integrate the various results obtained from our series of analyses into several broad areas of concern. These integrations relate to implications for development, theory, prevention, treatment, and methodology. Specific results of each analysis have already been discussed in the narrower, content-related integration at the end of each chapter. This information is not repeated here and the reader is referred to the appropriate chapter for more specific discussions of the individual results. Here we wish to step back and take a longer view of the meaning of our findings and relate them to more general topics of interest.

Developmental Implications

Adolescence is a period of development wherein far-reaching changes occur that affect virtually all aspects of teenagers' lives as they prepare for their roles as adults and contributing members of society. This developmental process involves a complex interaction between biological maturity, as reflected in changes resulting from puberty, and psychosocial transactions (e.g., Lerner, 1985). Each of these processes, of course, varies in its nature and timing, resulting in a range or diversity of outcomes generated by a fairly common set of developmental tasks and stressors.

Developmental Tasks

The notion of *developmental tasks* has been elaborated upon by Havighurst (1952, 1972), who defined such tasks as those that occur "at or about a certain period in the life of the individual, successful achievement of which leads to happiness and success with later tasks, while failure leads to unhappiness in the individual, disapproval by the society and difficulty with later tasks" (Havighurst, 1952, p. 2). Such tasks for adolescence typically include achieving mature relations with peers, emotional independence from parents, socially responsible behavior, personal values, appropriate social roles, and preparation for marriage and family life (Havighurst, 1972). Many of these tasks are not completed by the end of adolescence and carry over into young adult development (e.g., Roscoe & Peterson, 1984). Achievement of these tasks prepares the individual for confronting those developmental tasks characteristic of adulthood. These include finding a congenial social group, taking on civic responsibility, beginning an occupation, selecting a mate, managing a household, starting a family, and rearing children (Havighurst, 1972).

The adequate resolution or achievement of the adolescent tasks provides the maturity necessary to achieve success with the adult tasks. Thus if the adolescent tasks are not fully realized or accomplished, or are acquired in a nonnormative fashion (i.e., prematurely), the success of facing those tasks required as a young adult may suffer as a consequence.

Thus one defining feature of adolescence is a quest for or establishment of independence and autonomous identity and functioning. This may involve experimentation with a wide range of behaviors, attitudes, and activities before choosing a direction and way of life to call one's own. This process of testing attitudes and behavior may include drug use. In fact, experimental use of various types of drugs, both licit and illicit, may be considered a normative behavior among contemporary United States teenagers in terms of prevalence (e.g., Johnston et al., 1986; Kovach & Glickman, 1986), as well as from a developmental task perspective. As a consequence, our concern and effort must not be diverted toward pathologizing the occasional and experimental use of drugs among teenagers, because this reflects a manifestation of a normal developmental process. We must consider seriously, however, the regular use, committed use, or abuse of substances among teenagers and their effects on achieving both adolescent and adult developmental goals. This has been the mission of our book: To determine the specific effects of frequent drug use as a teenager (defined in relation to one's peers in our normal sample of adolescents) upon the quality, nature, and success of psychosocial functioning as a young adult.

Adolescent Drug Use Life-Style

Committed or frequent drug use (or, conversely, the avoidance or only experimental use of drugs) is one aspect of an integrated, but evolving, life-style of the teenager. Drug use does not occur in isolation, but is intimately interwoven with other behavior and attitudes (e.g., Castro, Newcomb, & Cadish, 1987; Donovan & Jessor, 1985). Drug use may be related more strongly to certain aspects of life-style than others, however. Table 15.1 presents the correlations between our teenage drug use latent factor and all other teenage constructs across our various analyses. These were taken from the final structural models in the various chapters, because these are the ones we are most concerned with interpreting.

Drug use was most highly correlated with a lack of social conformity or low traditionalism. Moderately large associations were apparent between drug use and other types of deviant behavior (Criminal Activities), frequent and precocious sexual involvement (Early Sexual Involvement and Frequency of Sexual Events), association with deviant peers (Deviant Friendship Network and Number of Sexually Active Friends), and a lack of educational concern. Smaller but significant relationships were found between drug use and increased Income, more Emotional Distress, more Parental Divorce, poor Family Support, and lowered Social Support.

From these patterns, we can characterize the adolescent life-style that includes regular use of drugs as one that also includes rebellion, nonconformity to traditional values, involvement with other deviant or illegal behaviors and with individuals engaged in such behavior, poor family connections, few educational interests, precocious involvement in sexual activities, experiences of emotional turmoil, lack of social connection, alienation, and precocious involvement with the work force and earning money. Our characterization of a typical drug-involved life-style does not imply that every youngster fits into this pattern—after all, the correlations are sufficiently low that many patterns exist and a few individuals will be quite average except for their level of drug involvement. Furthermore, our characterization is based on correlations,

TABLE 15.1

Correlates of Drug Use During Adolescence

Adolescent Factor	Correlation with General Drug Use		
Social Conformity		$-.69$**	
Family Support		$-.21$**	
Parental Divorce		$.17$**	
Criminal Activities		$.42$**	
Deviant Friendship Network		$.46$**	
Early Sexual Involvement	F:[a] $.52$** /	M: $.51$**	
Frequency of Sexual Events	F: $.31$** /	M: $.30$**	
Number of Seuxally Active Friends	F: $.40$** /	M: $.42$**	
Satisfaction with Opposite-Sex Relationships	F: $.00^b$ /	M: $.00^b$	
Academic Potential		$-.34$**	
Income		$.09$*	
Emotional Distress		$.16$**	
Social Support		$-.21$**	

a. F = female; M = male.
b. Fixed at zero in final structural model.
*$p < .05$; **$p < .001$.

and does not imply any causal priority (which we base on across-time analyses). Table 15.1, however, does provide a unified picture of the correlates of drug use and hence, implicitly, a prototype adolescent who is involved with drugs and the nature or quality of the developmental tasks he or she is facing in relation to his or her peers.

Many of the qualities differentially associated with teenage drug use are either extreme versions of those developmental tasks confronted in adolescence or else are ones that should normatively be faced as adults. For instance, earning income and sexual involvement with a partner represent tasks that should be addressed as young adults, but are more evident among teenagers who regularly use drugs than among those who do not. This finding supports our precocious development conception of teenage drug use. Precocious development does not imply the well-handling of typical tasks, rather, it implies a caricaturing and foreshortening of developmental sequences. Thus the independent behavior of adolescent drug users appears to be quite exaggerated, containing aspects of the rejection of traditional values and involvement in extreme deviant behavior (relative to their peers). Another aspect of precocious development involves failure at developmental tasks; for example, there may be a behavior deficit in drug users, compared to their non-drug-using peers. For instance, rather than developing mature relationships with their peers, drug users are feeling more disconnected and unsupported in their social relations. In terms of the adolescent developmental tasks identified by Havighurst (1972), drug-using teenagers appear to be achieving an independence from their parents (lowered Family Support). There are indications that this may not be a positive or maturing separation, however, because it may be related to Parental Divorce, accompanied by increased Emotional Distress, and a pattern of rejecting all traditional values (low Social Conformity). The pattern supports the concept of a pseudoemancipation, as suggested by Baumrind and Moselle (1985). Further, teenage drug users may not be acquiring socially responsible behavior or appropriate social roles, because they are engaging in Criminal Activities more than their non-drug-using peers. Thus, while precocious development could refer to an unusually gifted individual who is developmentally quite average except for showing a highly developed talent at an early age (e.g., a musical prodigy), to someone who is intellectually gifted ahead of the chronological age but emotionally at that age (e.g., an adolescent college graduate), or to a young entrepreneur who is determined to make a fortune on his or her own, the general picture we see does not have these positive features.

We are not suggesting that there is a single common pathway or explanation for teenage drug use. Just as there are several different causal factors related to drug use initiation (e.g., Newcomb, Maddahian, & Bentler, 1986), drug use maintenance no doubt involves a complex of correlated factors, specific components of which may or may not characterize a particular individual.

Trajectories of Teenage Drug Use

Drug use creates a developmental trajectory that progresses into young adulthood and can be observed as the impact of teenage drug use. In fact, because, in our research, we have controlled for baseline associations between teenage drug use and the many characteristics discussed above, the significant impacts we have found for teenage drug use on young adult functioning represent an increased divergence from the adolescent life-style patterns we have noted.

Table 15.2 summarizes results from each of our empirical analyses regarding the impact of teenage drug use on all of the young adult outcomes we have considered. The table is organized with all young adult outcome variables listed in the right-hand column, theoretically segregated into the content areas discussed in the previous chapters. The left-hand column lists those adolescent drug predictors that made a significant impact on the outcome variables; where no variable is listed, no significant drug predictor was found. The left-hand column also provides information on the direction of the effects (+ or –), and indicates where the given effect was located (in the small model of previous chapters, not italicized; in the large model of Chapter 14, italicized). These impacts represent changes over and above those life-style patterns characteristic of teenage drug users. The effects presented in Table 15.2 represent direct impacts of teenage drug use. They do not include the indirect effects of teenage drug use that also result from adolescent life-style variables (the baseline or control constructs) as mediating factors on later behavior. Discussions of indirect effects have been provided in the individual chapters on specific aspects of drug use consequences.

A brief perusal of Table 15.2 indicates that teenage drug use differentially influences or affects certain life areas as a teenager matures into a young adult. Similarly, there are differing effects for various types of substances. For instance, only the specific use of alcohol (and not other types of drugs) decreased Social Conformity and religious commitment from levels reported as a teenager. Aside from these effects, however, there were no other influences of drugs on attitudes toward or away from conformity or traditionalism beyond those already present as a teenager.

From Table 15.2, it can be seen that teenage drug use did have an influence on development into young adulthood. Teenage drug use appears to be associated with, if not propel, early involvement in family creation (marriage and having

TABLE 15.2

Summary of Drug Effects Across All Analyses

Types of Adolescent Drug Use Predictors[a]	*Young Adult Outcomes*
alcohol (R) −	Social Conformity
	law abidance
	liberalism
alcohol (R) −	religious commitment

Family Formation

	Relationship Satisfaction
	happy with relationship
Hard Drug Use +	trouble with relationship
General Drugs +; *Hard Drugs (R)* +; *PCP (R)* +	Family Formation
liquor (R) +; *inhalant (R)* +	marriage past 4 years
	number of children
General Drugs +	Relationship Importance
	current level of involvement
	dating importance
	Cohabitation History
General Drugs +; *cocaine (R)* +; *inhalants (R)* +	Divorce (past 4 years)

Deviant Behavior[b]

General Drugs +	Drug Crime Involvement
hypnotics (R) −	driving while intoxicated
liquor (R) −	selling or possessing drugs
General Drugs −	Violent Crime Involvement
	vandalism
	carrying a deadly weapon
	assault
alcohol (R) −	Property Crime Involvement
	other infraction
	theft
	Criminal Activities
Alcohol (R) −; *cocaine (R)* +	confrontational acts
General Drugs +; *hashish (R)* +; *cocaine (R)* −	stealing episodes
hypnotics (R) −	property damage

Sexual Behavior

	Birth Control Effectiveness
	effectiveness of current birth control
	effectiveness of future birth control

Continued

TABLE 15.2   Continued

Types of Adolescent Drug Use Predictors[a]	Young Adult Outcomes
	Dating Competence
	dating competence 1
	dating competence 2
	dating competence 3
	Satisfaction with Intimacy
Alcohol (R) +	happy with sex life
cocaine (R) − (women) hard drugs (R) −	happy being close with someone
wine (R) −; *liquor (R)* −;	satisfaction with sexual intercourse
hypnotics (R) +	
(women) hard drugs +; *beer* +;	Number of Relationships
hypnotics +; *cocaine* +	
(men) cannabis (R) +; (women)	number of steady partners
alcohol (R) +; *PCP (R)* −	
	number of sexual partners
	Frequency of Intercourse
	intercourse frequency/week
	intercourse frequency/month
	Contracted Venereal Disease
	Abortion Occurrence (women only)
	ever had abortion
	number of abortions
	Educational Pursuits
	Educational Aspirations
	educational plans
	educational expectations
General Drugs −; *beer (R)* −;	College Involvement
liquor (R) −; *PCP (R)* −	
alcohol (R) +	college attendance
	part-time job and college
inhalants (R) +	part-time employment
	Work Force Involvement
alcohol +	full-time job or military
General Drugs +	income
	months worked
hard drugs (R) −	Graduated from High School
	Livelihood Pursuits
General Drugs +	Income
beer (R) +	salary 1
hard drugs (R) +	salary 2
	salary 3
General Drugs +; *hashish (R)* +:	Job Instability
inhalants (R) +	

TABLE 15.2 Continued

Types of Adolescent Drug Use Predictors[a]	*Young Adult Outcomes*
stimulants (R) +; PCP (R) +	times fired past 4 years
	times lost job past 4 years
marijuana (R) +	times collected unemployment
	past 4 years
	Job Satisfaction
hard drugs (R) +	happy with work
	trouble with work
	Amount Worked Past Year
	Collected Public Assistance
	collected welfare past 4 years
	collected foodstamps past 4 years

Mental Health Status

General Drugs +	Psychoticism
	magic ideation 1
	magic ideation 2
	magic ideation 3
	Depression
alcohol (R) +	positive affect
	negative affect
	impaired motivation
alcohol (R) −	impaired relationships
	Emotional Distress
General Drugs −	deliberateness
	diligence
	self-acceptance
	depression
	Purpose in Life
	PIL 1
	PIL 2
	PIL 3
hard drugs (R) +; *hypnotics (R) +;*	Suicide Ideation
stimulants (R) +; inhalants (R) +	
narcotics (R) +	think about killing self
beer (R) −	told someone kill self
hard drugs (R) +	life end with suicide

Social Integration

alcohol (R) −	Loneliness
	lonely 1
hard drugs (R) +; *beer (R) −*	lonely 2
	lonely 3
alcohol +; Hard Drugs (R) −	Social Support
alcohol (R) +	good relationship with parents

Continued

TABLE 15.2   Continued

Types of Adolescent Drug Use Predictors[a]	*Young Adult Outcomes*
	good relationship with family
	good relationship with adults
	good relationship with peers

a. Lower case indicates observed-variable drugs; capitalized indicates latent-variable drugs; (R) indicates residual of the variable; + indicates an increase in the outcome variable; − indicates a decrease in the outcome variable; non-italicized effects are from Chapters 6-13; italicized effects are from Chaper 14.
b. Results from Chapter 8 were taken from the AGLS model and *not* the ML model.

children), while at the same time predicting divorce and unhappiness in such relationships. General drug use apparently increased involvement with drug crimes, reduced involvement with violent crimes, such as vandalism and carrying a deadly weapon, and increased stealing. Cocaine had a specific effect of increasing confrontational acts as a young adult. Alcohol use, however, decreased confrontational acts and other Property Crime Involvement. Thus teenage drug use changed dispositions and tendencies toward criminal behavior, with the specific and exclusive use of alcohol limiting such behavior and general drug use and specific types of hard drugs escalating such involvement (except for Violent Crime Involvement, which is reduced by general teenage drug use).

There were very few effects in which drug use changed aspects of sexual behavior and satisfaction beyond those experienced as a teenager. Teenage drug use had no effect on Birth Control Effectiveness, Dating Competence, Frequency of Intercourse, Venereal Disease, or Abortions. On the other hand, various types of drugs (except for an opposite effect for PCP) increased the Number of Relationships and partners one has had in life. Mixed results were found for satisfaction; some drugs helping (Alcohol and hypnotics) and others hindering (hard drugs and liquor) one's enjoyment of intimate encounters.

Although teenage drug use does not reduce educational aspirations beyond the lowered levels already evident in adolescence, it does reduce College Involvement (with specific effects of beer, liquor, and PCP reducing College Involvement).

Use of hard drugs significantly lowered the chances of graduating from high school. Thus teenage drug use tends to accelerate a divergence from traditional educational pursuits such as attending college. This forsaking of a higher education may ultimately limit the opportunities available for career advancement and satisfaction with work.

These effects are not yet apparent in this group of young adults. In fact, teenage drug users earned significantly more money than their non-drug-using peers. Hard drug and beer use made specific contributions to increasing salary from adolescence to young adulthood. As discussed in Chapter 11 regarding Livelihood Pursuits, this effect is not expected to remain over a lengthier period of time. It indicates that those who used drugs as a teenager were more likely to drop out of high school, not continue in college, and begin full-time employment sooner than those who did not use drugs, graduated from high school, pursued a college education, and are not yet employed as a result. Once they acquire their college training, they should surpass their drug-using peers in income, because they will have received additional training that will raise the ceiling on their potential salaries. This pattern reflects a trajectory of adolescent drug use that yields immediate benefits (higher salary), but long-term limitations.

In concert with this pattern of early involvement in the work force, teenage drug use (and in particular hashish, inhalants, stimulants, and marijuana) is predictive of reduced job stability into young adulthood. Thus, even though adolescent drug use generates early involvement in work activities, it also creates difficulties in maintaining those activities. This effect should not be seen as an effect of pressures associated with the relatively poor economy of the early 1980s, in which many individuals, especially unskilled workers, have lost their jobs. The effect is differential, depending upon levels of drug use. From a developmental perspective, it appears that teenage drug use generates a life trajectory that is plagued by an inability to maintain gainful employment with all the potential long-range additional consequences, such as low self-esteem, that this might presage. It is impossible to determine, however, whether the process that creates this instability (i.e., immaturity, drug use on the job, irresponsibility, developmental lags) will be continued over time, or, on the other hand, whether this trajectory will be self-correcting and hence not followed throughout life. On the positive side, teenage drug use did not influence Job Satisfaction (except for one effect of hard drug use increasing happiness with work), Amount Worked, or utilization of public assistance. Thus we can conclude that drug use among normal teenagers does not create "lazy bums" who can only "mooch off the government" for subsistence.

In terms of emotional functioning, different drugs seem to have different effects into young adulthood. General use of all drugs as a teenager leads to increased Psychoticism and lack of deliberateness. Thus frequent users of many drugs develop disorganized thinking, bizarre thoughts, and unusual beliefs that may ultimately interfere with their problem-solving abilities and emotional functioning. There were no general effects of drug use on changing affective states (e.g., depression, emotional distress). The specific use of alcohol, however, decreased relationship problems and increased positive affect. This represents an apparently beneficial effect of adolescent alcohol use. Most disturbing, however, was that use of hard drugs as a teenager, and in particular hypnotics, stimulants, inhalants, and narcotics, generated Suicidal Ideation and thoughts of self-destruction. Thus hard drug use is a portent for a life trajectory that is plagued by futility, thoughts of suicide, and a belief that one's life would end with self-annihilation.

Compounding or reflecting this pattern of self-destruction is the fact that teenage hard drug use reduces social support and increases loneliness in young adulthood. Thus use of hard drugs as an adolescent predicts social isolation and deprivation, as well as generating thoughts of futility and self-destruction. On the other hand, the specific use of alcohol has an opposite effect. Teenage alcohol use reduces loneliness and increases Social Support. This is apparently another beneficial effect of alcohol use as a teenager. These effects were discussed more fully in the chapters on Mental Health and Social Integration.

**Impact on Young Adult
Developmental Tasks**

The patterns of impact or influences of teenage drug use on young adult functioning have a direct relation to the achievement of adult developmental tasks. It is apparent that drug use as a teenager disrupts several tasks typically faced by young adults.

For instance, hard drug use interferes with social integration by reducing social support and increasing loneliness. Thus the adult developmental task of finding a congenial social network or group is damaged by prior hard drug use. On the other hand, early alcohol use seems to help social integration, perhaps by reducing social inhibitions and permitting adequate and appropriate social competencies to be learned. This social competency is hindered by use of hard drugs.

Another example relates to the adult task of beginning an occupation. Drug use as a teenager apparently facilitates early involvement with the job market, while at the same time reduces chances of success in such pursuits. This is evidenced by the abandonment of traditional educational pursuits, which limits the range of career opportunities and possible levels of advancement. On the other hand, youthful drug use is also predictive of job instability, being fired, and an inability to hold a job. A similar consequence of adolescent girls' use of marijuana was reported by Kandel et al. (1986). Thus teenage drug use may have interfered with the learning of necessary job skills and responsibilities that assure long-term employment. It is also possible that youthful drug users will not have learned the proper environments in which to use drugs, and in fact, may use them in work situations resulting in job loss.

The adult life task of acquiring civic responsibility was not directly tested in our data. We have shown, however, that teenage use of drugs was not related to collecting public assistance in the form of food stamps or welfare, which may be construed as reduced civic responsibility. On the other hand, youthful drug use was differentially related to criminal or deviant behavior, which can be seen as aspects of civic responsibility. For instance, teenage use of all types of substances was predictive of increased drug law violations, which may be an example of flaunting civic responsibility. Similarly, various types of adolescent drug use were predictive of increases and decreases in certain criminal behaviors. As a result, teenage drug use appears to have some effect on reducing specific aspects of civic responsibility, primarily related to drug law violations and certain other crimes.

In regard to selecting a mate, managing a home, starting a family, and rearing children, which are other family-related aspects of adult developmental tasks, drug use had both an accelerating and a detrimental impact. We have shown that adolescent use of all drugs, as well as specific substances, leads to early if not premature involvement in family formation processes, such as getting married and bearing children. Problems with this family formation are evidenced by an effect of youthful drug use leading to divorce. Thus adolescent drug use propels early or precocious acquisition of family roles, which are subsequently not performed adequately as reflected in the higher divorce rates for these youthful drug users.

In conclusion, it is obvious that teenage drug use both disrupts the timing of, as well as competence with, handling many of the critical developmental tasks of adolescence and adulthood. The timing is affected by generating a premature involvement with many tasks, such as work, sexuality, and family, prior to the acquisition of adequate competence to handle these challenges. On the other hand, teenage drug use directly interferes with social integration and acceptance of adult civic and societal responsibilities. Finally, teenage drug use affects cognitive processes (making them more disorganized and bizarre), while somehow reducing the will to live as reflected in increased suicidal ideation (specifically as a result of hard drug use).

Theoretical Implications

The results obtained in our series of analyses have important implications for the theories of drug use consequences reviewed in Chapter 2. Unfortunately, our results cannot test adequately each of the theories discussed. Certain theories, such as developmental lag, cannot be easily tested in the type of data we have available and must await more appropriate data for confirmation (Baumrind & Moselle, 1985). Nonetheless, our results provide valuable empirical information on these theoretical formulations that can yield an initial test of some of their hypotheses.

One common process in several of these theories is that teenage drug use somehow interferes with or disturbs the normal maturational functioning of the adolescent. As a consequence, essential life tasks of adulthood suffer because they are based on successful completion of adolescent formative tasks. The theories vary in regard to how this interference occurs. In general, we found that teenage drug use interferes with family development (by increasing divorce), job stability (by increasing the number of times fired), educational pursuits (by reducing the chances of high school graduation and likelihood of continuing to college), cognitive functioning (by increasing psychoticism and reducing deliberateness), survival attitudes (by increasing suicide ideation), and social functioning (by hard drugs increasing loneliness and reducing social support). These provide clear examples of the types of areas that adolescent drug use interferes with or disturbs for the young adult. Thus the general theory that teenage drug use interferes with various kinds of life functioning is supported in our analyses.

Baumrind and Moselle (1985) have suggested that teenage drug use creates a developmental lag in the maturation of the adolescent. As such, an adolescent drug user will not have acquired the necessary life skills (normally learned during adolescence, but not learned as a consequence of drug use) to succeed with life tasks of an adult. This is partially supported by our data, because we found that teenage drug users had greater problems with developmental tasks characteristic of adulthood than non-drug users (e.g., job stability, marital success, social integration). We cannot isolate the exact reason for this greater difficulty, however, nor determine whether it was the result of a developmental lag.

In regard to the DOMAIN model of drug use (e.g., Huba et al., 1980), we found that teenage drug use led to increased socioeconomic resources (income; contrary to the expectations of the model), alterations of psychological states (reduced cognitive organization, increased suicidal ideation, but did not change emotional affect levels), shifts in intimate support system (increased divorce, family formation, number of relationships, loneliness, and reduced social support), and influenced the amount of environmental stress (by leading to job failure, divorce, and criminal violations). We have not presented data on self-perceived behavioral pressure or organismic status, although such analyses have been presented elsewhere (e.g., Newcomb & Bentler, 1987b; Stein, Newcomb, & Bentler, in press).

Some have suggested that the reasons for getting involved in drug use will determine the outcome or consequences of such use (e.g., Carman, 1979). Our analyses did not consider the reasons or etiological bases for beginning drug use, so we cannot address this hypothesis directly. Margulies, Kessler, and Kandel (1977), however, found that social and peer factors generated initiation into alcohol and marijuana use, whereas individual pathology or personality predicted transition to hard drugs. Thus we may infer that regular users of hard drugs tend to do so for reasons of distress and alienation, rather than for social or peer-conformity reasons. This may help explain the more negative effects we have found for hard drug use than for either alcohol (which had some beneficial effects) and cannabis (which had moderately negative consequences as reflected in the general factor of drug use). When interpreted in this manner, we can conclude that we have found some indirect support for the etiology predicts outcome theory of teenage drug use.

Hendin and Haas (1985) found that marijuana use tended to consolidate or exacerbate a regressive coping style that permitted an avoidance of adaptive problem confrontation and solving. We have no data that can test this hypothesis directly. If we infer, however, that job instability and divorce represent failures at problem solving and adaptive functioning, and that suicidal ideation reflects a regressive coping response, some partial support for this theory can be found in our results.

In regard to drug use creating an amotivational syndrome, we found that teenage drug use did not influence future desires for education or interest beyond levels already reported as an adolescent. Drug use did, however, reduce college attendance. Thus, although amotivational attitudes were not generated by drug use, amotivated behavior toward educational pursuits was influenced by drug use. When we broaden the standard definition of amotivation beyond only educational concerns (e.g., Kandel, 1978), however, a more definitive answer can be found. For instance, teenage drug users are more involved with earning money than their nonusing peers—certainly not an example of amotivation. Similarly, teenage drug use had no impact upon use of public assistance such as food stamps and welfare, which could also be construed as amotivated behavior. Thus we must conclude that in our analyses we found very little support for teenage drug use creating an amotivational syndrome in young adulthood.

On the other hand, we have found clear evidence that teenage drug use effects psychosocial functioning, as suggested by Baumrind and Moselle (1985). Differential effects were noted for different types of substances, however. Alcohol use seemed to enhance social functioning by improving relationships with one's family, reducing loneliness, and increasing social support. The exact opposite effects were found for use of hard drugs as a teenager. Thus psychosocial dysfunction seems to be a consequence of hard drug use as a teenager, but not a consequence of alcohol use. On the other hand, if we interpret the causes of divorce and job instability to be a failure in psychosocial functioning, we can conclude that general teenage drug use had an impact on psychosocial dysfunction in these areas of life.

Another theory predicts that simply using drugs as a teenager predisposes someone to abuse drugs later in life. In our outcome measures, we have not focused on the current use of drugs or problematic use of substances. Our conclusions regarding this hypothesis must be speculative rather than definitive, although Stein et al. (in press) have addressed directly this issue. In this study (Stein et al., in press), we found that there were different predictors of young adult drug use and problems associated with drug use. Teenage drug use was highly predictive of young adult drug use, whereas teenage deviant attitudes and drug use role models were most predictive of young adult problematic use of drugs. In the present analyses, we have shown that teenage drug use does increase problems with drug law violations, which can certainly be construed as at least misuse of drugs. The only other evidence that we have regarding this hypothesis relates to the speculation that marital problems and job instability may have occurred as a direct result of drug use in these specific contexts. We cannot, however, verify this speculation, although drug and alcohol problems certainly can be aspects of divorce and being fired from a job (e.g., Bentler & Newcomb, 1978; Cleek & Pearson, 1985; Gupta & Jenkins, 1984).

Problem Behavior Theory as developed by the Jessors (Jessor & Jessor, 1977, 1978) has been an important conceptual model for understanding many aspects of drug-using behaviors among teenagers. In general, the theory predicts that a syndrome of problem or deviant behavior underlies or predicts problem drinking, illicit drug use, precocious sexual involvement, rebellious attitudes, and other delinquent-type behavior. Because these different types of behavior are presumed to result from a single, underlying cause (Donovan & Jessor, 1985), causal priorities among these have not been explicitly postulated. Many of our results confirm this conception of drug use, particularly the high correlations found between drug use and other problem behaviors and attitudes in adolescence, such as a lack of social conformity, high sexual involvement, and frequent criminal behaviors. We have, however, been able to separate the effects of general deviant attitudes (lack of social conformity) from those of teenage drug use. So, although our results do support a syndrome notion of deviant behavior, one part of which is drug use, we have been able to isolate specific effects of drug use and identify specific cross-influences within the syndrome of problem behaviors. Thus we found that teenage drug use increased sexual involvement (as reflected in the number of sexual partners) and certain types of criminal behavior. This suggests that the unified syndrome observed during adolescence may, in fact, diverge into other patterns of behavior in the postteenage years.

Although we have not included an adequate range of

variables to test properly the consequence portions of self-derogation theory (e.g., Kaplan, 1985, 1986)—because we do not have detailed measures of peer involvement—some relevant results were noted. This theory predicts that feelings of self-rejection engendered from conventional social agents can be reduced by involvement with drugs and drug-using friends. Support was found for this effect for alcohol, because its use increased perceived social support, decreased loneliness, improved relationships with family and others, and in other analyses (Newcomb, Bentler, & Collins, 1986) reduced self-derogation. This effect seems specific to alcohol, however, because different outcomes were apparent from cannabis and hard drug use. The theory was designed to account for processes in adolescent peer cultures and may not account as well for processes in young adulthood. It is also true that alcohol is a socially and legally accepted drug substance for young adults, which may account for its more beneficial effects over this period in life. On the other hand, if we accept the premise that hard drugs are used for more problematic reasons, such as self-medication (i.e., not just because of peer pressure or to fit in), we would not expect positive outcomes as a result. Thus we conclude that we found some support for Kaplan's theory of self-derogation for alcohol use, but not other drugs from adolescence to young adulthood.

Turning next to role compatibility theory (e.g., Yamaguchi & Kandel, 1985a, 1985b), mixed support for this notion was found in our analyses. Contrary to expectations from this theory, we found that teenage drug users entered traditional roles of work and the family earlier than those who did not use drugs. Thus the role selection hypothesis that deviant teenagers (those who use drugs) will not choose traditionally valued social roles (such as work, marriage, and family) was not supported in our data. Possible reasons for this discrepancy have been suggested in Chapter 7. On the other hand, support was found for the role compatibility hypothesis, which predicts that if a behavior (i.e., drug use) is at odds with a particular role (i.e., worker, spouse, parent), a means of reducing the discrepancy is to change behavior (stop using drugs, as we have noted elsewhere: Newcomb & Bentler, 1987a) or else leave the role (get fired or divorced) as found in the current analyses.

The last theory we will consider is precocious development, which we have mentioned several times throughout this book. We have found substantial support for this theory, which predicts that those who use drugs as a teenager become precociously involved with other behaviors that are characteristic of an adult rather than adolescent. By doing so, the teenager does not gain the requisite maturity to engage in these roles or behaviors in a manner that will enhance success and fulfillment. Evidence for this notion has been found in our results in several areas. For instance, teenage drug users were more involved with sexual behavior and livelihood pursuits (earning money) than were teenagers not using drugs. On the other hand, teenage drug use (a sign of precocious development) predicted early involvement with marriage and family, as well as making a living at a young age. Early involvement in these activities or roles, however, led to failure with them (divorce, job instability), possibly as a result of not taking the time during adolescence to learn the necessary socioemotional skills and maturity to succeed in these endeavors. Other detrimental effects of youthful drug use could also be attributed to problems resulting from precocious development. For instance, cognitive organization and social integration were adversely influenced by teenage drug use (particularly hard drug use), which may be accounted for by the circumvention of the necessary cognitive and social processes, tasks, and learning experiences characteristic of adolescence.

Of course, the present results cannot be a definitive test of any of these theories, because they represent complex interactive processes that can only be addressed from a variety of studies and perspectives. We believe, however, that our current findings substantially help refine and test important aspects of many of these theories. Further empirical work and theoretical explication are, of course, still needed to yield a highly coherent and valid integration of theory and drug use data. For example, extant theories on drug use consequences are incomplete in their specification of the fine-grained details on the causal mechanism or process by which use of a drug leads to an important psychological or social consequence. This process will consist, in general, of various mediating mechanisms that intervene between drug use and the observed consequence. These mechanisms may include biochemical, psychological, or social components that have yet to be identified, and then measured appropriately (e.g., at the right time subsequent to drug use with relevant instruments). Such expanded process theories would also provide an impetus for new research that would include more frequent and more varied assessments than we have undertaken in this study.

Prevention and Treatment Implications

Education, prevention, intervention, and treatment of drug abuse have become top priority national issues (Bell & Battjes, 1985; Glynn, Leukefeld, & Ludford, 1983). Heavy use or abuse of drugs clearly has destructive effects on the individual, social relationships, and society. In our analyses, we have demonstrated this in regard to a wide range of different types of substances over several critical areas of life functioning. We have also shown here and elsewhere that drug use is a relatively common occurrence among today's teenagers. In fact, not experimenting or at least trying tobacco, alcohol, and cannabis as an adolescent can be considered unusual and deviant behavior, because use of these drugs is so widespread. Adolescence is a period of experimentation with new and different attitudes and behaviors, and for good or ill, drug use has become a part of this natural curiosity.

When viewed from this perspective and with appreciation for the nature of adolescence, it would seem that eliminating the trial use of drugs among teenagers is neither an easy nor a high priority goal. Delaying the onset of experimentation as long as possible would most likely have the beneficial effect that experimental drug use would not be as easily transformed to severe drug use, because general coping patterns will have been further developed (see, e.g., Fleming et al., 1982; Hawkins, Lishner, & Catalano, 1985; Robins & Przybeck, 1985; Shiffman & Wills, 1985). Completely avoiding experimentation with drugs, however, seems unlikely in today's society. Thus it would seem that an emphasis must be placed on reducing the abuse, regular use, and misuse of drugs among teenagers. The typical youngster who has a beer or some marijuana at a party is not the one who is going to develop long-term damage as a result of their drug use. It is those teenagers who develop a life-style of drug use to relieve emotional distress and other life stressors (including the natural discomfort of adolescence) who will suffer long-term negative consequences of their use. Such consequences include those that have been identified in our analyses. The negative effects we have found for teenage drug use are not the result of very occasional or infrequent use, but are based on frequent and committed drug use as a teenager over a four-year period from early to late adolescence. It is these youngsters who need to be the focus of prevention and treatment efforts, and not the occasional user who indulges in substance use within social situations.

An implication of this notion that has been substantiated in research findings is that peer influences tend to motivate nonproblematic experimental use of drugs typically in a social setting (e.g., Carman, 1979; Margulies et al., 1977). The real concern should not be directed toward eliminating experimental drug use as often generated in peer settings, but toward preventing abuse or problematic use of drugs, which has many other causes aside from peer pressure. While peer pressure is an important and subtle phenomenon (e.g., Newman, 1984), that can no doubt have the effect of enhancing pseudomaturity as emphasized in our precocious development theory, it may not be destructive unless combined with a psychological difficulty. The psychological causes for abuse of drugs are many, but can include emotional distress, lack of self-esteem, low self-efficacy, family problems, inherited vulnerabilities, dysfunctional coping styles, and other stressors faced by the teenager. Dealing with these issues—for example, by personal and social skills training (Botvin & Wills, 1985)—and showing that drug use does not solve these problems, should be one important message in drug prevention programs. Focusing simply on handling peer pressure, such as the "just say no" approaches, may placate concerned but naive parents, teachers, and funding sources, but is an incomplete approach to confronting the task of preventing drug abuse among this nation's youth.

It must also be remembered that alcohol, cannabis, and hard drugs are not the only substances used by adolescents. Cigarettes are the second most frequently used substance by teenagers, with only alcohol being more prevalent. The vast destructive effects of cigarette smoking have been well documented (e.g., Richmond, 1979) and greater effort must be directed at preventing regular use of this extremely hazardous substance among teenagers. The effects of smoking in adolescence on respiratory impairment are obvious within a few years (Adams et al., 1984) and, in fact, in the quantities used by teenagers in our sample, cigarettes had greater physically destructive effects over a four-year period than alcohol, cannabis, and hard drugs (Newcomb & Bentler, 1987a). The recent increase in smokeless tobacco use among teenagers, especially males, is also alarming (e.g., Marty, McDermott, & Williams, 1986; McCarthy, Newcomb, Maddahian, & Skager, 1986). Increased emphasis should be placed on always considering tobacco products when focusing on drug education, prevention, and treatment among teenagers. Such emphasis is a natural concomitant of an emphasis on health promotion (Perry & Jessor, 1985).

Although the best source of information regarding drug prevention comes from etiological studies, and the best information about drug treatment is found in intervention studies, data from our analyses can also be useful for these tasks. Unfortunately, there has not been a strong tendency to incorporate results of empirical research into education or prevention programming (e.g., Dembo, 1979, 1981), which may account for the less than successful impacts of such programs (e.g., Blum, Garfield, Johnstone, & Magistad, 1978; Braucht & Braucht, 1984; Flay, 1985; Kinder, Pape, & Walfish, 1980; Polich, Ellickson, Reuter, & Kahan, 1984). Although many programs have been proposed (e.g., LeCoq & Capuzzi, 1984; Richmond & Peeples, 1984), rarely do they take into account the multidimensional nature of teenage drug use and the need to integrate a range of divergent approaches (e.g., Segal, 1986).

Although the strictly scare tactics of previous decades are less a part of contemporary intervention effort, virtually all substance use education, prevention, and treatment programs

directed toward adolescents emphasize the negative and unde-
sirable consequences of ingesting drugs (e.g., Polich et al.,
1984). It is in this area that the current results can best be
utilized in such programs. We have been able to establish that
certain types of drugs are related to specific kinds of negative
outcomes for the teenager. Information regarding such consequences can be incorporated into programs to convey the
possible eventual results of abusing drugs as a teenager.
Specific examples will not be repeated here, but are available
elsewhere in this book. It must be remembered, however, that
information-only approaches to drug use education and
prevention have not been very effective (Tobler, 1986), but
need to be linked to other interventions such as coping skills
training and alternatives appreciation.

Another distinct implication of our present results for
prevention and treatment programs is the fact that drug use
among teenagers is one component of an integrated life-style
involving attitudes and other behaviors. Thus a strict focus on
teenage drug use will be too limited for effective prevention or
treatment. At an individual level, the surrounding and correlated aspects of drug use must also be carefully considered
and integrated in programs, as, indeed, at the social level, the
general community climate must be considered (e.g., Durell &
Bukoski, 1984; Manatt, 1986).

Finally, the theoretical hypotheses advanced to help understand the consequences of teenage drug use are quite interesting
and potentially useful in and of themselves. They provide
important perspectives on how drug use influences adolescent
psychosocial development. Even though we have not been able
to substantiate fully or deny any of these theories, many of the
propositions make intuitive sense and could help guide program development. They may help provide a richer background
against which to understand drug use among teenagers.

Methodological Implications

The series of analyses reported in this book provide the first
systematic use of nonstandard linear structural equation
models in which the effects of interest are not limited primarily
to the "inner" relations among latent variables (where the

"outer" measurement models relations between latent and observed variables function mainly to identify the latent variables). In the context of longitudinal panel research, the inner latent variable relations, after all, serve only to highlight the common factor (general) consequences of previous (general) common factors. While such general effects are probably of primary importance—both theoretically and empirically— in the area of consequences of drug use and perhaps in wider areas of program evaluation, these should not be the only consequences of interest. More specific effects of particular variables must also be determined, especially if there are reasons to believe that all indicators of a given factor may not be equivalent except for error variance. In the area of drug use, this is certainly the case: While alcohol, cannabis, and hard drug use may contain an important common component (general drug use), there is certainly no a priori reason to believe that these substances are equivalent in their effects. In addition to the standard effects, this research project aimed to isolate potential effects of adolescent measured drug variables, or residuals in those measured variables, on factors or variables assessed during young adulthood, as well as the longitudinal consequences of residuals in adolescent first-order factors.

The modeling strategy we utilized yielded some interesting and interpretable effects, such as that early family formation was not the consequence of general drug use, but rather the effect of specific use of hard drugs (i.e., the factor residual). Thus we were able to achieve a goal that had to be abandoned by Kandel et al. (1986). Relying on more standard method-ologies, they were not able to assess exclusive effects of specific classes of drugs. Our methodology, however, is also not perfect, especially when it must be directed to evaluate small effects. It yielded some effects that were hard to interpret, for example, why the beer frequency residual should predict subsequent salary 1, but not the conceptually equivalent salary 2 or salary 3. Of course, as with all statistical methods, some of the specific effects we have isolated will be significant merely by chance and are thus not true effects. A more serious problem may also have occurred as a result of capitalizing on chance due to the use of the forward-stepping Lagrange Multiplier test. Although we used specific hypothesized sequences for as many of these tests as possible, inevitably there was an empirical component to the tests. That is, some parameters were included in a model due to their being significant in an empirical specification search procedure. As shown by Steiger, Shapiro, and Browne (1985), sequentially adding parameters to an incomplete model is not as safe a procedure as is sequentially deleting parameters from a more complete model; the results are correlated with one's starting position. Although we tried to overfit and then remove unnecessary parameters (by the Wald test), as would be implied by Steiger et al. (see also MacCallum, 1986), our theoretical specification was sufficiently incomplete that we were never able to start with a completely a priori, theoretically overparameterized model. Nonstandard models simply permit too many potential effects, and prior research and theory were insufficient to narrow down precisely only a few effects to test. Clearly, applications of this approach in future research will benefit by more explicitness in hypotheses on the range of specific effects to be anticipated.

Many of the specific cross-time effects that we found were quite small in terms of the size of the standardized coefficients involved. Perhaps this is inevitable in a study of a basically normal population in which drug abuse is not rampant. As noted by Kandel et al. (1986, p. 749), "In a general random sample of young people, patterns of involvement in certain drugs may not be sufficiently high to detect drug effects." Some of the effects we found, especially the effects of residuals in observed variables on other observed variables, act pretty much like "correlated errors" and may well reflect a variety of violation of assumptions underlying the method, such as nonlinearity of relations or nonnormal distributions (in addition to chance associations as noted above). Thus they may basically be "junk" parameters. Luckily, as we saw in the very high correlations between the factor intercorrelations of models that were developed completely a priori and those that included an empirical model modification component, the general latent variable influences seem to be quite free of such potential junk parameters. Such an optimistic conclusion may not, however, be true of the specific effects, especially the small a posteriori effects, which may be much more fragile in nature. Nonetheless, in the absence of more general methods and more complete theories, the effects we reported could not be statistically omitted from the models. It would have been ideal if our sample had been large enough to permit splitting the sample and verifying that the effects obtained in one subsample also held in the other subsample (e.g., Cliff, 1983), but we judged the sample not to be large enough to permit such a procedure in the context of the relatively large models we were evaluating. Consequently, future research will have to validate these results. Of course, we welcome the development of alternative methodological approaches to separating specific from general drug effects—especially, latent variable effects— but we know of no others at this time.

Conclusions

In sum, we have been able to provide some new information regarding the impact of teenage drug use on later psychosocial outcomes as young adults. We have attempted to integrate these results into available theories and provide implications for prevention and treatment of drug abuse. Our innovative methodological approach has permitted us to separate out effects of general drug use from types of specific substances, so that a very detailed picture of drug use consequences emerged.

The study of consequences of teenage drug use represents not only an empirical challenge, but also a challenge to the natural integration of adolescent development theories with theories on the life-span consequences of developmental patterns. This is an old topic in psychology, going back to Freud at least. In contrast to the global consequences of early childhood experiences, which remains a most difficult and abstract area to study, the effects of adolescent drug use would appear to be more narrow in nature and more empirically verifiable. Furthermore, such effects have potentially important consequences in modern society and merit study because drug use is an integral aspect of growing up as a teenager in American society. Consequently, the dynamics of drug involvement and outcomes of drug use are important aspects of maturational or developmental processes occurring between adolescence and young adulthood. It is our hope that this book has laid a foundation of theory and empirical results on which future research and theory development can be built. In addition, our results should have value to health professionals and those people concerned with guiding the psychosocial development of maturing teenagers and young adults, such as educators and therapists.

The results we have presented represent effects over a maximum of an eight-year period. Thus we can make no claims regarding the longer-term impacts of teenage drug use, although these must certainly be studied when data from lengthier periods are available. At this time, we do not know if use of drugs as a teenager represents a life-style that will be problematic during one's entire life, or whether the negative effects we have identified for adolescent drug use can be reversed over time. At this point, we can claim that teenage drug use, particularly of cannabis and hard drugs, has measurably negative effects on several critical areas of life functioning as a young adult. How these young adults will turn out once they reach full adulthood can only be guessed at this time.

This book represents one of the most comprehensive series of studies on consequences of teenage drug use to date. Of course, we have not been able to answer all of the crucial questions. We have, however, been able to provide some clear conclusions that should be useful to a wide range of professionals. Continued research will help bolster and supplement our initial attempts, and yield an even more complete picture of the consequences of teenage drug use. Several research projects have appropriate long-term data to address these vital issues from different perspectives and we must await analyses from these data sets to substantiate or challenge our current findings.

Appendix:
Detailed Description of Measures

The presentation below is organized according to chapter, to facilitate locating a description whenever necessary. Careful attention has been given to the choice of variable names so that they reflect the measures adequately and, in many cases, can be understood at face value. Where this is not clear, the discussion should provide sufficient additional information.

Aside from the description of all measures, this Appendix also provides univariate statistics and mean sex differences for all items or scales. These are summarized in Table A.1. Information is provided regarding the mean, range, number of items in each scale, variance, skew, and kurtosis. Mean sex differences are tested with point-biserial correlations with men scored as "1" and women scored as "2." Thus a positive correlation would indicate that the women had the larger value, whereas a negative correlation would indicate that the men had the larger value. The test of mean differences based on the point-biserial correlation is identical to the standard t-statistic, but it has the added advantage of yielding, when squared, a proportion of variance accounted for by the difference.

Chapter 6:
Drug Use and Social Conformity

Young Adulthood

Measures identical to those used during late adolescence were used to assess young adult Drug Use (measured scales of alcohol frequency, cannabis frequency, and hard drug frequency) and Social Conformity (law abidance, liberalism, and religious commitment). See Chapter 4 for a detailed description of these measures. Univariate statistics for these scales among young adults are given in Table A.1.

Sex Differences

During young adulthood, men reported drinking alcohol significantly more frequently than women, while there were no significant differences on frequency of use for cannabis or hard drugs. Paralleling the adolescent sex differences, women were significantly more law abiding and reported more religious commitment than men.

Chapter 7:
Family Formation

Adolescence

Family support. A latent construct of Family Support was reflected in two multi-item scales assessed during adolescence. These scales included good relationship with parents and good relationship with family. These are two scales, specific to the family, from a larger Social Support construct (see Newcomb & Bentler, 1986e). Each scale consists of four bipolar items rated on five-point scales anchored at each end by opposing descriptions. For instance, an item on the good relationship with parents scale had end points of "parents don't think my ideas are worth much" and "parents usually respect my ideas." Similarly, end points of an item on the good relationship with family scale were "family is very close to each other" and "family is not very close to each other." The items typically assess the amount of respect, support, and inclusion experienced with parents and family.

Parental divorce. Parent divorce or family disruption was assessed with one measured variable that determined whether the adolescent's parents were still married to each other. An intact family was scored "0" and was defined as "mother married to father." Any other parental configurations were considered a disrupted or divorced family and were scored "1." As evident in Table A.1, 24% of the sample reported having divorced parents. Although this question was asked in year 5 of the study, when subjects were in late adolescence, it is quite likely that an unknown percentage of the sample who reported living in a disrupted home at that time also lived in a disrupted home earlier in their lives as well.

Young Adulthood

Relationship satisfaction. Two single-item variables were used to reflect a Relationship Satisfaction latent construct: Happy with relationship and trouble with relationship. The happy with relationship item asked the subject to indicate how he or she felt during the past six months about the relationship with his or her date, mate, or spouse on a seven-point anchored rating scale that ranged from terrible (1) to delighted (7). The trouble with relationship item asked the respondent to indicate the amount of difficulty he or she had experienced during the past three months with a relationship

(Text continues on page 253)

TABLE A.1
Summary of Variable Characteristics According to Chapter

Latent Construct/ Measured Variable	Mean	Range	Number of Items	Variance	Skew	Kurtosis	Sex Difference[a] r_{pb}
Chapter 6—Drug Use and Social Conformity							
Young Adulthood							
Drug Use							
alcohol frequency	3.00	1-5.67	3	4.59	.00	-1.03	-.12**
cannabis frequency	1.70	1-6.50	2	2.31	1.52	1.39	-.04
hard drug frequency	1.11	1-2.67	15	.65	3.14	13.54	-.03
Social Conformity							
law abidance	14.19	4-20	4	11.70	-.41	-.42	.14***
liberalism	9.49	4-18	4	6.05	.40	.26	.01
religious commitment	15.62	4-20	4	15.92	-.88	.11	.14***
Chapter 7—Family Formation							
Adolescence							
Family Support							
good relationship with parents	15.87	5-20	4	11.90	-.76	-.17	.03
good relationship with family	14.27	4-20	4	17.64	-.47	-.61	-.01
Parental Divorce	.24	0-1	1	.19	1.19	-.60	-.04
Young Adulthood							
Relationship Satisfaction							
happy with relationship	5.22	1-7	1	2.50	-.75	-.09	.02
trouble with relationship	2.15	1-5	1	1.39	.83	-.18	.05

Continued

TABLE A.1 Continued

Latent Construct/ Measured Variable	Mean	Range	Number of Items	Variance	Skew	Kurtosis	Sex Difference[a] r_{pb}
Young Adulthood (cont.)							
Family Formation							
marriage past 4 years	.35	0-2	4	3.48	2.60	6.43	.16***
number of children	.17	0-3	1	1.83	2.79	8.93	.19***
Relationship Importance							
current level of involvement	3.63	1-6	1	2.79	-.20	-1.05	.16***
dating importance	2.95	1-4	1	3.89	-.45	-.94	.07
Cohabitation History	.33	0-1	1	.76	.74	-1.45	.05
Divorce Past 4 Years	.13	0-24	4	.58	6.32	43.60	.04
Chapter 8—Deviant Behavior							
Adolescence							
Criminal Activities							
confrontational acts	.35	0-9	4	.92	4.07	21.90	-.08*
stealing episodes	1.08	0-18	3	5.52	3.34	13.24	-.17***
property damage	.38	0-12	4	1.30	4.88	32.01	-.14***
Deviant Friendship Network							
confrontational friends	2.81	2-10	2	1.10	2.03	7.39	-.14***
friends deviant at school	6.20	4-17	4	8.24	1.86	3.49	.02
friends who steal	4.27	3-10	3	1.85	1.36	1.99	-.05
Young Adulthood							
Drug Crime Involvement							
driving while intoxicated	.05	0-4	4	.11	7.09	55.80	-.07

selling or possessing drugs	.02	0-2	4	.04	8.68	78.12	-.14***
Violent Crime Involvement							
vandalism	.01	0-2	4	.01	20.47	438.50	-.04
carrying a deadly weapon	.01	0-2	4	.01	15.06	248.11	-.08*
assault	.01	0-3	4	.02	18.34	375.84	-.11**
Property Crime Involvement							
other infraction	.08	0-6	4	.24	8.31	81.93	-.16***
theft	.03	0-4	4	.07	10.08	114.21	-.15***
Criminal Activities							
confrontational acts	.20	0-11	4	.59	7.11	73.06	-.13***
stealing episodes	.50	0-10	3	1.74	3.59	14.97	-.17***
property damage	.15	0-11	4	.55	9.92	124.21	-.15***

Chapter 9—Sexual Behavior

Adolescence

Early Sexual Involvement							
age of first sexual contact	14.65	3-22	1	9.61	-.83	1.20	.23***
age of first intercourse	16.79	6-22	1	5.34	-.60	2.51	.10*
Frequency of Sexual Events	1.67	0-6	7	1.51	.26	-.66	.08*
Number of Sexually Active Friends	3.49	1-5	1	1.44	-.66	.59	-.10*
Satisfaction with Opposite-Sex Relationships	4.05	1-5	1	1.00	-1.12	.80	.08*

Young Adulthood

Birth Control Effectiveness							
effectiveness of current birth control	2.34	1-3	1	.64	-.70	-1.11	.16***
effectiveness of future birth control	2.49	1-3	1	.52	-1.04	-.33	.25***

Continued

TABLE A.1 Continued

Latent Construct/ Measured Variable	Mean	Range	Number of Items	Variance	Skew	Kurtosis	Sex Difference[a] r_{pb}
		Young Adulthood (cont.)					
Dating Competence							
dating competence 1	8.81	4-13	3	3.13	-.07	-.35	-.07
dating competence 2	9.23	3-13	3	3.39	-.18	-.24	-.02
dating competence 3	9.98	4-14	3	3.46	-.14	-.16	-.03
Satisfaction with Intimacy							
happy with sex life	5.20	1-7	1	2.50	-.86	.22	.09*
happy being close with someone	5.75	1-7	1	1.77	-1.15	1.00	.09*
satisfaction with sexual intercourse	5.91	1-7	1	1.59	-1.77	3.45	-.01
Number of Relationships							
number of steady partners	3.82	0-40	1	27.98	10.45	165.24	-.01
number of sexual partners	5.98	0-40	1	101.61	5.37	39.36	-.02
Frequency of Intercourse							
intercourse frequency/week	2.25	0-9	1	5.76	1.21	.88	.08*
intercourse frequency/month	9.35	0-90	1	29.92	2.30	9.69	.08*
Contracted Venereal Disease	.07	0-1	1	.06	-3.45	9.90	-.07
Abortion Occurrence (women only)							
ever had abortion	.31	0-1	1	.21	.81	-1.32	—
number of abortions	.42	0-4	1	.55	1.91	3.40	—

Chapter 10—Educational Pursuits

Adolescence

	Mean	Range				
Academic Potential						
grade point average	2.62	0-4	.85	-.82	1.10	-.04
educational plans	3.92	1-6	1.23	-.18	-.33	-.03
Income						
salary 1	3.37	1-7	4.54	.27	-1.34	-.14***
salary 2	3.27	1-7	4.33	.35	-1.24	-.10*
salary 3	3.46	1-7	4.58	.29	-1.27	-.07
Young Adulthood						
Educational Aspirations						
educational plans	3.53	1-6	2.07	-.27	-.57	-.15***
educational expectations	3.88	1-7	1.02	.57	1.37	-.10*
College Involvement						
college attendance	.87	0-4	1.93	1.25	-.01	-.06
part-time job and college	1.98	0-4	2.34	.06	-1.44	-.08*
part-time employment	2.01	0-4	2.50	-.02	-1.51	-.02
Work Force Involvement						
full-time job or military	.49	0-1	.25	.03	-2.00	-.05
full-time employment	1.48	0-4	2.28	.50	-1.20	-.01
income	3.70	1-8	2.34	.03	-.48	-.15***
months worked	4.33	1-6	1.08	-.67	-1.27	-.11**
Graduated from High School	.93	0-1	.06	-3.45	9.90	-.03

Chapter 11—Livelihood Pursuits

Adolescence

Academic Potential—see Chapter 10 variables

Income—see Chapter 10 variables

Continued

TABLE A.1 Continued

Latent Construct/ Measured Variable	Mean	Range	Number of Items	Variance	Skew	Kurtosis	Sex Difference[a] r_{pb}
Young Adulthood							
Income							
salary 1	3.49	1-8	1	2.76	.31	.06	-.13***
salary 2	3.39	1-8	1	2.86	.42	.05	-.06
salary 3	3.53	1-8	1	2.99	.36	-.04	-.06
Job Instability							
times fired past 4 years	.18	0-3	4	.21	2.84	9.21	-.05
times lost job past 4 years	.19	0-3	4	.24	2.70	7.67	-.05
times collected unemployment past 4 years	.13	0-4	4	.17	3.87	20.13	-.01
Job Satisfaction							
happy with work	5.19	1-7	1	1.46	-.71	.43	-.02
trouble with work	1.91	1-5	1	.94	.92	.34	-.01
Collected Public Assistance							
collected welfare past 4 years	.11	0-4	4	.25	5.49	32.32	.12***
collected foodstamps past 4 years	.05	0-4	4	.10	7.70	67.51	.08*
Amount Worked Past Year	4.33	1-6	1	.06	-3.45	9.90	-.03
Chapter 12—Mental Health							
Adolescence							
Emotional Distress							
deliberateness	12.83	4-20	4	11.36	-.11	-.08	-.08*

diligence	14.32	4-20	4	10.11	−.23	−.21	.03
self-acceptance	15.86	4-20	4	9.92	−.66	.00	−.05
depression	7.69	4-18	4	10.63	.84	.00	.04

Young Adulthood

Psychoticism							
magic ideation 1	1.79	0-8	10	3.06	1.14	.94	.01
magic ideation 2	2.58	0-8	10	2.19	.60	.01	.03
magic ideation 3	2.46	0-9	10	4.04	.76	−.04	−.04
Depression (CES-D)							
positive affect	2.34	0-3	4	.40	−.94	.28	−.12**
negative affect	.63	0-3	5	.41	1.23	1.36	.16***
impaired motivation	.72	0-2.75	8	.21	.77	.84	.10*
impaired relationships	.33	0-3	3	.22	1.71	3.39	−.01
Emotional Distress							
deliberateness	13.00	4-20	4	10.05	−.15	−.21	−.10*
diligence	15.17	4-20	4	8.01	−.58	.69	−.05
self-acceptance	15.90	6-20	4	8.94	−.75	.20	−.10*
depression	7.51	4-20	4	9.67	1.03	.94	.06
Purpose in Life							
PIL 1	11.18	4.67-14	6	3.17	−.77	.08	−.04
PIL 2	10.63	4.75-14	7	3.24	−.60	.12	−.07
PIL 3	10.85	4.42-14	7	3.10	−.56	.06	−.05
Suicide Ideation							
think about killing self	1.35	1-4	1	.40	1.77	2.60	.00
told someone kill self	1.25	1-5	1	.34	2.72	8.73	−.02
life end with suicide	1.16	1-4	1	.23	3.40	12.11	−.02

Continued

TABLE A.1 Continued

Latent Construct/ Measured Variable	Mean	Range	Number of Items	Variance	Skew	Kurtosis	Sex Difference[a] r_{pb}
Chapter 13—Social Intergration							
Adolescence							
Social Support							
good relationship with parents	15.87	5-20	4	11.90	−.76	−.17	.03
good relationship with family	14.27	4-20	4	17.64	−.47	−.61	−.01
good relationship with adults	17.11	7-20	4	8.76	−.84	.88	.06
good relationship with peers	16.72	6-20	4	7.84	−1.08	1.02	.05
Young Adulthood							
Social Support							
good relationship with parents	16.54	4-20	4	10.30	−1.24	1.41	.07
good relationship with family	14.87	4-20	4	14.36	−.65	−.11	.07
good relationship with adults	17.28	8-20	4	4.45	−.89	1.03	.05
good relationship with peers	16.33	6-20	4	9.36	−1.09	.86	.02
Loneliness							
lonely 1	4.91	0-17	7	10.37	.60	.06	−.03
lonely 2	5.98	0-19	7	15.84	.60	−.11	−.01
lonely 3	4.91	0-13	6	8.82	.50	−.19	−.07
Chapter 14—Large Integrated Model of Specific Drug Effects							
Adolescence							

	Mean	Range					
Alcohol Use							
beer frequency	2.69	1-6	2	1.27	.18	-.98	-.16***
wine frequency	2.40	1-5	2	.92	.28	-.77	.05
liquor frequency	2.15	1-5	2	.98	.57	-.52	-.02
Cannabis Use							
marijuana frequency	1.98	1-6	2	1.49	1.15	.44	-.05
hashish frequency	1.34	1-4.5	2	.44	2.18	4.38	-.02
Hard Drug Use							
hypnotic frequency	1.09	1-4.8	5	.10	6.17	50.93	.03
cocaine frequency	1.21	1-3.5	2	.22	2.46	5.73	.03
stimulant frequency	1.15	1-4.33	3	.15	3.62	17.69	.08*
psychedelic frequency	1.07	1-3.67	3	.07	5.59	39.70	-.02
inhalant frequency	1.10	1-2.67	3	.07	3.14	10.30	.02
narcotic frequency	1.03	1-2.33	3	.02	6.30	46.89	.05
PCP frequency	1.09	1-5	1	.15	5.46	34.63	.05

Control Constructs

Social Conformity—three variables used in all chapters
Family Support—two variables from Chapter 7
Social Support—two unique variables from Chapter 13
Criminal Activities—three variables from Chapter 8
Early Sexual Involvement—two variables from Chapter 9
Academic Potential—two variables from Chapters 10 and 11
Income—three variables from Chapters 10 and 11
Emotional Distress—four variables from Chapter 12

Continued

TABLE A.1 Continued

Latent Construct/ Measured Variable	Mean	Range	Number of Items	Variance	Skew	Kurtosis	Sex Difference[a] r_{pb}
Young Adulthood							
Family Formation—two variables from Chapter 7							
Relationship Satisfaction—two variables from Chapter 7							
Drug Crime Involvement—two variables from Chapter 8							
Criminal Activities—three variables from Chapter 8							
Satisfaction with Intimacy—three variables from Chapter 9							
Number of Relationships—two variables from Chapter 9							
College Involvement—three variables from Chapter 10							
Job Instability—three variables from Chapter 11							
Income—three variables from Chapter 11							
Suicide Ideation—three variables from Chapter 12							
Psychoticism—three variables from Chapter 12							
Loneliness—three variables from Chapter 13							

a. A positive correlation indicates that the women had the larger value, whereas a negative correlation indicates the men had the larger value.
*p < .05; **p < .01; ***p < .001.

problem with a lover, spouse, or date, on a five-point anchored rating scale that ranged from no difficulty (1) to great difficulty (5).

Family formation. Two items were used to reflect a latent construct of Family Formation: marriage past 4 years and number of children. For each of the four years preceding the young adult assessment, the respondent indicated in a dichotomous manner whether they had been married (0 = no and 1 = yes). These four items were summed into the marriage past 4 years item. This measure captures one or multiple marriages during the four-year period. The number of children variable simply reflects the actual number of children the respondent acknowledged having.

Relationship importance. Two single-item measures were used to reflect a latent construct of Relationship Importance: Current level of involvement and dating importance. Current level of involvement was indicated on a six-point anchored rating scale with the following response categories: not dating (1), dating several people (2), dating one person regularly, but also dating others (3), going steady with one person (4), cohabiting (5), and married (6). Dating importance was rated on a four-point anchored rating scale that ranged from not important (1) to very important (4).

Cohabitation history. Each respondent indicated in a dichotomous manner (no = 0 and yes = 1) whether he or she had ever shared the same bedroom for an average of at least five (5) nights per week with someone he or she was sexually involved with but not married to (cohabitation). This represents a fairly standard definition of cohabitation (see Newcomb, 1981, 1983, 1986b; Newcomb & Bentler, 1980a). This single item was used as the indicator of Cohabitation History. As evident in Table 4.1, 33% of the sample admitted to cohabiting sometime in their life.

Divorce. For each of the four years preceding the young adult assessment, the respondent was asked to indicate whether or not he or she had obtained a divorce. As evident in Table A.1, approximately 13% of the sample had obtained a divorce since high school.

Sex Differences

There were significant sex differences on only three of the variables for the Family Formation model. These indicated that women were more likely to be married, have more children, and have a higher level of current relationship involvement than the men.

Chapter 8:
Deviant Behavior

Adolescence

Criminal activities. Three multi-item scales were used to reflect a Criminal Activities latent factor: confrontational acts, stealing episodes, and property damage. The adolescents were asked to indicate how often they had committed each of 16 different criminal acts ranging from minor fights to major acts of property destruction during the past six months. Confirmatory factor analyses revealed four factors (Huba & Bentler, 1984)—the three mentioned above and automobile theft, which was eliminated because of minimal variance. Responses to each item were summed within each scale. Confrontational acts included the number of times an individual got into serious fights, got into gang fights, caused a serious injury, and used a deadly weapon against someone. Stealing episodes included the number of times the adolescent had stolen something worth less than $50, stolen something worth more than $50, and shoplifted. Property damage included the number of times the teenager committed vandalism at school, committed vandalism at work, committed arson, or trespassed.

Deviant friendship network. Three multiple-item scales were used to reflect a latent construct of Deviant Friendship network: Confrontational friends, friends deviant at school, and friends who steal. Nine items were summed into these three scales. Each item asked for the number of friends who performed certain behaviors on a five-point anchored rating scale that ranged from none (1) to all (5). Confrontational friends included the number of friends who have carried a deadly weapon and get into fights. Friends deviant at school include the number of friends who regularly lie to their teachers, have been suspended from school, cut class-just don't go, and have cheated on an important exam. Friends who steal include the number of friends who have stolen money from their parents, take other kids' things in school, have been busted for burglary or robbery, and shoplift from stores.

Young Adulthood

Drug crime involvement. Two scales were used to represent a latent construct of Drug Crime Involvement: driving while intoxicated and selling or possessing drugs. These scales are the sum of the number of years in the past four years, between adolescence and young adulthood, that the individual has been arrested or convicted for each of these crimes. In other words, each respondent indicated whether he or she had (scored 1) or had not (scored 0) been arrested or convicted for a variety of criminal offenses during each of the previous four years. These responses were summed for each type of crime across the four years. For Drug Crime Involvement driving while intoxicated represents the number of years (of the previous four) that the respondent had been arrested or convicted for this crime. Selling or possessing drugs represents similar occurrences for that crime. Measured scales for Violent Crime Involvement and Property Crime Involvement (below) were created in a similar manner.

Violent crime involvement. Three scales were used to represent a latent construct of Violent Crime Involvement: vandalism, carrying a deadly weapon, and assault. Each of these three scales is the sum of the number of years in the past four years that the individual has been arrested or convicted for each of these crimes.

Property crime involvement. Two scales were used to reflect the Property Crime Involvement latent construct: other infraction and theft. Each of these two scales is the sum of the number of years in the past four years that the young adult has been arrested or convicted for each of these crimes.

Criminal activities. Three measures are used to represent a latent construct of Criminal Activities: confrontational acts, stealing episodes, and property damage. These were assessed in an identical fashion to those measured in adolescence.

Sex Differences

There were four significant mean differences between men and women on the adolescent measures and eight differences on the young adult measures. On all of the significant differences, men reported performing significantly more deviant acts than the women. There were no significant differences on friends deviant at school, friends who steal, driving while intoxicated, and vandalism. It should be noted that these deviant behavior variables are the most extremely nonnormal of the data set (large skews and kurtoses). As a result, in our analyses of these variables, we confirm our standard maximum likelihood results and estimates with those obtained using a method appropriate for nonnormal data (distribution-free method: e.g., Browne, 1984).

Chapter 9:
Sexual Behavior

Adolescence

Early sexual involvement. Two items are used to reflect a latent construct of Early Sexual Involvement: age of first sexual contact and age of first sexual intercourse. The actual age reported by the respondent was used as a datum for these items. Although these two items were actually assessed at the young adult follow-up, the ages reported pertain to the adolescent age period and are included there for conceptual reasons, even though they are retrospective measures.

Frequency of sexual events. This is a multi-item scale that is used as a single-variable factor. The subject was asked to indicate in a dichotomous manner (no = 0 and yes = 1) whether seven events had occurred to him or her during the past year (Newcomb, Huba, & Bentler, 1981, 1986a, 1986b). These seven events included falling deeply in love, getting pregnant or getting someone pregnant, getting or giving venereal disease, going out on dates regularly, breaking up with boyfriend or girlfriend, having a gay or lesbian experience, and losing virginity. Responses to these seven items were summed.

Number of sexually active friends. This is a single-item scale that is used as a single-variable factor. The subject was asked to indicate the number of their friends who were not virgins on a five-point anchored rating scale that ranged from none (1) to all (5).

Satisfaction with opposite-sex relationships. This is a single-item scale that is used as a single-variable factor. The teenager was asked to indicate his or her degree of happiness with his or her relations with opposite-sexed friends on a five-point anchored rating scale that ranged from very unhappy (1) to very happy (5).

Young Adulthood

Birth control effectiveness. Two variables are used as indicators of a Birth Control Effectiveness construct: effectiveness of current birth control and effectiveness of future birth control. Respondents were presented with a list of 10 birth control methods and were asked to indicate which they currently used and which they planned to use in the future. Based on previous research, these 10 modes of birth control were grouped into three categories of effectiveness for current and future use (Geis & Gerrard, 1984): low (0—nothing, withdrawal, and rhythm), moderate (1—spermicide, diaphragm, and condom), and high (3—birth control pills, intrauterine device, hysterectomy or vasectomy, and not sexually active). These two three-point scales were then used as the measured-variable indicators for this factor.

Dating competence. This factor was created from a nine-item dating competence or dating skills inventory developed by Levenson and Gottman (1978). Items were presented in two formats. One format asked the respondent to indicate on a four-point scale (never = 1 to always = 4) how often they were able to do certain dating behaviors, that is, get a second date with someone dated once or have an intimate physical relationship with someone of the opposite sex. The second format asked the young adult to indicate how much difficulty he or she would experience handling a variety of different situations on a five-point anchored scale (avoid if possible = 1 to very comfortable = 5), that is, start a conversation at a party with a member of the opposite sex. These nine items were randomly summed into three scales (dating competence 1, dating competence 2, and dating competence 3) and are used as indicators of the Dating Competence factor. This measure has proven useful in a variety of other research on sexual responsiveness (Newcomb, 1984) and cohabitation (Newcomb, 1986b).

Satisfaction with intimacy. Three single-item variables are used to reflect a latent construct of Satisfaction with Intimacy: happy with sex life, happy being close with someone, and satisfaction with sexual intercourse. For the first two items (sex life and being close), respondents indicated their amount of satisfaction with these areas of life during the past six months on seven-point anchored rating scales that ranged from terrible (1) to delighted (7). Satisfaction with sexual intercourse was also rated on a seven-point scale that ranged from very dissatisfied (1) to very satisfied (7).

Number of relationships. Two single-item measures were used as indicators of a latent construct of Number of Relationships: number of steady partners and number of sexual partners. The actual number of lifetime steady partners and sexual partners was used as a datum for these scales. On the average, the sample as a whole reported about four steady partners and six sexual partners during their lives (see Table A.1). Because these scales were so skewed, the modes did not coincide with the means, and in fact provide a reverse picture: most individuals had two sexual partners and three steadies.

Frequency of intercourse. Two single-items variables were used to reflect a latent construct of Frequency of Sexual Intercourse: intercourse frequency per week and intercourse frequency per month. The actual number reported by the young adult was used as a datum for these scales.

Contracted venereal disease. A single, dichotomous item was used for this single-variable factor. The item was scored "0" if they did not report ever having venereal disease and a "1" if they had. About 7% of the sample reported having venereal disease sometime in their lives.

Abortion occurrence. Two single-item measures were asked only of the women to reflect an Abortion Occurrence latent factor: ever had an abortion and number of abortions. Ever had an abortion was scored dichotomously (no = 0 and yes = 1) and the actual number was used for number of abortions. In all, 31% of the women reported having at least one abortion, with some reporting up to four.

Sex Differences

There were several significant mean differences between men and women on these sexual behavior items and scales. Compared to men, women were significantly older at first sexual contact and intercourse, had a higher frequency of sexual events, had fewer sexually active friends, had greater satisfaction with opposite-sex relationships during adolescence, used more effective birth control methods (both currently and planned for the future), were happier with their sex lives and being close with someone, and had higher rates of intercourse. Because of these many mean differences, as well as an expectation that the processes of sexual development, and the potential impact of drug use on these processes, may be different for men than women, separate models are generated for men and women.

Chapter 10:
Educational Pursuits

Adolescence

Academic potential. Two single-item variables are used as indicators of an Academic Potential latent construct: grade point average and educational plans. Grade point average for the past year was indicated in the standard manner (F = 0, D = 1, C = 2, B = 3, and A = 4). Educational plans were provided on a six-point anchored rating scale that ranged from some high school (will drop out before completion) (1) to doctor's degree (6).

Income. Three single-item measures were used as indicators of an Income latent construct: salary 1, salary 2, and salary 3. For three separate months during the previous year (July, October, and January), the respondent indicated his or her amount of earned income before taxes on seven-point anchored rating scales that ranged from none (1) to more than $500 (7). Salary 1 was the July amount, Salary 2 was the October amount, and Salary 3 was the January amount.

Young Adulthood

Educational aspirations. Two single-item scales are used to represent a latent construct of Educational Aspirations: educational plans and educational expectations. Educational plans was rated on a six-point anchored scale that asked the respondent to indicate their long-range educational plans from no more formal education (1) to doctor's degree (6). The educational expectations item asked the young adult to indicate the highest level of education they expected to complete in the next few years. Responses were given on a seven-point anchored rating scale that ranged from some high school (will not finish) (1) to doctor's degree (7).

College involvement. Three multi-item scales were used to reflect a College Involvement latent construct: college attendance, part-time job and college, and part-time employment. For each of the four years preceding the young adult assessment, the respondent indicated in a yes (1) or no (0) manner whether he or she had done any of these activities. Each type of activity was summed across the four years yielding the three measures, each of which ranged from 0 to 4.

Work force involvement. Four items or scales were used to reflect a latent construct of Work Force Involvement: full-time job or military, full-time employment, income, and months worked. Full-time job or military was scored "1" if the respondent indicated that either of the activities best characterized his or her employment situation for the past six months. Otherwise it was scored as "0." Of the sample, 49% reported that they had been engaged in full-time employment or the military during the past six months. Full-time employment represents the number of years of the four preceding the young adult follow-up that the respondent indicated that he or she was engaged in full-time employment. This variable ranged from 0 to 4. Income was the amount of money earned before taxes in the year preceding the young adult assessment. Responses were given on an eight-point anchored rating scale that ranged from none (1) to more than $30,000. Finally, months worked represent the number of months spent in full-time employment during the year preceding the young adult assessment. This was rated on a six-point scale that ranged from none (1) to more than nine months (6).

Graduated from high school. This is a single-item, dichotomous measure that is used as a single-variable factor. The respondent indicated in a yes (1) or no (0) manner whether they had ever completed high school. Of this total sample, 93% had completed high school by the time they were young adults.

Sex Differences

There were seven significant mean sex differences on the items or scales measuring educational pursuits. Compared to the men, women earned less money during adolescence (on salary 1 and salary 2), had lower educational plans and expectations as young adults, less often had a part-time job and college, had a lower income, and worked fewer months as young adults.

Chapter 11:
Livelihood Pursuits

Adolescence

Academic potential. This is the same construct as described above for Chapter 10.

Income. This is the same construct as described in the Educational Pursuits variables (Chapter 10).

Young Adulthood

Income. Three single-item measures were used as indicators of an Income latent construct: salary 1, salary 2, and salary 3. For three separate months during the previous year (August, October, and December), when the subjects were young adults, the respondent indicated his or her amount of earned income before taxes on eight-point anchored rating scales that ranged from none (0) to more than $2500 (7). Salary 1 was the August amount, Salary 2 was the October amount, Salary 3 was the December amount.

Job instability. Three multi-item scales were used to reflect a Job Instability latent factor: times fired past 4 years, times lost job past 4 years, and times collected unemployment past 4 years. For each of the four years preceding the young adult assessment, the respondent indicated in a yes (1) or no (0) manner whether any of these had happened to them. Each type of event or activity was summed across the four years yielding the three measures, each of which could range from 0 to 4.

Job satisfaction. Two single-item measures were used as indicators of a Job Satisfaction latent construct: happy with work and trouble with work. The respondent indicated his or her overall satisfaction with work (happy with work) during the past six months on a seven-point anchored rating scale that ranged from terrible (1) to delighted (7). Amount of trouble or difficulty with work was rated on a five-point anchored scale that ranged from no difficulty (1) to great difficulty (5).

Collected public assistance. Two multi-item scales were used to reflect a latent construct of Collected Public Assistance: collected welfare past 4 years and collected food stamps past 4 years. These two measured variables represent the number of years of the four preceding the young adult follow-up that the respondent indicated that he or she had collected assistance from these two sources (welfare and food stamps). These variables ranged from 0 to 4.

Amount worked past year. This is a single-variable factor. This variable is the amount worked measure described above in the Educational Pursuits section (Chapter 10) as one indicator of the Work Force Involvement construct.

Sex Differences

There were only five significant mean differences between men and women on these livelihood pursuit variables. Compared to men, women earned significantly less money during adolescence (on salary 1 and salary 2), earned less money during young adulthood on salary 1, more often collected welfare, and more often collected food stamps.

Chapter 12:
Mental Health

Adolescence

Emotional distress. Four multi-item scales were used to represent an Emotional Distress latent factor: (lack of) deliberateness, (lack of) diligence, (lack of) self-acceptance, and depression. Deliberateness, diligence, and self-acceptance are four-item scales taken from the Bentler Psychological Inventory (Bentler & Newcomb, 1978; Huba & Bentler, 1982; Stein et al., 1986a). The depression scale is from the Bentler Medical-Psychological Inventory (Newcomb et al., 1981, 1986b). These scales have good face validity and internal consistency (Newcomb et al., 1986b; Stein et al., 1986a) and when keyed in the direction of Emotional Distress represent dysphoric mood, self-dislike, lack of exactness and forethought, and little joy or excitement in life.

Young Adulthood

Psychoticism. Three multi-item scales were used to reflect a latent construct of Psychoticism: magic ideation 1, magic ideation 2, and magic ideation 3. The Magic Ideation Scale (MIS) was used to assess degree of Psychoticism. The MIS has been found to be a reliable indicator of schizotypy and predisposition to psychosis (Eckblad & Chapman, 1983). The MIS is composed of 30 dichotomous items, which elicit agreement or disagreement to a variety of beliefs conventionally considered invalid, as well as numerous bizarre or unusual experiences. Examples of items include "Some people can make me aware of them just by thinking about me" and "I have had the momentary feeling I might not be human." Items were randomly scored into three 10-item MIS subscales called magic ideation 1, magic ideation 2, and magic ideation 3 for use as indicators of a latent-variable called Psychoticism.

Depression (CES-D). Four multi-item scales were used to represent a Depression latent factor: (lack of) positive affect, negative affect, impaired motivation, and impaired relationships. These four scales contained 20 self-report items that constitute the Center for Epidemiologic Studies—Depression Scale (CES-D) constructed by Radloff (1977). Subjects were asked to report how often during the past week they felt sad, depressed, fearful, lonely, happy, hopeful, and so on, on a four-point anchored scale, that ranged from rarely (0) to most of the time (4). Based on our own and previous factor analytic examinations of the CES-D (Aneshensel, Clark, & Frerichs, 1983), the 20 items were grouped into four manifest indicators of a CES-D Depression latent factor. The four indicators, representing the average of their respective item clusters, were positive affect (four items), negative affect (five items), impaired motivation (eight items), and impaired relationships (three items).

Emotional distress. The same four measures as described for the adolescent period were used to assess Emotional Distress in young adulthood.

Purpose in life. Three multi-item scales were used to reflect a Purpose in Life construct: PIL 1, PIL 2, and PIL 3. These three scales contain the 20 items from Crumbaugh and Maholick's (1964, 1969) Purpose in Life test (PIL). Each item was rated on a seven-point anchored rating scale that ranged from strongly disagree (1) to strongly agree (7). Subjects were asked to indicate their amount of agreement with such items as "I am usually completely bored," and "I regard my ability to find a meaning, purpose, or mission in life as very great." Eleven of the items were negatively worded and nine reflected a positive outlook, with the final scores evaluated such that higher values indicated greater purpose in life. Based on a confirmatory factor analysis of the PIL (Newcomb, Harlow, & Bentler, 1985; Harlow, Newcomb, & Bentler, 1986, 1987), three scales were created and used as indicators of a Purpose in Life factor: PIL 1 (six items), PIL 2 (seven items), and PIL 3 (seven items).

Suicide ideation. Three single-item scales were used as indicators of a Suicide Ideation latent factor: think about killing self, told someone kill self, and life end with suicide. Each item was rated on a five-point anchored scale that ranged from never (1) to always (5). Two of these items were taken from Petrie and Chamberlain's (1983) Suicide Behavior Subscale: "I have been thinking about ways to kill myself" (think about killing self) and "I have told someone I want to kill myself" (told someone kill self). The remaining item was created for this project: "I imagine my life will end with suicide" (life end with suicide). Higher scores were indicative of a greater amount of suicide ideation. The three items were used as separate indicators of a Suicide Ideation construct or factor.

Sex Differences

There were only five significant mean sex differences between men and women on these measures of mental health. Compared to men, women were significantly less deliberate (in both adolescence and young adulthood), and reported less positive affect, more negative affect, more impaired motivation, and less self-acceptance during young adulthood.

Chapter 13:
Social Integration

Adolescence

Social support. Four multi-item scales were used to reflect a latent factor of Social Support: good relationship with parents, good relationship with family, good relationship with adults, and good relationship with peers. The parents and family scales are the same as those used for the Family Support construct in the Family Formation section (Chapter 7). The other two scales were measured in a similar fashion (i.e., four bipolar items each) and assess the amount of connection, support, and respect experienced with adults and peers.

Young Adulthood

Social support. The identical four measures of Social Support used during adolescence were also administered during young adulthood.

Loneliness. Three multi-item scales were used to represent a Loneliness latent construct: lonely 1, lonely 2, and lonely 3. These three scales consist of 20 items collectively called the UCLA Loneliness scale, which was developed by Russell, Peplau, and Cutrona (1980). The respondent was asked to indicate how often he or she felt each of 20 different ways on four-point anchored rating scales that ranged from never (1) to often (4). Sample items include lack companionship, feel left out, and no one really knows me. Controversy exists regarding the factor structure of the UCLA Loneliness scale (Hays & DiMatteo, in press; Hojat, 1982). Thus we performed our own factor analyses to establish its factor structure in the current sample. Four eigenvalues were greater than 1.0, although there was a huge drop between the first and second, suggesting the existence of one large general factor (first four eigenvalues = 7.18, 1.38, 1.24, 1.14). This was supported by the high loadings on the first unrotated factor: all except one item loaded higher than .35, and 14 of the 20 items had loadings of .50 or greater. Although several additional smaller factors may exist, the general nature of the scale appears to be unidimensional. Thus the items were randomly assigned to three scales that are used as manifest indicators of a latent construct of the UCLA Loneliness scale (Lonely 1, 2, and 3).

Sex Differences

There were no significant sex differences on any of the Social Integration scales.

Chapter 14:
Large Integrated Model of
Specific Drug Effects

Adolescence

Alcohol use. Three measures are used to reflect a latent construct of Alcohol Use: beer frequency, wine frequency, and liquor frequency. Each of these scales are the average of ratings given during early adolescence (year 1 of the study) and late adolescence (year 5 of the study) for each of the specific substances. See description on the Drug Use construct for all chapters for more details on how these items, and the others presented below, were measured.

Cannabis use. Two measures were used as indicators of a Cannabis Use latent factor: marijuana frequency and hashish frequency. Each of these was an average of responses given during early adolescence and late adolescence.

Hard drug use. Seven measures were used to represent a latent factor of Hard Drug Use: hypnotic frequency, cocaine frequency, stimulant frequency, psychedelic frequency, inhalant frequency, narcotic frequency, and PCP frequency. Hypnotic frequency was the average of five items (sedatives from early adolescence and major and minor tranquilizers, sedatives, and barbiturates from late adolescence). Cocaine frequency was the average of two items (cocaine at both early and late adolescence). Stimulant frequency was the average of three items (stimulants from early adolescence and amphetamines and nonamphetamine uppers from late adolescence). Psychedelic frequency was the average of three items (psychedelics from early adolescence and LSD and other psychedelics from late adolescence). Inhalant frequency was the average of three items (inhalants from early adolescence and amyl nitrate and other inhalants from late adolescence). Narcotic frequency was the average of three items (heroin from early adolescence and heroin and other narcotics from late adolescence). Finally, PCP frequency was a single item assessed in late adolescence (use of this drug was not assessed in early adolescence).

Other control variables. A total of 21 other variables from the adolescent age period were used to control for baseline levels of the young adult outcome constructs. Due to the extremely large size of the model, however, these variables were not included as actual constructs, but rather their influence on the entire system of adolescent and young adult variables was removed by partialing these variables out using multiple partial regression. These variables included law abidance, liberalism, religious commitment (the

Social Conformity construct from all chapters), good relationship with parents, good relationship with family, good relationship with adults, good relationship with peers (the Family Support construct from Chapter 7 and the Social Support construct from Chapter 13), confrontational acts, stealing episodes, property damage (the Criminal Activities construct from Chapter 8), age of first sexual contact, age of first sexual intercourse (the Early Sexual Involvement factor from Chapter 9), grade-point average, educational plans (the Academic Potential construct from Chapters 10 and 11), salary 1, salary 2, salary 3 (the Income factor from Chapters 10 and 11), deliberateness, diligence, self-acceptance, and depression (the Emotional Distress factor from Chapter 12).

Young Adulthood

All constructs from the young adult data have already been described above and are only summarized here with the chapter they were taken from as reference to their full description. They were selected for inclusion in this large model on the basis that they had been influenced by teenage drug use in the smaller models. In addition, at least one construct was taken from each of the smaller specific life area models. These constructs included Family Formation (with indicators of marriage past 4 years and number of children, from Chapter 7), Relationship Satisfaction (with indicators of happy with relationship and trouble with relationship, from Chapter 7), Drug Crime Involvement (with indicators of driving while intoxicated and selling or possessing drugs, from Chapter 8), Criminal Activities (with indicators of confrontational acts, stealing episodes, and property damage, from Chapter 8), Satisfaction with Intimacy (with indicators of happy with sex life, happy being close with someone, and satisfaction with intercourse, from Chapter 9), Number of Relationships (with indicators of number of steady partners and number of sexual partners, from Chapter 9), College Involvement (with indicators of college attendance, part-time job and college, and part-time employment, from Chapter 10), Job Instability (with indicators of times fired past 4 years, times lost job past 4 years, and times collected unemployment past 4 years, from Chapter 11), Income (with indicators of salary 1, 2, and 3, from Chapter 11), Suicide Ideation (with indicators of think about killing self, told someone kill self, and life end with suicide, from Chapter 12), Psychoticism (with indicators of magic ideation 1, 2, and 3, from Chapter 12), and Loneliness (with indicators of Lonely 1, 2, and 3, from Chapter 13).

Sex Differences

Only the individual drug substance mean differences by sex have not been presented above. On the 12 different substances, there were only two significant differences between adolescent boys and girls. Boys drank significantly more beer than girls. On the other hand, girls reported more frequent use of stimulants than boys. No other significant sex differences on specific drug substances were evident.

References

Adams, B. N. (1985). The family: Problems and solutions. *Journal of Marriage and the Family, 47*, 525-529.

Adams, E. H., Gfroerer, J. C., Rouse, B. A., & Kozel, N. J. (1986). Trends in prevalence and consequences of cocaine use. *Advances in Alcohol & Substance Abuse, 6*, 49-71.

Adams, L., Lonsdale, D., Robinson, M., Rawbone, R., & Guz, A. (1984). Respiratory impairments induced by smoking in children in secondary schools. *British Medical Journal, 288*, 891-895.

Adelson, J. (1980). *Handbook of adolescent psychology.* New York: John Wiley.

Akers, R. (1984). Delinquent behavior, drugs, and alcohol: What is the relationship? *Today's Delinquent, 3*, 19-48.

Akers, R., Krohn, M., Lanza-Kaduce, L., & Radosevich, M. (1979). Social learning and deviant behavior: A specific test of a general theory. *American Sociological Review, 44*, 635-655.

Amemiya, Y., & Anderson, T. W. (1985). *Asymptotic chi-square tests for a large class of factor analysis models.* Technical Report No. 12. Stanford, CA: Stanford University.

Anderson, T. W., & Amemiya, Y. (1985). *The asymptotic normal distribution of estimators in factor analysis under general conditions.* Technical Report No. 12. Stanford, CA: Stanford University.

Aneshensel, C. S., Clark, V. A., & Frerichs, R. R. (1983). Race, ethnicity, and depression: A confirmatory analysis. *Journal of Personality and Social Psychology, 44*, 385-398.

Aneshensel, C. S., & Huba, G. J. (1983). Depression, alcohol use, and smoking over one year: A four-wave longitudinal causal model. *Journal of Abnormal Psychology, 92*, 134-150.

Anglin, M. D., & Speckart, G. (1986). Narcotics use, property crime, and dealing: Structural dynamics across the addiction career. *Journal of Quantitative Criminology, 2*, 355-375.

Bachman, J. G., Johnston, L. D., & O'Malley, P. M. (1981). Smoking, drinking, and drug use among American high school students: Correlates and trends, 1975-1979. *American Journal of Public Health, 71*, 59-69.

Bachman, J. G., O'Malley, P. M., & Johnston, L. D. (1984). Drug use among young adults: The impacts of role status and social environment. *Journal of Personality and Social Psychology, 47*, 629-645.

Bahr, S. J., & Galligan, R. J. (1984). Teenage marriage and marital stability. *Youth and Society, 15*, 387-400.

Barrett, F. M. (1980). Sexual experience, birth control usage, and sex education of unmarried Canadian university students: Changes between 1968 and 1978. *Archives of Sexual Behavior, 9*, 367-390.

Baumrind, D. (1983). Spacious causal attributions in the social sciences: The reformulated stepping-stone theory as exemplar. *Journal of Personality and Social Psychology, 45*, 1289-1298.

Baumrind, D., & Moselle, K. A. (1985). A developmental perspective on adolescent drug use. *Advances in Alcohol and Substance Use, 5*, 41-67.

Beary, J. F., Mazzuchi, J. F., & Richie, S. I. (1983). Drug use in the military: An adolescent misbehavior problem. *Journal of Drug Education, 13*, 83-93.

Beauvais, F., & Oetting, E. R. (1986). Drug use in an alternative high school. *Journal of Drug Education, 16*, 43-50.

Becker, H. S. (1963). *Outsiders: Studies in the sociology of deviance.* New York: Free Press.

Beckman, L. (1980). Perceived antecedents and effects of alcohol consumption in women. *Journal of Studies on Alcohol, 41*, 518-530.

Bell, C. S., & Battjes, R. (Eds.). (1985). *Prevention research: Deterring drug abuse among children and adolescents* (Research Monograph #63). Rockville, MD: National Institute on Drug Abuse.

Bennett, T., & Wright, R. (1984). The relationship between alcohol use and burglary. *British Journal of Addiction, 79*, 431-437.

Bentler, P. M. (1978). The interdependence of theory, methodology, and empirical data: Causal modeling as an approach to construct validity. In D. B. Kandel (Ed.), *Longitudinal research on drug use: Empirical findings and methodological issues* (pp. 267-302). Washington, DC: Hemisphere.

Bentler, P. M. (1980). Multivariate analysis with latent variables: Causal modeling. *Annual Review of Psychology, 31*, 419-456.

Bentler, P. M. (1983). Some contributions to efficient statistics in structural models: Specification and estimation of moment structures. *Psychometrika, 48*, 493-517.

Bentler, P. M. (1986a). Structural modeling and Psychometrika: An historical perspective on growth and achievements. *Psychometrika, 51*, 35-51.

Bentler, P. M. (1986b). *Theory and implementation of EQS: A structural equations program.* Los Angeles: BMDP Statistical Software.

Bentler, P. M. (1986c). *Lagrange multiplier and Wald tests for EQS and EQS/PC.* Los Angeles: BMDP Statistical Software.

Bentler, P. M. (1987a, April). *Latent variable structural models for separating specific from general effects.* Prepared for Health Services Research Conference: Strengthening Causal Interpretations of Non-experimental Data, Tucson.

Bentler, P. M. (1987b). Drug use and personality in adolescence and young adulthood: Structural models with nonnormal variables. *Child Development, 58*, 65-79.

Bentler, P. M., & Bonett, D. G. (1980). Significance tests and goodness of fit in the analysis of covariance structures. *Psychological Bulletin, 88*, 588-606.

Bentler, P. M., & Chou, C.-P. (1986, April). *Statistics for parameter expansion and construction in structural models.* Paper presented at the American Educational Research Association meeting, San Francisco.

Bentler, P. M., & Chou, C.-P. (1987). Practical issues in structural modeling. In J. S. Long (Ed.), *Common problems in quantitative social research.* Newbury Park, CA: Sage.

Bentler, P. M., & Huba, G. J. (1979). Simple mini-theories of love. *Journal of Personality and Social Psychology, 37*, 124-130.

Bentler, P. M., & Newcomb, M. D. (1978). Longitudinal study of marital success and failure. *Journal of Consulting and Clinical Psychology, 46*, 1053-1070.

Bentler, P. M., & Newcomb, M. D. (1986a). Personality, sexual behavior, and drug use revealed through latent variable methods. *Clinical Psychology Review, 6*, 363-385.

Bentler, P. M., & Newcomb, M. D. (1986b, June). *A longitudinal study of social support, drug use, and health: Linear structural equation modeling with nonnormal variables.* Paper presented at the conference on Longitudinal Methods in Health Research, Berlin.

Bentler, P. M., & Newcomb, M. D. (in preparation). *A structural modeling approach to studying drug use consequences: Partitioning the effects of different substances.*

Bentler, P. M., & Peeler, W. H. (1979). Models of female orgasm. *Archives of Sexual Behavior, 8*, 405-423.

Bentler, P. M., & Speckart, G. (1979). Models of attitude-behavior relations. *Psychological Review, 86*, 452-464.

Bentler, P. M., & Speckart, G. (1981). Attitudes "cause" behaviors: A structural equation analysis. *Journal of Personality and Social Psychology, 40*, 228-238.

Bentler, P. M., & Weeks, D. G. (1980). Linear structural equations with latent variables. *Psychometrika, 45*, 289-308.

Berkman, L. F. (1985). The relationship of social networks and social support to morbidity and mortality. In S. Cohen & S. L. Syme (Eds.), *Social support and health* (pp. 241-262). New York: Academic Press.

Beschner, G., & Friedman, A. (1979). *Youth drug abuse: Problems, issues, and treatment.* Lexington, MA: Lexington Books, D. C. Heath.

Bielby, W. T. (1986). Arbitrary matrices in multiple-indicator models of latent variables. *Sociological Methods and Research, 15*, 3-23, 62-63.

Blum, R. H., Garfield, E. F., Johnstone, J. L., & Magistad, J. G. (1978). Drug education: Further results and recommendations. *Journal of Drug Issues, 8*, 379-426.

Booth, A., & Edwards, J. N. (1985). Age at marriage and marital instability. *Journal of Marriage and the Family, 47*, 67-75.

Botvin, G. J., & Wills, T. A. (1985). Personal and social skills training: Cognitive-behavioral approaches to substance abuse prevention. In C. S. Bell & R. Battjes (Eds.), *Prevention research: Deterring drug abuse among children and adolescents* (pp. 8-49) (Research Monograph #63). Rockville, MD: National Institute on Drug Abuse.

Braucht, G. N., & Braucht, B. (1984). Prevention of problem drinking among youth: Evaluation of educational strategies. In P. M. Miller & T. D. Nirenberg (Eds.), *Prevention of alcohol abuse* (pp. 253-279). New York: Plenum.

Brennan, T., & Auslander, N. (1979). *Adolescent loneliness: An exploratory study of social and psychological predisposition and theory.* Unpublished manuscript, Behavioral Research Institute, Boulder, CO.

Briar, S., & Piliavin, I. (1965). Delinquency, situational inducements, and commitment to conformity. *Social Problems, 13*, 35-45.

Broadhead, W. E., Kaplan, B. H., James, S. A., Wagner, E. H., Schoenbach, V. J., Grimson, R., Heyden, S., Tibblin, G., & Gehlbach, S. H. (1983). The epidemiologic evidence for a relationship between social support and health. *American Journal of Epidemiology, 117*, 521-537.

Brook, J. S., Whiteman, M., & Gordon, A. S. (1985). Father absence, perceived family characteristics and stage of drug use in adolescence. *British Journal of Developmental Psychology, 2*, 87-94.

Brook, J. S., Whiteman, M., Gordon, A. S., & Cohen, P. (1986). Dynamics of childhood and adolescent personality traits and adolescent drug use. *Developmental Psychology, 22*, 403-414.

Brooks-Gunn, J., Petersen, A. C., & Eichorn, D. (1985). The study of maturational timing effects in adolescence. *Journal of Youth and Adolescence, 14*, 149-161.

Browne, M. W. (1984). Asymptotically distribution-free methods for the analysis of covariance structures. *British Journal of Mathematical and Statistical Psychology, 37*, 62-83.

Brunswick, A. F., & Messeri, P. (1984a). Gender differences in the processes leading to cigarette smoking. *Journal of Psychosocial Oncology, 2*, 49-69.

Brunswick, A. F., & Messeri, P. (1984b). Causal factors in onset of adolescents' cigarette smoking: A prospective study of urban Black youth. *Addictive Behaviors, 9*, 35-52.

Brunswick, A. F., & Messeri, P. (1986). Drugs, lifestyle, and health: A longitudinal study of urban Black youth. *American Journal of Public Health, 75*, 52-57.

Bry, B. H. (1983). Predicting drug abuse: Review and reformulation. *International Journal of the Addictions, 18*, 223-233.

Bry, B. H., McKeon, P., & Pandina, R. J. (1982). Extent of drug use as a function of number of risk factors. *Journal of Abnormal Psychology, 91*, 273-279.

Burgess, R. L. (1981). Relationships in marriage and the family. In S. Duck & R. Gilmour (Eds.), *Personal relationships 1: Studying personal relationships* (pp. 179-196). London: Academic Press.

Carman, R. S. (1979). Motivations for drug use and problematic outcomes among rural junior high school students. *Addictive Behaviors, 4*, 91-93.

Castro, F. G., Maddahian, E., Newcomb, M. D., & Bentler, P. M. (1987). A multivariate model of the determinants of cigarette smoking among adolescents. *Journal of Health and Social Behavior, 28*, 273-289.

Castro, F. G., McCreary, C., Newcomb, M. D., Beazconde-Garbanati, L., & Cervantes, R. C. (in press). Cigarette smokers: They do more than just smoke cigarettes. *Health Psychology*.

Castro, F. G., Newcomb, M. D., & Cadish, K. (1987). Lifestyle differences between young adult cocaine users and their nonuser peers. *Journal of Drug Education, 17*, 89-111.

Chassin, L. (1984). Adolescent substance use and abuse. *Advances in Child Behavioral Analysis and Therapy, 3*, 99-152.

Check, J.V.P., Perlman, D., & Malamuth, N. M. (1983, August). *Loneliness and aggressive behavior*. Paper presented at the American Psychological Association, Anaheim, CA.

Cherry, N., & Kiernan, K. (1976). Personality and smoking behavior: A longitudinal study. *British Journal of Preventive and Social Medicine, 30*, 123-131.

Clayton, R. R., & Bokemeier, J. L. (1980). Premarital sex in the seventies. *Journal of Marriage and the Family, 42*, 759-775.

Clayton, R. R., & Lacey, W. B. (1982). Interpersonal influences on male drug use and drug use intentions. *International Journal of the Addictions, 17*, 655-666.

Clayton, R. R., & Ritter, C. (1985). The epidemiology of alcohol and drug abuse among adolescents. *Advances in Alcohol and Substance Abuse, 4*, 69-97.

Clayton, R. R., & Tuchfeld, B. S. (1982). The drug-crime debate: Obstacles in understanding the relationship. *Journal of Drug Issues, 12*, 153-165.

Clayton, R. R., & Voss, H. L. (n.d.). *Smoking and health, marijuana and use of other illicit drugs: Causal relationships.* Unpublished manuscript, University of Kentucky.

Cleek, M. G., & Pearson, T. A. (1985). Perceived causes of divorce: An analysis of interrelationships. *Journal of Marriage and the Family, 47*, 179-183.

Cliff, N. (1983). Some cautions concerning the application of causal modeling methods. *Multivariate Behavioral Research, 18*, 115-128.

Cloward, R. A., & Ohlin, L. E. (1960). *Delinquency and opportunity.* New York: Free Press.

Cohen, A. K. (1955). *Delinquent boys.* New York: Free Press.

Cohen, S. (1985). Reinforcement and rapid delivery systems: Understanding adverse consequences of cocaine. In N. J. Kozel & E. H. Adams (Eds.), *Cocaine use in America: Epidemiologic and clinical perspectives* (pp. 151-157). Rockville, MD: National Institute on Drug Abuse.

Cohen, S., & Wills, T. A. (1985). Stress, social support, and the buffering hypothesis. *Psychological Bulletin, 98*, 310-357.

Coleman, J. C. (1978). Current contradictions in adolescent theory. *Journal of Youth and Adolescence, 7*, 1-11.

Connell, J. P., & Tanaka, J. S. (Eds.). (1987). Special section on structural equation modeling. *Child Development, 58*, 1-175.

Coombs, R. H., Fawzy, F. I., & Gerber, B. E. (1984). Patterns of substance use among children and youth: A longitudinal study. *Substance and Alcohol Actions/Misuse, 5*, 59-67.

Coombs, R. H., Fawzy, F. I., & Gerber, B. E. (1986). Patterns of cigarette, alcohol, and other drug use among children and adolescents: A longitudinal study. *International Journal of the Addictions, 21*, 897-913.

Coombs, R. H., Wellisch, D. K., & Fawzy, F. I. (1985). Drinking patterns and problems among female children and adolescents: A comparison of abstainers, past users, and current users. *American Journal of Alcohol Abuse, 11*, 315-348.

Crumbaugh, J. C., & Maholick, L. T. (1964). An experimental study in existentialism: The psychometric approach to Frankl's concept of noogenic neurosis. *Journal of Clinical Psychology, 20*, 200-207.

Crumbaugh, J. C., & Maholick, L. T. (1969). *Manual of instructions for the purpose in life test.* Munster, IN: Psychometric Affiliates.

Cullen, K., Stenhouse, N. S., & Wearne, K. L. (1982). Alcohol and mortality in the Busselton Study. *International Journal of Epidemiology, 11*, 67-70.

Cunningham, J. D., & Antill, J. K. (1981). Love in developing romantic relationships. In S. Duck & R. Gilmour (Eds.), *Personal relationships 2: Developing personal relationships* (pp. 27-51). London: Academic Press.

D'Augelli, J. F., & Cross, H. J. (1975). Relationship of sex guilt and moral reasoning to premarital sex in college women and in couples. *Journal of Consulting and Clinical Psychology, 43*, 40-47.

DeLamater, J. D., & MacCorquodale, P. (1979). *Premarital sexuality: Attitudes, relationships, behavior.* Madison: University of Wisconsin Press.

Dembo, R. (1979). Substance abuse prevention programming and research: A partnership in need of improvement. *Journal of Drug Education, 9*, 189-208.

Dembo, R. (1981). Critical issues and experiences in drug treatment and prevention evaluation. *International Journal of the Addictions, 16*, 1399-1414.

Dembo, R., Blount, W. R., Smeidler, J., & Burgos, W. (1985). Methodological and substantive issues involved in using the concept of risk in research into the etiology of drug use among adolescents. *Journal of Drug Issues, 15*, 537-553.

Diamant, L., & Windholz, G. (1981). Loneliness in college students: Some therapeutic considerations. *Journal of College Student Personnel, 22*, 515-522.

Diepold, J., & Young, R. Y. (1979). Empirical studies of adolescent sexual behavior: A critical review. *Adolescence, 14*, 45-64.

Dohrenwend, B. P., Shrout, P. E., Egri, G., & Mendelsohn, F. S. (1980). Nonspecific psychological distress and other dimensions of psychopathology. *Archives of General Psychiatry, 37*, 1229-1236.

Donovan, J. E., & Jessor, R. (1983). Problem drinking and the dimensions of involvement with drugs: A Guttman scalogram analysis of adolescent drug use. *American Journal of Public Health, 73*, 543-552.

Donovan, J. E., & Jessor, R. (1985). Structure of problem behavior in adolescence and young adulthood. *Journal of Consulting and Clinical Psychology, 53*, 890-904.

Donovan, J. E., Jessor, R., & Jessor, L. (1983). Problem drinking in adolescence and young adulthood: A follow-up study. *Journal of Studies on Alcohol, 44*, 109-137.

Dornbusch, S. M., Carlsmith, J. M., Gross, R. T., Martin, J. A., Jennings, D., Rosenberg, A., & Duke, P. (1981). Sexual development, age, and dating: A comparison of biological and social influences upon one set of behaviors. *Child Development, 52*, 179-185.

Downey, L. (1980). Intergenerational changes in sex behavior: A belated look at Kinsey's males. *Archives of Sexual Behavior, 9*, 267-318.

Durell, J., & Bukoski, W. (1984). Preventing substance abuse: The state of the art. *Public Health Reports, 99*, 23-31.

Eckblad, M., & Chapman, L. J. (1983). Magical ideation as an indicator of schizotypy. *Journal of Consulting and Clinical Psychology, 51*, 215-225.

Elliott, D. S., Huizinga, D., & Ageton, S. S. (1985). *Explaining delinquency and drug use*. Newbury Park, CA: Sage.

Ellis, E. H. (1979). Some problems in the study of adolescent development. *Adolescence, 14*, 101-109.

Erikson, E. H. (1959). Identity and the life cycle. *Psychological Issues, 1*, 1-171.

Erikson, E. H. (1963). *Childhood and society*. New York: Norton.

Erikson, E. H. (1968). *Identity: Youth and crisis*. New York: Norton.

Eward, A. M., Wolfe, R., Moll, P., & Harburg, E. (1986). Psychosocial and behavioral factors differentiating past drinkers and life-long abstainers. *American Journal of Public Health, 76*, 68-70.

Fawzy, F. I., Coombs, R. H., & Gerber, B. (1983). Generational continuity in the use of substances: The impact of parental substance use on adolescent substance use. *Addictive Behaviors, 8*, 109-114.

Fillmore, K. M. (1974). Drinking and problem drinking in early adulthood and middle age: An exploratory 20-year follow-up study. *Quarterly Journal of Studies on Alcohol, 35*, 819-840.

Fillmore, K. M. (1975). Relationship between specific drinking problems in early adulthood and middle age: An exploratory 20-year follow-up study. *Journal of Studies on Alcohol, 36*, 882-907.

Fischman, M. W. (1984). The behavioral pharmacology of cocaine in humans. In J. Grabowski (Ed.), *Cocaine: Pharmacology, effects, and treatment of abuse* (pp. 72-91). Rockville, MD: National Institute on Drug Abuse.

Fischman, M. W., & Schuster, C. R. (1981). Acute tolerance to cocaine in humans. In L. S. Harris (Ed.), *Problems of drug dependence, 1980*. Rockville, MD: National Institute on Drug Abuse.

Fisher, D. G., MacKinnon, D. P., Anglin, M. D., & Thompson, J. P. (1987). Parental influences on substance use: Gender differences and stage theory. *Journal of Drug Education, 17*, 69-85.

Flay, B. R. (1985). Psychosocial approaches to smoking prevention: A review of findings. *Health Psychology, 4*, 449-488.

Fleming, J. P., Kellam, S. G., & Brown, C. H. (1982). Early predictors of age at first use of alcohol, marijuana, and cigarettes. *Drug and Alcohol Dependence, 9*, 285-303.

Freeman, E. W., Rickels, K., Huggins, G. R., Mudd, E. H., Garcia, C., & Dickens, H. O. (1980). Adolescent contraceptive use: Comparison of male and female attitudes and information. *American Journal of Public Health, 70*, 790-797.

Freud, A. (1958). Adolescence. In R. S. Eissler et al. (Eds.), *Psychoanalytic study of the child* (Vol. 13). New York: International Universities Press.

Freud, A. (1969). Adolescence as a developmental disturbance. In G. Caplan & S. Lebovici (Eds.), *Adolescence*. New York: Basic Books.

Friedman, A., Glickman, N., & Utada, A. (1985). Does drug and alcohol use lead to failure to graduate from high school? *Journal of Drug Education, 15*, 353-364.

Funder, D. C., Block, J. H., & Block, J. (1983). Delay of gratification: Some longitudinal personality correlates. *Journal of Personality and Social Psychology, 44*, 1198-1213.

Geis, B. D., & Gerrard, M. (1984). Predicting male and female contraceptive behavior: A discriminant analysis of groups high, moderate, and low in contraceptive effectiveness. *Journal of Personality and Social Psychology, 46*, 699-680.

Glick, P. C., & Lin, S. (1986). More young adults are living with their parents: Who are they. *Journal of Marriage and the Family, 48*, 107-112.

Glynn, T. J., Leukefeld, C. G., & Ludford, J. P. (Eds.). (1983). *Preventing adolescent drug abuse: Intervention strategies* (Research Monograph #47). Rockville, MD: National Institute on Drug Abuse.

Gold, M. S., Washton, A. M., & Dakis, C. A. (1985). Cocaine abuse: Neurochemistry, phenomenology, and treatment. In N. J. Kozel & E. H. Adams (Eds.), *Cocaine use in America: Epidemiologic and clinical perspectives*. Rockville, MD: National Institute on Drug Abuse.

Gollob, H. F., & Reichardt, C. S. (1987). Taking account of time lags in causal models. *Child Development, 58*, 80-92.

Gordon, T., & Kannel, W. B. (1984). Drinking and mortality: The Framingham Study. *American Journal of Epidemiology, 120*, 97-107.

Gossett, J. T., Lewis, J. M., & Phillips, V. A. (1972). Psychological characteristics of adolescent drug users and abstainers: Some implications for preventive education. *Bulletin of the Menninger Clinic, 36*, 425-435.

Goswick, R. A., & Jones, W. H. (1981). Loneliness, self-concept, and adjustment. *Journal of Psychology, 107*, 237-240.

Gupta, N., & Jenkins, G. D. (1984). Substance use as an employee response to the work environment. *Journal of Vocational Behavior, 24*, 84-93.

Halikas, J. A., Weller, R. A., Morse, C. L., & Hoffman, R. G. (1983). Regular marijuana use and its effect on psychosocial variables: A longitudinal study. *Comprehensive Psychiatry, 24*, 229-235.

Harlow, L. L. (1985). *Behavior of some elliptical theory estimators with nonnormal data in a covariance structures framework: A Monte Carlo study*. Doctoral dissertation, University of California, Los Angeles.

Harlow, L. L., Newcomb, M. D., & Bentler, P. M. (1986). Depression, self derogation, substance use, and suicide ideation: Lack of purpose in life as a mediational factor. *Journal of Clinical Psychology, 42,* 5-21.

Harlow, L. L., Newcomb, M. D., & Bentler, P. M. (1987). Purpose in life test: A psychometric assessment using latent variable methodology. *British Journal of Clinical Psychology.*

Hass, A. (1981). *Teenage sexuality: A survey of teenage sexual behavior.* Los Angeles: Pinnacle Books.

Havighurst, R. J. (1952). *Developmental tasks and education.* New York: McKay.

Havighurst, R. J. (1972). *Developmental tasks and education* (3rd ed.). New York: McKay.

Hawkins, J. D., Lishner, D. M., & Catalano, R. F. (1985). Childhood predictors and the prevention of adolescent substance abuse. In C. L. Jones & R. J. Battjes (Eds.), *Etiology of drug abuse: Implications for prevention* (pp. 75-125) (Research Monograph #56). Rockville, MD: National Institute on Drug Abuse.

Hays, R. D., & DiMatteo, M. R. (in press). A short-term measure of loneliness. *Journal of Personality Assessment.*

Hays, R. D., Widaman, K. F., DiMatteo, M. R., & Stacy, A. W. (1987). Structural equation models of current drug use: Are appropriate models so simple(x)? *Journal of Personality and Social Psychology, 52,* 134-144.

Healthy people: The surgeon general's report on health promotion and disease prevention. (1979). Washington, DC: Government Printing Office.

Hendin, H., & Haas, A. P. (1985). The adaptive significance of chronic marijuana use for adolescents and adults. *Advances in Alcohol and Substance Abuse, 5,* 99-115.

Hirschi, T. (1969). *Causes of delinquency.* Berkeley: University of California Press.

Hirschi, T., & Selvin, H. (1973). *Principles of survey analysis.* New York: Free Press.

Hogan, D. P. (1981). *Transitions and social change: The early lives of American men.* New York: Academic Press.

Hornick, J. P. (1978). Premarital sexual attitudes and behavior. *Sociological Quarterly, 19,* 534-544.

Hojat, M. (1982). Psychometric characteristics of the UCLA Loneliness Scales: A study with Iranian college students. *Educational and Psychological Measurement, 42,* 917-925.

Huba, G. J., & Bentler, P. M. (1980). The role of peer and adult models for drug taking at different stages in adolescence. *Journal of Youth and Adolescence, 9,* 499-465.

Huba, G. J., & Bentler, P. M. (1982). A developmental theory of drug use: Derivation and assessment of a causal modeling approach. In B. P. Baltes & O. G. Brim, Jr. (Eds.), *Life-span development and behavior* (Vol. 4, pp. 147-203). New York: Academic Press.

Huba, G. J., & Bentler, P. M. (1983a). Causal models of the development of law abidance and its relationship to psychosocial factors and drug use. In W. S. Laufer & J. M. Day (Eds.), *Personality theory, moral development, and criminal behavior* (pp. 165-215). Lexington, MA: D. C. Heath.

Huba, G. J., & Bentler, P. M. (1983b). Test of a drug use causal model using asymptotically distribution free methods. *Journal of Drug Education, 13,* 3-14.

Huba, G. J., & Bentler, P. M. (1984). Causal models of personality, peer culture characteristics, drug use, and criminal behaviors over a five-year span. In D. W. Goodwin, K. T. Van Dusen, & S. A. Mednick (Eds.), *Longitudinal research in alcoholism* (pp. 73-94). Boston: Klower-Nijhof.

Huba, G. J., & Harlow, L. L. (1986). Robust estimation for causal models: A comparison of methods in some developmental datasets. In R. M. Lerner & D. L. Featherman (Eds.), *Life-span development and behavior* (Vol. 6, pp. 69-111). New York: Academic Press.

Huba, G. J., & Harlow, L. L. (1987). Robust structural equation models: Implications for developmental psychology. *Child Development, 58*, 147-166.

Huba, G. J., Newcomb, M. D., & Bentler, P. M. (1986). Adverse drug experiences and drug use behaviors: A one-year longitudinal study of adolescents. *Journal of Pediatric Psychology, 11*, 203-219.

Huba, G. J., Newcomb, M. D., & Bentler, P. M. (1987). *The effects on drug use on health and psychological distress among adolescents.* Under editorial review for publication.

Huba, G. J., Wingard, J. A., & Bentler, P. M. (1980). Framework for an interactive theory of drug use. In D. J. Letticri, M. Sayers, & H. W. Pearson (Eds.), *Theories on drug abuse.* Rockville, MD: National Institute on Drug Abuse.

Huba, G. J., Wingard, J. A., & Bentler, P. M. (1981). A comparison of two latent variable causal models for adolescent drug use. *Journal of Personality and Social Psychology, 40*, 180-193.

Jessor, R. (1986). Adolescent problem drinking: Psychosocial aspects and developmental outcomes. In R. K. Silbereisen, K. Eyferth, & G. Rudinger (Eds.), *Development as action in context: Problem behavior and normal youth development* (pp. 241-264). Berlin: Springer-Verlag.

Jessor, R., Chase, J. A., & Donovan, J. E. (1980). Psychosocial correlates of marijuana use and problem drinking in a national sample of adolescents. *American Journal of Public Health, 70*, 604-613.

Jessor, R., Costa, F., Jessor, L., & Donovan, J. E. (1983). Time of first intercourse: A prospective study. *Journal of Personality and Social Psychology, 44*, 608-626.

Jessor, R., & Jessor, S. L. (1977). *Problem behavior and psychosocial development.* New York: Academic Press.

Jessor, R., & Jessor, S. L. (1978). Theory testing in longitudinal research on marijuana use. In D. B. Kandel (Ed.), *Longitudinal research on drug use: Empirical findings and methodological issues* (pp. 41-71). Washington, DC: Hemisphere.

Jessor, S. L., & Jessor R. (1975). Transition from virginity to nonvirginity among youth: A social-psychological study over time. *Developmental Psychology, 11*, 473-484.

Johnston, L. D., & O'Malley, P. M. (1985). Issues of validity and population coverage in student surveys of drug use. In B. A. Rouse, N. J. Kozel, & L. G. Richards (Eds.), *Self-report methods of estimating drug use: Meeting current challenges to validity* (pp. 31-54) (Research Monograph #57). Rockville, MD: National Institute on Drug Abuse.

Johnston, L. D., O'Malley, P. M., & Bachman, J. G. (1986). *Drug use among American high school students, college students, and other young adults: National trends Through 1985.* Rockville, MD: National Institute on Drug Abuse.

Johnston, L. D., O'Malley, P. M., & Eveland, L. K. (1978). Drugs and delinquency: A search for causal connections. In D. B. Kandel (Ed.), *Longitudinal research on drug use: Empirical findings and methodological issues* (pp. 137-156). Washington, DC: Hemisphere.

Jones, C. L., & Battjes, R. J. (1985). *Etiology of drug abuse: Implications for prevention* (Research Monograph #56). Rockville, MD: National Institute on Drug Abuse.

Jones, M. C. (1968). Personality correlates and antecedents of drinking patterns in adult males. *Journal of Consulting and Clinical Psychology, 36*, 2-12.

Jones, M. C. (1971). Personality antecedents and correlates of drinking patterns in women. *Journal of Consulting and Clinical Psychology, 36*, 61-69.

Jones, R. T. (1984). The pharmacology of cocaine. In J. Grabowski (Ed.), *Cocaine: Pharmacology, effects, and treatment of abuse* (pp. 34-53). Rockville, MD: National Institute on Drug Abuse.

Jöreskog, K. G. (1977). Structural equation models in the social sciences: Specification, estimation, and testing. In P. R. Krishnaiah (Ed.), *Application of statistics* (pp. 265-287). North-Holland.

Jöreskog, K. G., & Sörbom, D. (1985). *LISREL VI: Users guide*. Mooreville, IN: Scientific Software.

Jorgensen, S. R., & Sontegard, J. S. (1984). Predicting adolescent sexual and contraceptive behavior: An application and test of the Fishbein model. *Journal of Marriage and the Family, 46*, 43-55.

Judd, C. M., Jessor, R., & Donovan, J. E. (1986). Structural equation models and personality research. *Journal of Personality, 54*, 149-198.

Jurich, A. P. (1979). Differential determinants of premarital sexual standards among college students. *Adolescence, 14*, 797-810.

Jurich, A. P., Polson, C. J., Jurich, J. A., & Bates, R. A. (1985). Family factors in the lives of drug users and abusers. *Adolescence, 20*, 142-159.

Kaestner, E., Frank, B., Marel, R., & Schmeidler, J. (1986). Substance use among females in New York State: Catching up with the males. *Advances in Alcohol and Substance Abuse, 5*, 29-49.

Kandel, D. B. (1973). Adolescent marijuana use: Role of parents and peers. *Science, 181*, 1067-1070.

Kandel, D. B. (1978). Convergences in prospective longitudinal surveys of drug use in normal populations. In D. Kandel (Ed.), *Longitudinal research on drug use: Empirical findings and methodological issues* (pp. 3-38). Washington, DC: Hemisphere.

Kandel, D. B. (1980). Drug and drinking behavior among youth. *Annual Review of Sociology, 6*, 235-285.

Kandel, D. B. (1984). Marijuana users in young adulthood. *Archives of General Psychiatry, 41*, 200-209.

Kandel, D. B. (1985). On processes of peer influences in adolescent drug use: A developmental perspective. *Advances in Alcohol and Substance Abuse, 4*, 139-163.

Kandel, D. B. (1986). Processes of peer influences in adolescence. In R. K. Silbereisen, K. Eyferth, & G. Rudinger (Eds.), *Development as action in context: Problem behavior and normal youth development* (pp. 203-227). Berlin: Springer-Verlag.

Kandel, D. B., Davies, M., Karus, D., & Yamaguchi, K. (1986). The consequences in young adulthood of adolescent drug involvement. *Archives of General Psychiatry, 43*, 746-754.

Kandel, D. B., Davies, M., & Raveis, V. H. (1985). The stressfulness of daily social roles for women: Marital, occupational, and household roles. *Journal of Health and Social Behavior, 26*, 64-78.

Kandel, D. B., & Faust, R. (1975). Sequence and stages in patterns of adolescent drug use. *Archives of General Psychiatry, 32*, 923-932.

Kandel, D. B., Murphy, D., & Karus, D. (1985). Cocaine use in young adulthood: Patterns of use and psychosocial correlates. In N. J. Kozel & E. H. Adams (Eds.), *Cocaine use in America: Epidemiologic and clinical perspectives* (pp. 76-110). Rockville, MD: National Institute on Drug Abuse.

Kandel, D. B., Simcha-Fagan, O., & Davies, M. (1986). Risk factors for delinquency and illicit drug use from adolescence to young adulthood. *Journal of Drug Issues, 16*, 67-90.

Kaplan, H. B. (1975). Increase in self-rejection as an antecedent of deviant responses. *Journal of Youth and Adolescence, 4*, 438-458.

Kaplan, H. B. (1980). *Deviant behavior in defense of self.* New York: Academic Press.

Kaplan, H. B. (1984). *Patterns of juvenile delinquency.* Newbury Park, CA: Sage.

Kaplan, H. B. (1985). Testing a general theory of drug abuse and other deviant adaptations. *Journal of Drug Issues, 15*, 477-492.

Kaplan, H. B. (1986). *Social psychology self-referent behavior.* New York: Plenum.

Kaplan, H. B., Martin, S. S., & Robbins, C. (1984). Pathways to adolescent drug use: Self-derogation, peer influence, weakening of social controls, and early substance use. *Journal of Health and Social Behavior, 25*, 270-289.

Kessler, R. C., & McLeod, J. D. (1985). Social support and mental health in community samples. In S. Cohen & S. L. Syme (Eds.), *Social support and health* (pp. 219-240). New York: Academic Press.

Khantzian, E. J., & Khantzian, N. J. (1984). Cocaine addiction: Is there a psychological predisposition. *Psychiatric Annals, 14*, 753-759.

Kim, J. O., & Ferree, G. D. (1981). Standardization in causal analysis. *Sociological Methods & Research, 10*, 187-210.

Kinder, B. N., Pape, N., & Walfish, S. (1980). Drug and alcohol education programs: A review of outcome studies. *International Journal of the Addictions, 7*, 1035-1054.

Kitsuse, J. I. (1962). Societal reaction to deviant behavior: Problems of theory and method. *Social Problems, 9*, 247-257.

Klatsky, A. L., Friedman, G., & Siegelaub, A. B. (1981). Alcohol and mortality: A ten-year Kaiser-Permanente experience. *Annals of Internal Medicine, 95*, 139-145.

Kovach, J. A., & Glickman, N. W. (1986). Levels and psychosocial correlates of adolescent drug use. *Journal of Youth and Adolescence, 15*, 61-77.

Labouvie, E. W. (1986). The coping function of adolescent alcohol and drug use. In R. K. Silbereisen, K. Eyferth, & G. Rudinger (Eds.), *Development as action in context: Problem behavior and normal youth development* (pp. 229-239). Berlin: Springer-Verlag.

Leavy, R. L. (1983). Social support and psychological disorder: A review. *Journal of Community Psychology, 11*, 3-21.

LeCoq, L. L., & Capuzzi, D. (1984, June). Preventing adolescent drug abuse. *Humanistic Education and Development*, pp. 155-169.

Lee, S.-Y. (1986). Analysis of conditional covariance structures. *Computational Statistics & Data Analysis, 4*, 41-59.

Lee, S.-Y., & Bentler, P. M. (1980). Some asymptotic properties of constrained generalized least squares estimation in covariance structure models. *South African Statistical Journal, 14*, 121-136.

Lerner, R. M. (1985). Adolescent maturational changes and psychosocial development: A dynamic interactional perspective. *Journal of Youth and Adolescence, 14*, 355-372.

Lettieri, D. J. (1985). Drug abuse: A review of explanations and models of explanations. *Advances in Alcohol and Substance Abuse, 4*, 9-40.

Lettieri, D. J., Sayers, M., & Pearson, H. W. (1980). *Theories on drug abuse: Selected contemporary perspectives.* Rockville, MD: National Institute on Drug Abuse.

Levenson, R. W., & Gottman, J. M. (1978). Toward the assessment of social competence. *Journal of Consulting and Clinical Psychology, 46*, 453-462.

Libby, R. W., Gray, L., & White, M. (1978). A test and reformulation of reference group and role correlates of premarital permissiveness theory. *Journal of Marriage and the Family, 40*, 79-82.

Long, J.V.F., & Scherl, D. J. (1984). Developmental antecedents of compulsive drug use: A report on the literature. *Journal of Psychoactive Drugs, 16*, 169-182.

Loper, R., Kammier, M., & Hoffman, H. (1973). MMPI characteristics of college freshmen who later become alcoholics. *Journal of Abnormal Psychology, 82*, 159-162.

Lowe, G. D., & Witt, D. D. (1984). Early marriage as a career contingency: The prediction of educational attainment. *Journal of Marriage and the Family, 46*, 689-698.

MacCallum, R. (1986). Specification searches in covariance structure analyses. *Psychological Bulletin, 100*, 107-120.

Maddux, J. F., & Desmond, D. P. (1984). Heroin addicts and nonaddicted brothers. *American Journal of Drug and Alcohol Abuse, 10*, 237-248.

Magnusson, D., Stattin, H., & Allen, V. L. (1985). Biological maturation and social development: A longitudinal study of some adjustment processes from mid-adolescence to adulthood. *Journal of Youth and Adolescence, 14*, 267-283.

Manatt, M. (1986). *Parents, peers and pot II: Parents in action.* Rockville, MD: National Institute on Drug Abuse.

Margulies, R. Z., Kessler, R. C., & Kandel, D. B. (1977). A longitudinal study of onset of drinking among high school students. *Journal of Studies on Alcohol, 38*, 897-912.

Marty, P. J., McDermott, R. J., & Williams, T. (1986). Patterns of smokeless tobacco use in a population of high school students. *American Journal of Public Health, 76*, 190-192.

Matarazzo, J. D. (1982). Behavioral health's challenge to academic, scientific, and professional psychology. *American Psychologist, 37*, 1-14.

McCarthy, W. J., Newcomb, M. D., Maddahian, E., & Skager, R. (1986). Use of smokeless tobacco among adolescents: Demographic differences, use of other substances, and psychological correlates. *Journal of Drug Education, 16*, 383-402.

Mellinger, G. D., Somers, R. H., Bazell, S., & Manheimer, D. I. (1978). *Drug use, academic performance, and career indecision: Longitudinal data in search of a model.* In D. B. Kandel (Ed.), *Longitudinal research on drug use* (pp. 157-177). Washington, DC: Hemisphere.

Mellinger, G. D., Somers, R. H., Davidson, S. T., & Manheimer, D. I. (1976). The amotivational syndrome and the college student. *Annals of the New York Academy of Science, 282*, 37-55.

Miller, J. D., Cisin, I. H., Gardner-Keaton, H., Harrell, A. V., Wirtz, P. W., Abelson, H. I., & Fishburne, P. M. (1983). *National survey on drug abuse: Main findings 1982.* Rockville, MD: National Institute on Drug Abuse.

Miller, L. L. (1979). Cannabis and the brain with special reference to the limbic system. In G. G. Nahas & W. D. Patton (Eds.), *Marijuana: Biological effects.* Elmwood, NY: Pergamon.

Miller, W. B. (1958). Lower class culture as a generating milieu of gang delinquency. *Journal of Social Issues, 14*, 5-19.

Mills, C. J., & Noyes, H. L. (1984). Patterns and correlates of initial and subsequent drug use among adolescents. *Journal of Consulting and Clinical Psychology, 52*, 231-243.

Miranue, A. C. (1979). Marihuana use and achievement orientations of college students. *Journal of Health and Social Behavior, 20*, 194-199.

Mitchell, R. E., Billings, A. G., & Moos, R. H. (1982). Social support and well-being: Implications for prevention programs. *Journal of Primary Prevention, 3*, 77-98.

Mooijaart, A., & Bentler, P. M. (1987). *Robustness of normal theory statistics in structural equation models.* Manuscript under editorial review.

Mott, F. L., & Moore, S. F. (1979). The causes of marital disruption among young American women: An interdisciplinary perspective. *Journal of Marriage and the Family, 41*, 355-365.

Mulaik, S. (1987). Toward a conception of causality applicable to experimentation and causal modeling. *Child Development, 58*, 18-32.

Murstein, B. I., & Holden, C. C. (1979). Sexual behavior and correlates among college students. *Adolescence, 14*, 625-639.

Muthen, B., & Kaplan, D. (1985). A comparison of methodologies for the factor analysis of non-normal Likert variables. *British Journal of Mathematical and Statistical Psychology, 38*, 171-180.

Naditch, M. P. (1974). Acute adverse reaction to psychoactive drugs, drug usage, psychopathology. *Journal of Abnormal Psychology, 83*, 394-403.

Naditch, M. P. (1975). Ego mechanisms and marihuana usage. In D. J. Lettieri (Ed.), *Predicting adolescent drug abuse: A review of issues, methods, and correlates* (pp. 207-222). Rockville, MD: National Institute on Drug Abuse.

Naditch, M. P., Alker, P. C., & Joffe, P. (1975). Individual differences and settings as determinants of acute adverse reactions to psychoactive drugs. *Journal of Nervous and Mental Disease, 161*, 326-335.

Newcomb, M. D. (1981). Heterosexual cohabitation relationships. In S. Duck & R. Gilmour (Eds.), *Personal relationships 1: Studying personal relationships* (pp. 131-164). London: Academic Press.

Newcomb, M. D. (1983). Relationship qualities of those who live together. *Alternative Lifestyles, 6*, 78-102.

Newcomb, M. D. (1984). Sexual behavior, responsiveness, and attitudes among women: A test of two theories. *Journal of Sex and Marital Therapy, 10*, 272-286.

Newcomb, M. D. (1985). Sexual experience among men and women: Associations within three independent samples. *Psychological Reports, 56*, 603-614.

Newcomb, M. D. (1986a). Nuclear attitudes and reactions: Associations with depression, drug use, and quality of life. *Journal of Personality and Social Psychology, 50*, 906-920.

Newcomb, M. D. (1986b). Sexual behavior of cohabitors: A comparison of three independent samples. *Journal of Sex Research, 22*, 492-513.

Newcomb, M. D. (1986c). Cohabitation, marriage, and divorce among adolescents and young adults. *Journal of Social and Personal Relationships, 3*, 473-494.

Newcomb, M. D. (in press). *Drug use in the workplace: Risk factors for disruptive substance use among young adults.* Dover, MA: Auburn House.

Newcomb, M. D., & Bentler, P. M. (1980a). Cohabitation before marriage: A comparison of couples who did and did not cohabit. *Alternative Lifestyles, 3*, 65-85.

Newcomb, M. D., & Bentler, P. M. (1980b). Assessment of personality and demographic aspects of cohabitation and marital success. *Journal of Personality Assessment, 44*, 11-24.

Newcomb, M. D., & Bentler, P. M. (1981). Marital breakdown. In S. Duck & R. Gilmour (Eds.), *Personal relationships 3: Personal relationships in disorder* (pp. 57-94). London: Academic Press.

Newcomb, M. D., & Bentler, P. M. (1983). Dimensions of subjective female orgasmic responsiveness. *Journal of Personality and Social Psychology, 44*, 862-873.

Newcomb, M. D., & Bentler, P. M. (1985). The impact of high school substance use on choice of young adult living environment and career direction. *Journal of Drug Education, 15*, 253-261.

Newcomb, M. D., & Bentler, P. M. (1986a). Drug use, educational aspirations, and workforce involvement: The transition from adolescence to young adulthood. *American Journal of Community Psychology, 14*, 303-321.

Newcomb, M. D., & Bentler, P. M. (1986b). Cocaine use among adolescents: Longitudinal associations with social context, psychopathology, and use of other substances. *Addictive Behaviors, 11*, 263-273.

Newcomb, M. D., & Bentler, P. M. (1986c). Frequency and sequence of drug use: A longitudinal study from early adolescence to young adulthood. *Journal of Drug Education, 16*, 101-120.

Newcomb, M. D., & Bentler, P. M. (1986d). Cocaine use among young adults. *Advances in Alcohol and Substance Abuse, 6*, 73-96.

Newcomb, M. D., & Bentler, P. M. (1986e). Loneliness and social support: A confirmatory hierarchical analysis. *Personality and Social Psychology Bulletin, 12*, 520-535.

Newcomb, M. D., & Bentler, P. M. (1987a). Changes in drug from high school to young adulthood: Effects of living arrangement and current life pursuit. *Journal of Applied Developmental Psychology*.

Newcomb, M. D., & Bentler, P. M. (1987b). The impact of late adolescent substance use on young adult health status and utilization of health services: A structural-equation model over four years. *Social Science and Medicine, 24*, 71-82.

Newcomb, M. D., & Bentler, P. M. (in press). The impact of family context, deviant attitudes, and emotional distress on adolescent drug use: Longitudinal latent variable analyses of mothers and their children. *Journal of Research in Personality*.

Newcomb, M. D., Bentler, P. M., & Collins, C. (1986). Alcohol use and dissatisfaction with self and life: A longitudinal analysis of young adults. *Journal of Drug Issues, 16*, 479-494.

Newcomb, M. D., & Harlow, L. L. (1986). Life events and substance use among adolescents: Mediating effects of perceived loss of control and meaninglessness in life. *Journal of Personality and Social Psychology, 51*, 564-577.

Newcomb, M. D., Harlow, L. L., & Bentler, P. M. (1985, April). *The purpose in life test: Exploratory, confirmatory, and validational analyses.* Paper presented at the Western Psychological Association, San Jose, CA.

Newcomb, M. D., Huba, G. J., & Bentler, P. M. (1981). A multidimensional assessment of stressful life events among adolescents: Derivation and correlates. *Journal of Health and Social Behavior, 22*, 400-415.

Newcomb, M. D., Huba, G. J., & Bentler, P. M. (1983). Mother's influence on the drug use of their children: Confirmatory tests of direct modeling and mediational theories. *Developmental Psychology, 19*, 714-726.

Newcomb, M. D., Huba, G. J., & Bentler, P. M. (1986a). Desirability of various life change events among adolescents: Effects of exposure, sex, age, and ethnicity. *Journal of Research in Personality, 20*, 207-227.

Newcomb, M. D., Huba, G. J., & Bentler, P. M. (1986b). Life change events among adolescents: An empirical consideration of some methodological issues. *Journal of Nervous and Mental Disease, 174*, 280-289.

Newcomb, M. D., Huba, G. J., & Bentler, P. M. (1986c). Determinants of sexual and dating behavior among adolescents. *Journal of Personality and Social Psychology, 50*, 428-438.

Newcomb, M. D., Maddahian, E., & Bentler, P. M. (1986). Risk factors for drug use among adolescents: Concurrent and longitudinal analyses. *American Journal of Public Health, 76*, 525-531.

Newcomb, M. D., Maddahian, E., Skager, R., & Bentler, P. M. (1987). Substance abuse and psychosocial risk factors among teenagers: Associations with sex, age, ethnicity, and type of school. *American Journal of Drug and Alcohol Abuse, 13*, 413-433.

Newman, I. M. (1984). Capturing the energy of peer pressure: Insights from a longitudinal study of adolescent cigarette smoking. *Journal of School Health, 54*, 146-148.

Nicholi, A. M. (1983). The college student and marijuana: Research findings concerning adverse biological and psychological effects. *Journal of American College Health, 32*, 73-77.

Nicholi, A. M. (1984). Cocaine use among the college age group: Biological and psychological effects—clinical and laboratory research findings. *Journal of American College Health, 32*, 258-261.

NIDA (National Institute on Drug Abuse). (1986). *Capsules: Overview of the 1985 national household survey on drug abuse.* Rockville, MD: Author.

Nye, F. I. (1976). *Role structure and analysis of the family.* Newbury Park, CA: Sage.

Nye, F. I. (1982). *Family relationships: Rewards and costs.* Newbury Park, CA: Sage.

Orford, J., & O'Reilly, P. (1981). Disorders in the family. In S. Duck & R. Gilmour (Eds.), *Personal relationships 3: Personal relationships in disorder* (pp. 123-140). London: Academic Press.

Osgood, D. W. (1985). *The drug-crime connection and the generality and stability of deviance.* Paper presented at the meetings of the American Society of Criminology.

Paton, S., Kessler, R. C., & Kandel, D. B. (1977). Depressive mood and illegal drug use: A longitudinal analysis. *Journal of Genetic Psychology, 131*, 267-289.

Peele, S. (1986). The life study of alcoholism: Putting drunkenness in biographical context. *Bulletin in the Society of Psychologists in Addictive Behaviors, 5*, 49-53.

Penning, M., & Barnes, G. E. (1982). Adolescent marijuana use: A review. *International Journal of the Addictions, 17*, 749-791.

Pentz, M. A. (1985). Social competence and self-efficacy as determinants of substance use in adolescence. In S. Shiffman & T. A. Wills (Eds.), *Coping and substance use* (pp. 117-142). Orlando, FL: Academic Press.

Peplau, L. A., & Perlman, D. (1982). Perspectives on loneliness. In L. A. Peplau & D. Perlman (Eds.), *Loneliness: A sourcebook of current theory, research, and therapy* (pp. 1-20). New York: Wiley-Interscience.

Perry, C. L., & Jessor, R. (1985). The concept of health promotion and the prevention of adolescent drug abuse. *Health Education Quarterly, 12*, 169-184.

Petrie, K., & Chamberlain, K. (1983). Hopelessness and social desirability as moderating variables in predicting suicide behavior. *Journal of Consulting and Clinical Psychology, 51*, 485-487

Piaget, J. (1962). *Play, dreams, and imitation in childhood.* New York: Norton.

Piaget, J. (1972). Intellectual evolution from adolescence to adulthood. *Human Development, 15*, 1-12.

Polich, J. M., Ellickson, P. L., Reuter, P., & Kahan, J. P. (1984). *Strategies for controlling adolescent drug use.* Santa Monica, CA: Rand.

Polk, K., & Halferty, D. (1966). Adolescence, commitment, and delinquency. *Journal of Research in Crime and Delinquency, 4*, 82-96.

Pope, H., & Mueller, C. W. (1979). The intergenerational transmission of marital instability: Comparisons by race and class. In G. Levinger & O.C. Moles (Eds.), *Divorce and separation*. New York: Basic Books.

Quayle, D. (1983). American productivity: The devastating effect of alcoholism and drug abuse. *American Psychologist, 38*, 454-458.

Raboch, J., & Bartak, V. (1980). Changes in the sexual life of Czechoslovakian women born between 1911 and 1958. *Archives of Sexual Behavior, 9*, 494-502.

Radloff, L. S. (1977). The CES-D scale: A self-report depression scale for research in the general population. *Applied Psychological Measurement, 1*, 385-401.

Ralph, N., & Spigner, C. (1986). Contraceptive practices among female heroin addicts. *American Journal of Public Health, 76*, 1016-1017.

Reader's Digest (1987). Can cocaine conquer America? *Reader's Digest, 130*, 30-38.

Reckless, W. C. (1967). *The crime problem*. New York: Appleton-Century-Crofts.

Reeder, L. G. (1977). Sociocultural factors in the etiology of smoking behaviors: An assessment. In M. E. Jarvik, J. W. Cullen, E. R. Gritz, & L. J. West (Eds.), *Research on smoking behavior* (Research Monograph #17, pp. 186-201). Rockville, MD: National Institute on Drug Abuse.

Reichardt, C. S., & Gollob, H. F. (1986). Satisfying the constraints of causal modeling. In W.M.K. Trochim (Ed.), *Advances in quasi-experimental design and analysis* (pp. 91-107). San Francisco: Jossey-Bass.

Reiss, I. L. (1981). Some observations on ideology and sexuality in America. *Journal of Marriage and the Family, 43*, 271-283.

Richman, A., & Warren, R. A. (1985). Alcohol consumption and morbidity in the Canada Health Survey: Inter-beverage differences. *Drug and Alcohol Dependence, 15*, 255-282.

Richmond, J. H. (1979). *Smoking and health: A report of the Surgeon General*. Washington, DC: Government Printing Office.

Richmond, J., & Peeples, D. (1984). Rural drug abuse prevention: A structured program for middle schools. *Journal of Counseling and Development, 63*, 113-114.

Rittenhouse, J. D., & Miller, J. D. (1984). Social learning and teenage drug use: An analysis of family dyads. *Health Psychology, 3*, 329-346.

Robins, L. N. (1984). The natural history of adolescent drug use. *American Journal of Public Health, 74*, 656-657.

Robins, L. N., Darvish, H. S., & Murphy, G. E. (1970). The long-term outcome for adolescent drug users: A follow-up study of 76 users and 146 non-users. In J. Zubin & A. M. Freedman (Eds.), *The psychopathology of adolescence* (pp. 159-178). New York: Grune & Stratton.

Robins, L. N., & Przybeck, T. R. (1985). Age of onset of drug use as a factor in drug and other disorders. In C. L. Jones & R. J. Battjes (Eds.), *Etiology of drug abuse: Implications for prevention* (Research Monograph #56, pp. 178-192). Rockville, MD: National Institute on Drug Abuse.

Rook, K. S. (1984). The functions of social bonds: Perspectives from research on social support, loneliness, and social isolation. In I. G. Sarason & B. R. Sarason (Eds.), *Social support: Theory, research, and application* (pp. 243-267). The Hague: Martinu Nijhof.

Roscoe, B., & Petersen, K. L. (1984). Older adolescents: A self-report of engagement in developmental tasks. *Adolescence, 19*, 391-396

Rubenstein, C., & Shaver, P. (1980). Loneliness in two northeastern cities. In J. Hartog, J. R. Audy, & Y. A. Cohen (Eds.), *The anatomy of loneliness*. New York: International Universities Press.

Russell, D., Peplau, L. A., & Cutrona, C. E. (1980). The revised UCLA loneliness scale: Concurrent and discriminant validity evidence. *Journal of Personality and Social Psychology, 39,* 472-480.

Sack, A. R., Billingham, R. E., & Howard, R. D. (1985). Premarital contraceptive use: A discriminant analysis approach. *Archives of Sexual Behavior, 14,* 165-182.

Sadava, S. W. (1985). Problem behavior theory and consumption and consequences of alcohol use. *Journal of Studies on Alcohol, 46,* 392-397.

Sadava, S. W. (1987). Interactional theories. In H. T. Blane & K. E. Leonard (Eds.), *Psychological theories of drinking and alcoholism*. New York: Guilford.

Sadava, S. W., & Thompson, M. M. (in press). Loneliness, social drinking, and vulnerability to alcohol problems. *Canadian Journal of Science.*

Sarason, I. G., Levine, H. M., Basham, R. B., & Sarason, B. R. (1983). Assessing social support: The social support questionnaire. *Journal of Personality and Social Psychology, 44,* 127-139.

Sarbin, T. R., & Allen, V. L. (1968). Role theory. In G. Lindzey & E. Aronson (Eds.), *Handbook of social psychology*. Reading, MA: Addison-Wesley.

Satorra, A. (1987). *Alternative test criteria in covariance structure analysis: A unified approach*. Under editorial review for publication.

Satorra, A., & Bentler, P. M. (1986). *Robustness properties of ML statistics in covariance structure analysis*. Under editorial review for publication.

Schultz, R., Bohrnstedt, G. W., Borgatta, E. F., & Evans, R. R. (1977). Explaining premarital sexual intercourse among college students: A causal model. *Social Forces, 56,* 148-163.

Seeman, M., & Anderson, C. S. (1983). Alienation and alcohol: The role of work, mastery, and community in drinking behavior. *American Sociological Review, 48,* 60-77.

Segal, B. (1986). Intervention and prevention of drug-taking behavior: A need for divergent approaches. *International Journal of the Addictions, 21,* 165-173.

Sermat, V. (1980). Some situational and personality correlates of loneliness. In J. Hartog, J. R. Audy, & Y. A. Cohen (Eds.), *The anatomy of loneliness*. New York: International Universities Press.

Shapiro, A. (1986). Asymptotic theory of overparameterized structural models. *Journal of the American Statistical Association, 81,* 142-149.

Shiffman, S., & Wills, T. A. (1985). *Coping and substance use*. Orlando, FL: Academic Press.

Simons, R. L., & Murphy, P. I. (1985). Sex differences in the causes of adolescent suicide ideation. *Journal of Youth and Adolescence, 14,* 423-434.

Singh, B. K. (1980). Trends in attitudes toward premarital sexual relations. *Journal of Marriage and the Family, 42,* 387-393.

Smart, R. G., & Adlaf, E. M. (1982). Adverse reactions and seeking medical treatment among student cannabis users. *Drug and Alcohol Dependence, 9,* 201-211.

Smith, D. E., Wesson, D. R., & Apter-Marsh, M. (1984). Cocaine- and alcohol-induced sexual dysfunction in patients with addictive disease. *Journal of Psychoactive Drugs, 16,* 359-361.

Smith, G. M., & Fogg, C. P. (1978). Psychological predictors of early use, late use and non-use of marijuana among teenage students. In D. B. Kandel (Ed.), *Longitudinal research on drug use: Empirical findings and methodological issues* (pp. 101-113). Washington, DC: Hemisphere.

Sobel, M. E., & Arminger, G. (1986). Platonic and operational true scores in covariance structure analysis. *Sociological Methods & Research, 15*, 44-58.

Speckart, G., & Anglin, M. D. (1985). Narcotics and crime: A causal modeling approach. *Journal of Quantitative Criminology, 2*, 3-28.

Speckart, G., & Anglin, M. D. (1986). Narcotics use and crime: An analysis of existing evidence for a causal relationship. *Behavioral Science and the Law, 3*, 259-283.

Spotts, J. V., & Shontz, F. C. (1983). Psychopathology and chronic drug use: A methodological paradigm. *International Journal of the Addictions, 18*, 633-680.

Starr, J. M. (1986). American youth in the 1980s. *Youth & Society, 17*, 323-345.

Steiger, J. H., Shapiro, A., & Browne, M. W. (1985). On the multivariate asymptotic distribution of sequential chi-square statistics. *Psychometrika, 50*, 253-263.

Stein, J. A., Newcomb, M. D., & Bentler, P. M. (1986a). Stability and change in personality: A longitudinal study from early adolescence to young adulthood. *Journal of Research in Personality, 20*, 276-291.

Stein, J. A., Newcomb, M. D., & Bentler, P. M. (1986b). The relationship of gender, social conformity, and substance use: A longitudinal study. *Bulletin of the Society of Psychologist in Addictive Behaviors, 5*, 125-138.

Stein, J. A., Newcomb, M. D., & Bentler, P. M. (1987). An eight-year study of multiple influences on drug use and drug use consequences. *Journal of Personality and Social Psychology, 53*, 1099-1105.

Suwaki, H. (1983). A follow-up study of adolescent glue-sniffers in Japan. *British Journal of Addiction, 78*, 409-413.

Tanaka, J. S., & Bentler, P. M. (1985). Quasi-likelihood estimation in asymptotically efficient covariance structure models. In. *1984 Proceedings of the American Statistical Association* (Social Statistics Section, pp. 658-662).

Tanaka, J. S., & Huba, G. J. (1984). Confirmatory hierarchical factor analyses of psychological distress measures. *Journal of Personality and Social Psychology, 46*, 621-635.

Tobler, N. S. (1986). Meta-analysis of 143 adolescent drug prevention programs: Quantitative outcome results of program participants compared to a control or comparison group. *Journal of Drug Issues, 16*, 537-568.

Udry, J. R. (1980). Changes in the frequency of marital intercourse from panel data. *Archives of Sexual Behavior, 9*, 319-326.

Vicary, J. R., & Lerner, J. V. (1986). Parental attributes and adolescent drug use. *Journal of Adolescence, 9*, 115-123.

Vingilis, E., & Smart, R. (1981). Physical dependence on alcohol in youth. In Y. Israel, F. Glaser, H. Kalent, R. Popham, W. Schmidt, & R. Smart (Eds.), *Research advances in alcohol and drug problems* (Vol. 6). New York: Plenum.

Voss, H. (1969). Differential association and containment theory: A theoretical convergence. *Social Forces, 47*, 381-391.

Voss, H. L., & Clayton, R. R. (1984). "Turning on" other persons to drugs. *International Journal of the Addictions, 19*, 633-652.

Washton, A. M., & Gold, M. S. (1984). Chronic cocaine abuse: Evidence for adverse effects on health and functioning. *Psychiatric Annals, 14*, 733-739.

Wertheim, E. H., & Schwartz, J. C. (1983). Depression, guilt, and self-management of pleasant and unpleasant events. *Journal of Personality and Social Psychology, 45*, 884-889.

Wheaton, B. (in press). Assessment of fit in overidentified models with latent variables. In J. S. Long (Ed.), *Common problems in quantitative social research*. Newbury Park, CA: Sage.

White, C. B. (1982). Sexual interest, attitudes, knowledge, and sexual history in relation to sexual behavior in the institutionalized age. *Archives of Sexual Behavior, 11*, 11-21.

Williams, R., & Thomson, E. (1986). Normalization issues in latent variable modeling. *Sociological Methods & Research, 15*, 24-43, 64-68.

Wortman, C. B., & Conway, T. W. (1985). The role of social support in adaptation and recovery from physical illness. In S. Cohen & S. E. Syme (Eds.), *Social support and health* (pp. 281-302). New York: Academic Press.

Yamaguchi, K., & Kandel, D. B. (1985a). On the resolution of role incompatibility: A life event history analysis of family roles and marijuana use. *American Journal of Sociology, 90*, 1284-1325.

Yamaguchi, K., & Kandel, D. B. (1985b). Dynamic relationships between premarital cohabitation and illicit drug use: An event history analysis of role selection and role socialization. *American Sociological Review, 50*, 530-546.

Young, J. E. (1982). Loneliness, depression, and cognitive therapy: Theory and application. In L. A. Peplau & D. Perlman (Eds.), *Loneliness: A sourcebook of current theory, research, and therapy* (pp. 379-405). New York: Wiley-Interscience.

Zabin, L. S. (1984). The association between smoking and sexual behavior among teens in US contraceptive clinics. *American Journal of Public Health, 74*, 261-263.

Zelnik, M., Kantner, J. F., & Ford, K. (1981). *Sex and pregnancy in adolescence.* Newbury Park, CA: Sage.

Zucker, R. A., & Gomberg, E. S. L. (1986). Etiology of alcoholism reconsidered: The case for a biopsychosocial approach. *American Psychologist, 41*, 783-793.

About the Authors

Michael D. Newcomb received his Ph.D. in clinical psychology from the University of California, Los Angeles, in 1979. He is currently an Adjunct Associate Professor and Associate Research Psychologist in the Department of Psychology at UCLA. He has recently joined the Counseling Psychology Department faculty at the University of Southern California as an Associate Professor. He is a licensed clinical psychologist with a private practice in Santa Monica, California. He is principal investigator on several federally funded grants for the study of drug abuse among teenagers and adults. This support is primarily from the National Institute on Drug Abuse.

His research interests include etiology and consequences of adolescent drug abuse; methodology and multivariate analysis; human sexuality; stress, social support, and health; attitudes and affects related to nuclear war; and cohabitation, marriage, and divorce. He has over 70 publications in these areas of interest. He is currently working on a book about drug abuse in the workplace, which should be released shortly.

He is a native of Southern California and was raised in the art colony town of Laguna Beach. His current personal interests include music, fine wines, gardening, backpacking, and living near the beach. He is happily married to Kathleen Andrews and lives in Santa Monica with several cats, two rabbits, and perhaps a basset hound in the future.

Peter M. Bentler received his Ph.D. in clinical psychology from Stanford University in 1964, spent a postdoctoral year at the Educational Testing Service in Los Angeles (UCLA), where he has been ever since. He is now Professor of Psychology at UCLA, and Director of the NIDA/UCLA Drug Abuse Research Center established with the support of the National Institute on Drug Abuse (NIDA). Formerly a practicing clinician doing clinical research in gender identity, especially transvestism, his current research interests include social science methodology, especially psychometrics, and the substantive areas of drug abuse, attitude-behavior relations, personality assessment, and sexual behavior. He has over 225 publications in these and related areas.

He is a past president of the Psychometric Society and the Society of Multivariate Experimental Psychology. Currently, he is president of the Division of Evaluation and Measurement, American Psychological Association, as well as the recipient of a Research Scientist Award from the NIDA. He is on the editorial board of nine scientific journals, and editorial consultant to many others.

NOTES

NOTES

NOTES